To Hans W. Frei

John A. Hoober
Professor of Religious Studies
Yale University

in gratitude and affection
on the occasion of his
sixty-fifth birthday
29 April 1987

Scriptural Authority and Narrative Interpretation

Edited by
GARRETT GREEN

Fortress Press
Philadelphia

**Library of Congress
Cataloging-in-Publication Data**

Scriptural authority and narrative interpretation.

    Essays on the occasion of the sixty fifth birthday
of Hans W. Frei.
    Bibliography: p.
    Includes index.
    1. Bible—Hermeneutics. 2. Bible—Evidences,
authority, etc. 3. Narration in the Bible. 4. Frei,
Hans W. I. Green, Garrett. II. Frei, Hans W.
BS476.S37 1987   220.6'01   86–46416
ISBN 0–8006–0839–9

2992C87   Printed in the United States of America   1–839

Contents

Contributors

Stephen Crites
  Professor of Religion and
  Hedding Professor of Moral Science,
  Wesleyan University
Garrett Green
  Professor of Religious Studies,
  Connecticut College
Stanley Hauerwas
  Professor of Theological Ethics,
  The Divinity School,
  Duke University
David H. Kelsey
  Professor of Theology,
  Yale Divinity School
George Lindbeck
  Pitkin Professor of Historical Theology,
  Yale University
Gene Outka
  Timothy Dwight Professor of Philosophy
  and Christian Ethics,
  Yale University
Kathryn E. Tanner
  Assistant Professor of Religious Studies,
  Yale University
Ronald F. Thiemann
  John Lord O'Brian Professor
  of Divinity and Dean,
  Harvard Divinity School
Maurice Wiles
  Regius Professor of Divinity,
  Oxford University
Charles M. Wood
  Associate Professor of Theology,
  Perkins School of Theology,
  Southern Methodist University

Editor's introduction

A good case can be made that interpretation of the Bible has remained the focal point of controversy in Christian theology throughout the modern era. The reason lies not simply in the dogmatic import that the Protestant Reformers attributed to scripture but even more in the fact that so many of the peculiarly modern challenges faced by Christian thinkers have impinged on traditional faith at the point where it appeals to the canon of scripture. The rise of the modern natural sciences; the development of historical-critical method; the discovery of a multitude of other religious and cultural traditions, each making ultimate claims; the transformation of humanity's sense of its own origins through revolutions in biology and geology—all these developments challenged the self-understanding of Christians, and none of them could be dealt with by a straightforward appeal to the authoritative text of the Bible, since it was precisely that claim to authority that was being called into question. The result has been a fascinating, if often bewildering, series of attempts by Christian thinkers over several centuries to say how the Bible ought to be read in a postcritical age and to account for its authoritative status in new and more plausible ways.

Over the past decade or so this modern preoccupation with the nature and authority of scripture has taken a surprising turn, as theologians have discovered new significance in the fact that the Bible can be read as a narrative. What might appear self-evident to the naive outsider—the fact that the Bible tells a story—has recently become a focus of interest for many theologians. The neglect of this obvious fact by modern theology has been best accounted for by a book that is also a principal cause of its rediscovery: Hans W. Frei's *Eclipse of Biblical Narrative*. Through a painstaking analysis of hermeneutical theory in the eighteenth and nineteenth centuries, Frei shows how what had once been most obvious about the Bible—that it offers a narrative depiction of reality—was almost entirely overlooked by those very thinkers who specialized in its interpretation. Since the publication of Frei's book in 1974 there has been no shortage of responses to its implicit challenge, as proposals for "narrative interpretation" and "narrative theology" have abounded. Despite this renewed interest in narrative, however, no consensus has emerged about its implications for Christian theology.

The authors of the present volume—students, colleagues, and friends of Professor Frei—could think of no more fitting way to honor him than by contributing to the theological conversation that his work has been so largely responsible for initiating. The way in which *The Eclipse of Biblical Narrative* has influenced theological discussion exemplifies what Professor Frei does best: he brings the results of patient and rigorous historical scholarship to bear on systematic theology. It is not just happenstance that a work that on its face appears to be nothing but a *historical* study, thoroughly researched and compellingly presented, has fostered an outpouring of *theological* reflection. For Frei's historical work is motivated by a concern for theological questions. As Stephen Crites points out in his contribution to this volume, Frei has done for theologians something akin to what Freud attempted in another venue. By recovering for us a portion of our own intellectual history, he has discovered the roots of some contemporary quandaries and unleashed new energies for our continuing work. The complement is likewise true: when Professor Frei does theology, his work is informed by historical awareness, the best evidence for which is another influential book, *The Identity of Jesus Christ*.

A major source of Frei's influence as a theologian has been his resolute pursuit of his own vision. In this trait he resembles the theologian from whom he has learned the most, Karl Barth. Frei is far too perceptive a student of Barth's theology to try to emulate it. Yet like Barth, he has remained committed through thick and thin to what Barth would have called *die Sache*, and this *Sachlichkeit*, this stubborn refusal to be seduced by current trends or other people's programs—even if called narrative theology—is what gives his work its integrity. It is therefore not surprising that Frei has a healthy suspicion of disciplemaking. On that score at least, this volume should cause him no embarrassment, for it is not the product of any one theological program or school of thought. Its unity has more to do with common questions than common answers. All the contributors share a conviction that certain issues urgently demand the attention of Christian theologians in our time, and all have found Professor Frei's articulation of those issues to be especially astute and helpful in their own work, whether they have agreed or disagreed with his attempted solutions. This shared agenda, as indicated by the title of the volume, focuses on the Bible, and particularly on the point at which theological concern with its authority as scripture intersects with hermeneutical questions about its character as narrative.

The essays grouped in the first part of the volume address various theoretical aspects of this common focus on scripture and narrative. Charles M. Wood's contribution sets the keynote for the discussion by raising the question of what difference a text's scriptural status ought to make in its interpretation, and noting how attention to narrative can change the terms in which this question has traditionally been posed. Ronald F. Thiemann, responding to arguments by literary critics such as Frank Kermode and some of the deconstructionists that narrative texts are irreducibly obscure, shows through examples from the Old and New Testaments how biblical narratives depict a "followable world." Maurice Wiles, though appreciative of Frei's work in clarifying the issue of scriptural authority, expresses some reservations about how the category of narrative is being applied theologically. Drawing his examples chiefly from Wood, Thiemann, and Lindbeck, Wiles warns against the dangers of using narrative to impose an unwarranted unity on the canon; he proposes instead a "soft" view of scriptural authority, in which the Bible functions as basic resource rather than binding norm. Kathryn E. Tanner's contribution, developing recent suggestions by Frei, employs a social-science approach to scripture in order to argue that, far from locking Christian practice into a rigid conservatism, the linking of scriptural authority to the Bible's "plain sense," understood as its narrative meaning, has encouraged a flexible and self-critical use of the Bible. The essays by Garrett Green and Stephen Crites each raise—in quite different ways—the issue of the truth of scriptural narratives. According to the former, Frei's unraveling of the modern confusion of historical reference with textual meaning invites a reconsideration of what it means to call a text fiction and makes possible a "literalism of the second naiveté," affirming the truth of fictionlike narratives. Crites, likewise eschewing the identification of narrative truth with historical reference, explores the dimensions of narrative space in order to discover what it means to say that stories tell the truth.

The second part of the volume comprises essays that develop the implications of a narrative reading of scripture for particular theological topics. David H. Kelsey, starting from remarks by Frei about narrative and human identity, distinguishes between "foundationalist" and "nonfoundationalist" uses of narrative in theology and argues that the latter provides a sounder approach for theological *anthropology*. Drawing on some of the same anthropological and christological insights from Frei's work, Gene Outka develops their specifically *ethical* implications, stressing particularly the relationship between Jesus' unique identity and that of Christians seeking to follow him. The last two contributions focus on the implications of a narrative approach for the topic of the *church*. George Lindbeck's essay outlines an ecclesiology based on a unified narrative reading of Old and New Testaments and shows how even nonbiblical conceptions of the church may under certain historical circumstances remain faithful to the story. Finally, Stanley Hauerwas employs an actual sermon to bring home the importance of an ecclesial context in appropriating the insights of narrative interpretation for theology.

To all the contributors, the editor acknowledges his profound gratitude. Each of the essays has been written expressly for this volume and has not previously appeared in print. The alacrity with which the authors accepted the challenge and their enthusiasm and promptness in carrying it out bear witness to the esteem in which they hold Professor Frei. A special note of thanks is due to David Kelsey, George Lindbeck, and Gene Outka, who—along with Charles Wood by long distance—have served as an informal editorial committee since the inception of the project. The theme of the volume grew out of our common discussions, and without the early commitment and ongoing support of my colleagues it would never have become a reality. Acknowledgment is due also to Connecticut College for aiding the project by reducing the teaching responsibilities of the editor during its concluding stages and by providing secretarial and technical support in the preparation of the manuscript.

We hope that Professor Frei will find reflected in these essays some of the qualities that all of us have learned from him—not only from his published writings but also from his gentle prodding not to lose sight of *die Sache,* conveyed so affably (often with a twinkle in the eye) and yet so seriously. It is to him that we acknowledge the greatest debt and to whom we gratefully dedicate this volume.

GARRETT GREEN

PART ONE

Theoretical
considerations

1

Hermeneutics and the authority of scripture

Charles M. Wood

What bearing, if any, ought the fact that a given text or body of texts is scripture, that is, authoritative writing, to have upon the principles governing its interpretation? Two opposing answers to this question—one typically "liberal," the other typically "conservative"—come readily to mind. According to the first, the fact that texts have authoritative status within a religious community ought to have no bearing at all on their interpretation. There should be no "sacred hermeneutics," no privilege given these texts on account of their supposed authority; they should be treated like any other. Of course, the fact that they are *religious* texts may indicate that they should be approached with the resources of a particular "regional" hermeneutics, just as texts of other sorts may require their own particular hermeneutical considerations. But valid interpretation requires that one disregard the ways in which the community or communities for which these texts are scripture have described and approached them as such. The interpreter who happens to be a member of such a community must also prescind from any consideration of the authority of these texts for his or her own life, and must approach them as free as possible from any prior commitment to their normativeness. Only thus will the texts be able to speak for themselves rather than being made to say something that corresponds to the interpreter's dogmatic preunderstanding. On this view, giving questions of scriptural authority any role in hermeneutics is a sure way to subvert the aims of interpretation. The question of what authority the scriptural texts should possess can be taken up *after* interpretation, if at all—certainly not before.

According to the opposing view, a prior commitment to the authority of the scriptural text is the only way to a proper understanding of it. The text functions to disclose or to teach something that may not be otherwise accessible to us and that we are not predisposed to receive. If we approach it as we would other materials, subjecting it to scrutiny and testing it by our ordinary reason and experience, we will only miss its message, because that message transcends our ordinary reason and experience. The interpreter must submit to the text, accepting its authority and being instructed and shaped by it, if he or she is to understand it. Scripture should not be treated like any other writing, because it is not like any other writing. (The advocate of this view is ordinarily a member of a particular community, and it is that community's scripture, and not sacred writings in general, that he or she has in mind when making such claims. But one might envision a more generic version of this position, in which it is claimed that any religious text can only be understood by an insider to its community.) Furthermore, that prior commitment to the authority of the text must be of the right sort: we must understand what this text is and how it is authoritative before we will know how to submit our understanding to it. In other words, a proper doctrine of the authority of scripture— a doctrine derived, perhaps, from scripture itself, or from some other authorized source in the community (a magisterium)—is the necessary precondition for valid interpretation and must have a prominent role in hermeneutical reflection.

The adherents of each of these views are understandably suspicious of the adherents of the other. From the standpoint of the first answer, those who advocate the second wrongly allow extrinsic considerations (e.g., a particular community's judgments concerning the nature and content of a text) to determine their understanding of it, rather than letting the text speak for itself. Further, they tend to hold confused or mistaken ideas concerning judgments of truth—perhaps maintaining, in precritical fashion, that one may simply assume the truth of what scripture teaches, or perhaps offering some sort of fideistic view according to which there can be no appeal to truth criteria beyond the circle of faith constituted by a given community's relation to its scripture. From the standpoint of the second answer, the advocates of the first view are simply imposing their own authority upon the text, under the guise of a freedom from dogmatic constraints. By disregarding the scriptural status and context of a given text, they are refusing to let it be what it is. Further, they do not recognize that their refusal to take seriously the normative character of the text gives an unwarranted normativity to their own standards of reasonableness, meaningfulness, and truth, and does not allow these standards to be challenged and corrected by what the text has to say.

Recent hermeneutical developments have led to refinements of these two opposing positions, and to some attempts to mediate between them. Nevertheless, they remain effectively in place. Like some political positions, each is sustained by a sort of coalition of interests, and differences within each coalition can threaten the stability and coherence of the position. (Currently, for example, fundamentalists and liberation theologians may find themselves uneasily allied in criticizing certain aspects of the "liberal" position, and liberals may find some of their own arguments against the "conservative" position co-opted by neoconservatives who apply them to liberation theologians.) But despite the shakiness of the coalitions holding at any given time, the positions have an inherent power because each embodies certain valid insights.

My aim in this essay is to propose and defend an answer to our opening question which combines the strengths of these two opposing positions while avoiding their weaknesses. I hope to show that the scriptural status of texts is hermeneutically relevant for certain purposes, and that a doctrine of the authority of scripture may have a proper hermeneutical function. At the same time, I will argue that an acknowledgment of these points is eminently compatible with an insistence that the questions of the meaning and truth of scriptural texts not be begged. The answer will be worked out here specifically in terms of Christian scripture; mutatis mutandis, it might be applied to scriptures in other traditions.

NONSCRIPTURAL USES OF SCRIPTURE

Scripture is writing that is authoritative for some community. As David Kelsey puts it, " 'Authoritative' is part of the meaning of 'scripture' "'; the notion of authority is analytic to the concept of scripture.[1] Of course, the fact that scripture is authoritative for a community does not mean that it must be regarded as authoritative by its interpreters, or that it must be interpreted as an authoritative text. Interpreters within or outside the community whose scripture it is may for various reasons disregard its authority—that is, disregard its character as scripture—on the grounds that for their particular purposes its authoritative character is either irrelevant or inadmissible. Historians of early Christianity, for example, are obliged to treat the texts of the New Testament as ordinary historical documents, in principle neither more nor less reliable than noncanonical texts as sources for historical investigation. The authority ascribed to New Testament texts by the Christian community has no bearing upon their historical reliability. (At the same time, the fact that the church has ascribed authority to certain texts, has preserved them, given them prominence, traditionally trusted them as historical records, and so on, is a fact of great historical significance that the historian must take into account—not because it is evidence for the texts' historical authenticity but because it helps explain such things as the state of the documentation for the early Christian movement.) Scriptural texts may also be put to other uses for which their scriptural status is irrelevant: they may, for example, be studied for their literary value, or analyzed as examples of Hebrew or Greek syntax, or combed for interesting vignettes of human behavior.

Among the nonscriptural uses of scripture are some we may call (for lack of a better term) *religious* uses. These are uses of scriptural texts in which their potential claim upon the life of their users is taken seriously but in which the text is regarded more as a resource than as an authority. Text and reader are in principle on the same level here. The reader is open to the text's influence and may well be affected, even deeply, by it; but the reader is also free to criticize and transcend the text. It is a resource, perhaps of great significance, but it is not a norm. Interpretation is a dialogue or conversation or (less irenically put) a struggle with the text, the desired outcome of which is not the reader's submission to or conformation with the text but rather the realization of some new insight or value beyond what the text itself contains—a new stage in the growth of the tradition in which both text and reader stand.

Elisabeth Schüssler Fiorenza frequently uses the contrast between "archetype" and "prototype" in advocating her own version of this nonauthoritative use of biblical texts: an archetype is a normative pattern, any deviation from which is an error; a prototype is a first attempt, from which one may learn both positively and negatively, and which may and probably should be surpassed.[2] In associating biblical texts with the latter rather than the former concept, Schüssler Fiorenza means in effect to reject the notion of Christian scripture, that is, of authoritative texts. Her canon is an extrabiblical one—the liberation of women, as that is defined in the struggle for liberation itself.[3]

Another recent exponent of this sort of use of scripture is Delwin Brown. He proposes a redefinition rather than a relocation of theological authority, but in doing so he uses a pair of contrasting concepts that are instructively similar in function to those used by Schüssler Fiorenza: he rejects an "authorization" model in favor of an "authoring" model of biblical authority. The Bible does not serve as a norm authorizing theological proposals; rather, it serves as a source that "authors" new life, giving its readers the power and freedom to realize new possibilities for existence. The text is powerful and empowering, but it is not normative. The conservatism of the authorization model, which binds us to a standard frozen in the past, must be overcome in favor of a model that opens us to novelty in the future.[4]

For both Brown and Schüssler Fiorenza, the texts of Christian scripture are best viewed as portions of tradition to which the community, for a mixture of reasons (not altogether creditable), has given normative status. If this bestowal of status were simply a way of acknowledging the superior natural life-giving or liberating power of the texts relative to other portions of the tradition, it might be regarded as benign in intention. But insofar as it involves an attempt by the community (or more accurately, by some segments of the community) to establish standards for belief and conduct and thus to set limits to the community's creative freedom with the tradition, it must be viewed with suspicion. Schüssler Fiorenza emphasizes the ways in which the formation of the New Testament involved the legitimizing of certain (especially sexist) interests and thus represented an ideological victory for cultural norms over the egalitarian tendencies of primitive Christianity. Brown argues that the very notion of normative tradition has no valid place in Christianity: to identify a standard in the past to which Christians are expected always to conform is to renounce that God-given creative freedom in which the tradition is summoned constantly to transcend itself so that human potential may be more fully realized. In any case, the church's ways of ascribing particular authority to these texts—of marking them off from ordinary tradition, rationalizing their status, and making them, in some sort of unity, the criterion for Christian faith and life—should have no bearing upon their interpretation. Valid interpretation requires an original and critical encounter with the texts in themselves, in which their own power and also their limitations may be discerned. The church's judgments about these texts—that is, doctrines of the authority of scripture—are at best irrelevant to this sort of encounter.

Though I have focused here upon two recent advocates of the view that a nonscriptural approach to biblical texts is theologically appropriate, the general position is widely shared. A good many contemporary theologians would acknowledge that the texts of Christian scripture have had a special role in the formation and maintenance of the Christian tradition and that they are therefore particularly worthy of attention if one is attempting to understand the substance and dynamics of that tradition. But, these theologians would argue, to take them as authoritative (i.e., normative) is unwarranted. At the beginning of my essay, I characterized this as a typically liberal response, because it has often been ingredient in treatments of theological authority developed in liberal theology—for example, the relocation of theological authority from "holy scripture" to the life and teachings of the historical Jesus or to some immanent principle of religious or cultural evolution, or the renunciation of the very notion of authority as incompatible with enlightened or responsible faith. For such positions, the concept of authoritative text or scripture as such is one with no place in serious theology, and one the church as a whole may in good time outgrow. In short, from this standpoint, the fact that these writings are regarded as scripture by a community ought to have no bearing on their interpretation, because this very designation is at best an anachronism, and one of the positive tasks of hermeneutics is to enable the community to overcome the unfortunate relationship to its texts which the designation "scripture" represents and to find or recover a more appropriate one.

HERMENEUTICAL IMPLICATIONS OF SCRIPTURAL STATUS

On the other hand, those who affirm rather than lament the scriptural status of biblical texts generally take this status to be hermeneutically significant. That is, where the texts are regarded not simply as a sample of early tradition, but as the *criterion* of tradition—as tradition that is somehow distinctively authoritative—this regard is normally (and rightly) thought to have hermeneutical implications. Although this position is for obvious reasons generally typical of conservative theologies, it is not found exclusively there and can in fact be developed in quite other directions. It is intrinsically conservative only in the formal sense that a historically prior reality (scripture) is given some sort of normative status over subsequent developments; but as Christian history has repeatedly shown, this conservatism can have radical consequences. To call something scripture is to affirm a critical principle: it is to identify something over against "tradition" (even if it is also *within* tradition) by which the authenticity of tradition may be evaluated and by which the development of tradition may be guided. It is to remove the presumption—which may be more characteristic of a conventionally conservative outlook—that tradition per se is valid, and to put in its place the principle that tradition must be tested.

Our concern in this essay is not to determine whether or not the texts constituting the Christian Bible—or, for that matter, any texts at all—ought to be regarded as scripture by the Christian church, or ought to function in any authoritative way in Christian theology. Rather, assuming their authority, our purpose is to ask whether that status has any proper bearing on their interpretation. Characteristically, those who answer this question in the negative also deny, explicitly or implicitly, that very assumption; that is, they typically claim that the texts ought not to be regarded as authoritative. Instead, they are to be treated as resources of one sort or another. Such positions are at least consistent in this regard. It would be inconsistent to affirm or assume the scriptural status of the texts and to deny that the status has hermeneutical implications. What sort of implications it has is what we must now investigate.

Ascribing authority to texts involves making certain judgments about them. Any well-developed normative account of the authority of scripture will make these judgments explicit by furnishing answers to three principal questions: First, for what is this material authoritative? Second, how does it exercise its authority? Third, why is it authoritative? The first question concerns the scope of scripture's authority; the second, its character; and the third, its source. The same questions might be addressed by a descriptive account of scripture's authority for a community—an account of what is sometimes called its de facto authority. In that case, attention of a social-scientific sort would be given to the actual functioning of scriptural authority in the community—its scope, its character, its source. Here, however, the concern is with a normative account, or a doctrine, of the authority of scripture, or with what can be called its de jure authority: What is the *proper* scope of scripture's authority? How *should* it function authoritatively? *Why* is it authoritative? What it means to take a particular body of texts as scripture depends upon the answers given to these questions.

For example, demarcations of the scope of scriptural authority have varied widely. Some religious believers have held that scripture is authoritative on any subject so far as a passage from scripture may be taken to convey any information about that subject. Scripture is then the final arbiter, in principle, on any question, whether of history, geology, cosmology, anthropology, or grammar, on which some part of scripture may touch. Others have made a distinction between what scripture happens to contain and what it teaches, and have restricted the scope of scriptural authority to the latter—often further specified as matters concerning faith and morals, as distinct (it may be) from history or natural science. (Of course, it may also be held that certain historical or scientific beliefs are matters of faith, in which case the scope of scriptural authority extends to these things. This claim, then, like the first position mentioned, raises questions concerning the relationship between such historical or scientific beliefs and critical scholarship in these fields, and more generally, questions concerning the relationship of biblical authority to secular inquiry, of faith to knowledge, and so on.)

The scope of scriptural authority has sometimes been further demarcated not with respect to the sorts of beliefs or activities upon which its authority bears but rather with respect to the sort of validity that may be adjudged by an appeal to scripture. It is widely held in contemporary theology that there are at least two basic questions, of different sorts, that theological reflection is obliged to raise concerning the validity of any instance of Christian witness: there is the question of its faithfulness to normative Christianity (what Schubert M. Ogden calls its "appropriateness," and David H. Kelsey its "Christianness"), and there is the question of its meaningfulness and truth. Those who make such a distinction frequently go on to affirm that although scriptural authority may bear upon the first of these questions, it cannot bear upon the second. That is, one may appeal to scripture to settle the question of whether a given stance is authentically Christian but not to settle the question of whether it is credible or true.[5]

Such decisions concerning the scope of scriptural authority, particularly as they are made more specific, are inevitably bound up with other judgments concerning both the character and the source of that authority. To say that scripture is authoritative in what it teaches concerning faith and morals, for instance, is to suggest a range of ways in which the character of its authority—that is, how it functions authoritatively—might be conceived. If the accent is on the *fides quae creditur*, scripture's authority will most likely be conceived in doctrinal terms: for example, scripture will be conceived to function as the repository of, or guide to, right doctrine. If the accent is rather on the *fides qua creditur*, attention might instead be concentrated on the ways in which scripture functions to evoke and shape faithful dispositions. Scripture as *teacher* rather than as *teachings* might be the motif, and the effects of scripture upon its readers or hearers, rather than its cognitive content, might be highlighted.

Similarly, certain accounts of the source of scriptural authority will comport more naturally with some options concerning its scope and character than with others. (The ultimate source of scriptural authority, on nearly any normative account, is God; what is at issue here is

the proximate source, the link between God and scripture, or—to put
it another way—the specific way in which scripture derives its authority from God.) If scripture's authority is essentially a doctrinal
authority, a theory of inspiration (plenary or otherwise) might come
into play as an account of scripture's authorization as the deposit of
divine teaching. Some other accounts of the source of scriptural
authority—for example, that it is the record of intense but basically
ineffable experiences of divine presence, or that it is the human
witness to God's might acts in history—might be more difficult to
reconcile with that view of the scope or character of its authority. A
depiction of scriptural authority as having to do primarily with its
normative role in shaping faithful dispositions, or in providing practical guidance for living, might well cohere with an account in which
scripture is portrayed as an instrument used by God for these purposes. God's present relation to and use of these texts would perhaps
be a more prominent feature of such an account than of some others,
where the emphasis is on how the texts came to be.

These examples are quite restricted. Their point has not been to
provide even a beginning inventory of accounts of scriptural authority but rather simply to indicate that to call certain texts authoritative—and still more obviously, to follow through by treating
them as authoritative—leads one to a number of decisions concerning the authority the texts are thought to bear. These decisions affect
one's view of the texts in hermeneutically significant ways. To take a
body of texts, such as the Bible, as "scripture" involves a set of related
judgments all of which generally cohere in an overall synoptic judgment of the texts' character, a basic construal (to use Kelsey's term) of
scripture as a whole. Such a construal is a complex imaginative
judgment, as Kelsey has argued.[6] But though imaginative, it is hardly
arbitrary or inexplicable, as a rule. It is ordinarily informed by certain
features of the scriptural texts themselves, by what are taken to be
significant aspects of the interpretive tradition in which the interpreter stands, and by the interpreter's own sense (however derived) of
what normative Christianity is, that is, of what it is that scripture is
supposed to authorize. None of these three factors—not the intrinsic
character of the component texts, the history of their interpretation in
the community, or the interpreter's vision of Christianity—has an
assured priority in the formation of a construal of scripture; the three

are intimately related, and the relative weight of each may vary from case to case. It should be clear from these considerations that scriptural authority can mean a number of different things. It would be a mistake to suppose that the only alternative to the sort of approach that Delwin Brown or Elisabeth Schüssler Fiorenza advocates is the rigid and restrictive view of scriptural authority which they themselves use as a foil to their proposals—that is, the view of scripture as an archetype binding and confining Christians to patterns of thought and behavior laid down once for all in the past. Certainly this has been a common view—arguably the standard view throughout most of Christian history—and as such, it has done incalculable harm. It deserves the sort of exposure and critique to which these authors and many others have subjected it. But it represents only one of several possibilities. It ordinarily results from a basic construal of scripture as a body of divine teachings that are to be accepted, believed, and obeyed. Prominent as this construal has been historically, there are others that may have far more warrant and that lead in other directions.

In this connection, one of the major values of the recent attention to biblical narrative which the work of Hans Frei has helped to promote is its potential for a reconception of the nature of biblical authority. If a text functions to teach truths that its readers are to believe and to which they are to conform, it will be fairly clear what it means to say that the text authorizes certain beliefs and actions. The text itself sets forth the paradigms. But if a text functions narratively, to disclose a world in which its readers are invited to dwell, or to depict a character in relation to whom the readers are asked to see themselves, then the logic of authorization is considerably different. The readers are brought into the narratives; it becomes a context for reflection and action. The insights, convictions, dispositions, and so forth that the readers achieve in their interaction with the text are, as Brown rightly maintains, the fruits of a struggle. What is achieved is not simply read off the text and accepted but is rather created through the engagement of the readers—who have their distinctive backgrounds and locations—with the text. It is (or may be) authorized by the text, insofar as it is in keeping with the sense of the story. (Not everything that springs from a reader's encounter with a text is thus authorized. The old distinction between what is simply derived from

scripture somehow and what is genuinely in accord with scripture
has not lost its usefulness.) But what is "in keeping with the sense of
the story" cannot be predetermined; it is not latent in the text itself
but must be produced through the readers' own engagement with the
text. Thus, although the text is normative, in that it is by the text that
the appropriateness of Christian belief and conduct is to be judged, its
normativeness does not stifle diversity and creativity. Indeed, it
positively mandates them.

Other basic construals of scripture—for example, a "kerygmatic"
construal according to which scripture functions to call forth existential decision—might also be shown to have their own distinctive
implications concerning the character of biblical authority, as different from those of the "authorization" model which Brown opposes as
are those of a narrative construal. My purpose, however, is not to
illustrate or to assess the variety of senses of "authority" and "authorize" that may be associated with various construals of scripture,
though the fact that there is such a variety is a point worth reiterating.
It is rather to show that the decisions one makes concerning scriptural
authority, and the basic construal of scripture in which they cohere,
have a great deal to do with how one interprets a given text within
scripture *as* scripture. How this is so might best be indicated by
pointing briefly to three considerations.

First, a text's status as a component of scripture, under some
definite construal of the latter, may inform an interpreter's judgment
as to the sort of text it is—that is, it may inform the initial decision as
to genre which furnishes the reader with a stock of interpretive
procedures and criteria to be applied to the task.

The term "genre" is employed here not in any technical sense but
only to signal the fact that we do have ways of distinguishing among
texts and utterances as belonging to different sorts, and of approaching those of each sort with certain expectations concerning how they
will work. Writing and speech are ordinarily governed by conventions, and some of the conventions have to do with distinctions
among sorts of discourse which enable speakers and hearers, or
writers and readers, to know how to operate. Sometimes the conventions dictate that a clear identifying signal be provided: "Once upon a
time . . ." But even these can be turned to different uses, and often it is
impossible to tell simply from the form or content of the text or

utterance itself to what genre it may belong. Further, speakers and writers are hardly imprisoned within established conventions; they are free to modify the given usages, to adapt literary forms to new purposes, or even to invent new forms (a move carrying with it the task of somehow initiating the audience into the novelty if there is the wish to be understood).

The texts of the Christian Bible are of a great many kinds. Many of the component documents are themselves composed of earlier texts and oral traditions, or of fragments of those. An interpreter interested in the origins of the traditions found in scripture will be concerned to find the earliest identifiable genres and, from that standpoint, might regard their later transformations as corruptions of an earlier purity. From another standpoint, the same transformations might be regarded more neutrally as transitions to (or the creation of) new genres, so that a given literary unit might be seen to belong to several different genres over the course of time. The historicizing of myth in the formation of Israel's primordial history and the creation of gospels out of earlier traditions are standard examples of such genre shifts, and interpreters increasingly recognize the importance of acknowledging them and of asking, for example, what it means to interpret a Gospel as a Gospel and not simply as a source from which earlier traditions might be recovered. To take that question seriously is not to deny the integrity and importance of the earlier traditions. It is rather to acknowledge that this material may now be read as a new sort of whole, and that this task may bring a new set of considerations into play.

To treat a text (such as a Gospel) as a component of *scripture*—that is, as a part of a still larger determinate whole—is to take this process one step further. It would be difficult to construe scripture as a whole as belonging to any single genre, and so it is not the absorption of earlier texts into a new genre, or a new single text of a certain genre, which is envisioned here. But certain basic construals of scripture lead one to take its component texts in certain ways—to read them for certain purposes, to identify certain features of them as significant—and this may have an impact on the way one approaches the component texts in their relative independence. The basic construal of scripture which one adopts may suggest specific construals of particular texts within it. It may lead one to apply a certain genre identification to a given text and read it as a text of that sort. It may be that, apart from the scriptural context, some other genre identification would be equally fitting or more fitting; but taking the text as scripture opens up the possibility of taking the text, for *this* purpose, according to this construal.

Second, taking a text as a component of scripture furnishes a new context for interpretation. In an essay on the New Testament canon, Harry Y. Gamble observes, "In the nature of the case, canonization entails a recontextualization of the documents incorporated into the canon. They are abstracted both from their generative and traditional settings and redeployed as parts of a new literary whole; henceforth, they are known and read in terms of this collection."[7] The basic construal of scripture with which one operates is likely to affect the resultant "intertextuality," influencing the way in which the texts are read in terms of one another and in terms of the whole that they are taken to constitute. Though the specific implications of such intertextuality will depend upon the basic construal employed, Gamble's claim regarding the New Testament canon is surely applicable to scripture generally: "Since the canon has such results, it cannot be regarded only as an anthology; in its actual effects, the canon is a hermeneutical medium which by its very nature influences the understanding of its contents."[8] From the standpoint of a normative doctrine of scriptural authority, such intertextuality is not simply a historical phenomenon—something that happens to texts when they are assembled into collections under certain conditions—but also a hermeneutical principle.

A third consideration has to do with the principle that George Lindbeck has discussed under the name of intratextuality.[9] Whereas "*inter*textuality" designates the way in which a body of scripture serves as an interpretive medium for its component texts, "*intra*textuality" designates the way in which the same body of scripture serves as an interpretive medium for the extratextual world. Rather than interpreting the text in terms of some other, extratextual frame of reference, one asks how the text's own uses of language constitute its distinctive meaning, and then uses the text as an instrument through which to interpret the world. As Frei puts it in summarizing Lindbeck, "The direction in the flow of intratextual interpretation is that of absorbing the extratextual universe into the text, rather than the reverse (extratextual) direction."[10] Lindbeck himself articulates the basic understanding of language and meaning underlying this principle in this way:

Meaning is constituted by the uses of a specific language rather than being distinguishable from it. Thus the proper way to determine what "God" signifies, for example, is by examining how the word operates in a religion and thereby shapes reality and experience rather than by first establishing its propositional or experiential meaning and reinterpreting or reformulating its uses accordingly.[11]

One function of a basic construal of scripture, and of the specific understanding of authority that accompanies it, is to show how and why this principle of intratextuality is to be followed. The principle itself would seem to be a natural corollary to any adequate doctrine of the authority of scripture, since it simply asserts the hermeneutical priority of scripture over its interpreter. The task of interpretation is to learn the sense of scripture, undertaking whatever development of one's own capacities is requisite to that end, rather than to submit scripture to explanation in terms of one's present knowledge and capacities ("making sense of it") on the assumption that the latter are essentially adequate to whatever scripture may contain.[12] To recognize the authority of scripture is, among other things, to submit one's understanding to it: to be willing to be guided by it, and to allow one's previous understandings to be challenged, extended, and transformed by it. Whether this sort of approach is uniquely pertinent to the understanding of *authoritative* texts is, of course, debatable. Lindbeck's judgment (which I share) is that the principle of intratextuality is rooted in more general features of language learning and conceptual growth, so that the procedures would be similar if, say, one were trying seriously to understand a religious faith, or a political perspective, other than one's own. If this is the case, a doctrine of scriptural authority might serve more as a reminder of good interpretive procedure generally than as an injunction to give these texts special treatment.

THE LIMITS OF
SCRIPTURAL AUTHORITY

These three considerations—that a text's scriptural status may properly affect the interpreter's initial judgment as to what sort of text

it is; that it provides a context for interpretation; and that it supports
the hermeneutical priority of the text—reflect the principal ways in
which scriptural status may be taken to be hermeneutically pertinent.
It is worth noting, in conclusion, that none of the considerations
obliges the interpreter to surrender his or her critical freedom vis-à-
vis the text. In the first place, the decision to take a text as scripture,
and to allow that status and context to affect one's interpretation,
might well be regarded as a provisional, heuristic decision. It does not
prohibit one from also taking the text in other ways, for other
purposes; it represents a desire to investigate what this text, taken as
scripture under a certain construal of scripture, might mean. (The
necessity of reflecting upon one's concept of scripture, and of working
out some understanding of the various aspects of its authority, as a
prelude to interpretation might in fact help an interpreter to avoid
letting untested assumptions and attitudes shape the process.)

In the second place, the three considerations in no way oblige the
interpreter to accept whatever scriptural texts teach (or disclose, or
evoke, or whatever scriptural texts do) as true. Although understanding scriptural texts may require existential engagement, and one may
need to grow in certain ways in order to get their point or to inhabit
the world they open up, there is still a useful distinction between the
logic of discovery and the logic of justification—or otherwise put,
between coming to see how things might be and coming, on reflection, to accept that vision as true. The procedure commended by the
principle of intratextuality, or the hermeneutical priority of the text, is
then also best understood as a heuristic procedure, and not as involv-
ing a prior commitment to the truth of what scripture conveys. The
point is that one will not be in a position to make an informed
judgment concerning the truth of a passage if one does not submit
one's understanding, provisionally, to the text.

In the third place, to be guided hermeneutically by the three
considerations does not even commit the interpreter to the proposition that what scripture, thus construed, conveys is normatively
Christian. One of the ways in which a doctrine of the authority of
scripture for the community's life and thought can be tested is by
trying it out and discovering what it yields. If it is true that the
authority of scripture is not established but rather only acknowledged
by the church and that this acknowledgment must be continually

renewed, then clearly a doctrine of scripture's authority can play at best only a secondary and instrumental role—principally by suggesting some hermeneutical principles whereby the church's engagement with the scriptural texts might be guided. Whether that engagement leads to a reaffirmation of the texts as the church's scripture or to the deepening of some serious questions over whether they can or should so serve is a question only time and practice can settle.

NOTES

1. David H. Kelsey, *The Uses of Scripture in Recent Theology* (Philadelphia: Fortress Press, 1975), 97. There are, of course, other definitions of "scripture," but this one best serves my purposes here. In most of the occurrences of "scripture" in this essay, the term "canon" might serve as well. For other purposes, the terms are not synonymous.

2. See, e.g., Elisabeth Schüssler Fiorenza, *Bread Not Stone: The Challenge of Feminist Biblical Interpretation* (Boston: Beacon Press, 1984), 61, et passim. As Schüssler Fiorenza acknowledges (161 n. 39), she borrows the contrast from Rachel Blau DuPlessis.

3. Ibid., 13–14, et passim. Just how this alternative, extrabiblical canon is to be identified and understood is less clear from Schüssler Fiorenza's essays than is her critique of biblical authority. The question of whether the feminist canon is to be understood also as the *Christian* canon—and if so, on what grounds—is especially intriguing.

4. Delwin Brown, "Struggle till Daybreak: On the Nature of Authority in Theology," *Journal of Religion* 65 (1985):15–32, esp. 20–26. Brown's "authoring model" trades on the sense of *exousia* that is closer to "power" than to "authority" when these terms are distinguished. The model has so little to do with the latter concept that his attempt to offer it as a *redefinition* of biblical and theological authority faces some significant difficulties. Whether an alternative approach is able to escape his strictures against the "authorization model" is another question.

5. See, e.g., Schubert M. Ogden, "What Is Theology?" *Journal of Religion* 52 (1972): 22–40; and Kelsey, *Uses of Scripture*, 153–54. Ogden has since refined his account of theological inquiry, with reference to Jürgen Habermas's analysis of the "validity claims" made or implied in discourse and action; see, e.g., Schubert M. Ogden, "The Service of Theology to the Servant Task of Pastoral Ministry," in *The Pastor as Servant*, ed. Earl E. Shelp and Ronald H. Sunderland (New York: Pilgrim Press, 1986), 87–93. For yet another account of the sorts of questions involved in theological inquiry, see Charles M. Wood, *Vision and Discernment: An Orientation in Theological Study* (Atlanta: Scholars Press, 1985), chap. 3.

6. Kelsey, *Uses of Scripture*, chap. 8.

7. Harry Y. Gamble, *The New Testament Canon: Its Making and Meaning* (Philadelphia: Fortress Press, 1985), 75.

8. Ibid. The whole of Gamble's essay, and especially the last chapter, is instructive for our topic. See also Brevard S. Childs, *The New Testament as Canon: An Introduction* (Philadelphia: Fortress Press, 1984), chap. 4.

9. George A. Lindbeck, *The Nature of Doctrine: Religion and Theology in a Postliberal Age* (Philadelphia: Westminster Press, 1984), 113–24.

10. Hans W. Frei, "The 'Literal Reading' of Biblical Narrative in the Christian Tradition: Does It Stretch or Will It Break?" in *The Bible and the Narrative Tradition*, ed. Frank McConnell (New York: Oxford Univ. Press, 1986), 72. Frei goes on to argue that the "literal sense is the paradigmatic form of such intratextual interpretation in the Christian community's use of its scripture."

11. Lindbeck, *Nature of Doctrine*, 114. Cited in Frei, " 'Literal Reading' of Biblical Narrative," 72.

12. E. D. Watt, in one of the more discriminating and helpful of recent treatments of the concept of authority, writes, "Authority is never egalitarian. An authority is always a superior of some kind, to be obeyed in some cases, in other cases to be followed, consulted, attended to, deferred to, or conformed to. . . . Authority in all its forms is associated with, and is a constant reminder of, some human limitation, weakness, or dependency" (*Authority* [New York: St. Martin's Press, 1982], 7).

2

Radiance and obscurity in biblical narrative

In Kafka's *The Trial* a priest recounts to K a tale about a man seeking entrance to the law.[1] But the door to the law is guarded by a series of terrible doorkeepers determined to turn away all who would seek entrance. The man, undeterred by these obstacles, resolves to wait, and so sits on his stool, cajoling and even bribing the doorkeeper, but to no avail. Finally, after many years of waiting, the man begins to slip into death. In his final moments he notes a beautiful light streaming from the door, and seeks from the doorkeeper some explanation for these strange occurrences. The keeper replies, "This door was intended only for you. Now I am going to shut it." With that the parable ends.

Frank Kermode has made a great deal of this story, using it in his book *The Genesis of Secrecy*[2] to argue that all interpreters of narratives are finally outsiders, readers who seek to discover a tale's radiant mystery but always fail. Our efforts to understand run up against an "uninterpretable radiance,"[3] and so they die, like the seeker of the law, frustrated and unfulfilled. "All narratives are essentially dark,"[4] Kermode argues, and the worlds they cast up before us are finally "unfollowable." "World and book," Kermode writes, "are hopelessly plural, endlessly disappointing.... [O]ur sole hope and pleasure is in the perception of a momentary radiance, before the door of disappointment is finally shut on us."[5]

Ronald F. Thiemann

21

Kermode states with particular eloquence what has become a commonplace of contemporary hermeneutics: that literary texts are indeterminable and thus inevitably yield multiple, irreducibly diverse, interpretations. Some theorists have readily drawn a further conclusion, one that does not necessarily follow from the fact of multiple interpretations, namely, that there can be no criteria for preferring one reading to another, and that we are therefore cast into the darkest of hermeneutical nights in which all readings are indistinguishably gray. Such hermeneutical relativism surely does suggest that both text and world are hopelessly unfollowable, that the brief glimmer of light emitted by shadowy narratives is hardly sufficient to light the path of interpretation, much less to illumine an entire world of experience. And so we are left to stumble about in the dark, making our way as best we can.

THE POLITICS OF
NARRATIVE OBSCURITY

This view of interpretation and of the human condition has been powerfully and persuasively presented by contemporary literary critics. Many critics, the deconstructionists chief among them, recognize the important political implications of their hermeneutical arguments. By loosing interpretation from the authoritative grasp of the "metaphysics of presence" they hope to revive the freedom necessary for a critical humanism.[6] The world created by Christendom, ruled by the Christian God, and governed by the philosophers of being must fall if freedom, difference, and playfulness are to flourish.

The hermeneutical position represented by Kermode and others has become persuasive in part because we have many confirming experiences of relativism within our own cultural situation. American public life exhibits many of the vices and virtues of our current cultural pluralism. The national political debate has been greatly enriched by the lively positions and arguments put forward by women, blacks, Hispanics, native Americans, and others who had been previously excluded from political influence. Advances in the areas of civil and economic rights would have been inconceivable without the feisty pressure of such diverse groups. The American constitutional system has demonstrated its resilience by including

these competing parties within the political process without ruptur-
ing the tender bonds holding the nation together. And yet it cannot be
denied that the fabric of our common national life has come under
increasing pressure and may not long withstand the opposing tugs of
competing interest groups.

Even more distressing is the fact that we seem to be losing our
ability to engage in common discourse about the important political
and moral issues facing the republic. The debates concerning abortion
provide the most evident and painful example of the collapse of any
apparent consensus on the most basic ethical questions. Do we call
that which the woman carries a fetus or an unborn child? Do we call
the act of abortion a "termination of pregnancy" or a "taking of
innocent life"? Our failure to reach even linguistic consensus on
these matters indicates that a deep moral pluralism underlies the
current debate about abortion.

Moral pluralism can too easily connote not just a fruitful diversity
of opinion but the belief that such diversity is irreducible, that is, that
there can be no rational decision procedures for adjudicating not only
conflicting interpretations of texts but also the deep moral and political disagreements within our culture. This new pluralism will be
sustained by the conviction that opposing positions regarding abortion or nuclear disarmament or social welfare programs are simply
equally unjustifiable opinions that express the personal preferences of
those who hold them—that there are no reasons or arguments that
can ultimately decide such matters and that they must thus be decided simply by the exercise of power (a position clearly illustrated by
the recent bombings of abortion clinics). To believe that ethical positions are nothing more than expressions of personal preference or
cultural differences, to believe that our deepest beliefs and convictions are simply nonrational opinions, is to despair of the possibility
of any significant common life within the republic. People who hold
these beliefs have no motivation to participate in the common good
of the nation. They have no reason to listen to the arguments of those
with whom they disagree. And finally they have no reason to curb
their own excesses in defending the positions that most accord with
their own personal preferences—no matter how harmful the positions may be to the community as a whole.

Political and cultural diversity is a gift to be nurtured and celebrated. The freedom upon which such diversity is based is particularly precious and must be preserved and extended to those who have been excluded from full participation in a free society. But like all gifts of God's creation these blessings have been touched by the distorting power of sin. Freedom yoked to selfishness becomes avarice, and diversity contemptuous of the common good yields a nation of isolated individuals.

The consequences of unbridled pluralism are not as evident in hermeneutics as they are in political life, but as the avant-garde critics rightly remind us, the interpretive positions we adopt in the academy ultimately have political implications. Too often, however, these critics assume that their deconstruction of text and world is an occasion. for pure celebration. But there is another, darker side to their exuberant subversion of that tradition which has sought to use texts to enlighten a world, a side seen clearly by one of the fathers of deconstruction, Friedrich Nietzsche.

In a famous scene from *The Gay Science* a madman runs into a crowded marketplace crying, "I seek God! I seek God!" As the crowd taunts and ridicules him the madman jumps into their midst and "pierce[s] them with his glances":

> "Whither is God," he cried. "I shall tell you. *We have killed him*—you and I. All of us are his murderers. But how have we done this? . . . Who gave us the sponge to wipe away the entire horizon? What did we do when we unchained this earth from its sun? Whither is it moving now? Whither are we moving now? Away from all suns? Are we not plunging continually? . . . God is dead. God remains dead. And we have killed him. How shall we, the murderers of all murderers, comfort ourselves? . . . Is not the greatness of this deed too great for us? Must not we ourselves become gods simply to seem worthy of it?"[7]

Nietzsche recognized clearly that the end of the authoritative tradition that Christianity had spawned and nurtured meant not only a bracing new freedom but a profound sense of intellectual and ethical vertigo. A world without a horizon is a world without balance. A world without illumination is a world plunging away from all suns into cold and darkness. The only way to regain our balance in such a disorienting situation is for us to become gods ourselves.[8]

NARRATIVE OBSCURITY AND
THE BIBLE

It is important to remember that Kermode grounds his case about "narrative obscurity" in an analysis of the Gospel of Mark. Thus he raises his hermeneutical challenge to textual enlightenment by deconstructing one of the texts that for almost two millenniums has been central to the self-understanding of the Christian community and, through that community, to much of Western culture. The Gospel narratives continue to be the central formative texts of Christianity, whatever their more uncertain fate within our broader culture. Consequently the claim that narrative texts can depict and illumine a followable world is one that Christians are concerned to defend not as a general principle but as a proposition true with reference to the Bible. Yet Christians must take care to define clearly the claims they wish to defend, or they may find themselves committed to positions that are ultimately indefensible.

In my subsequent remarks I will argue that biblical narratives do illumine a followable world for the readers of the scriptural texts. But before I launch into the development of that argument, I want to engage in a little deconstruction of my own, by attempting to subvert an erroneous assumption that has haunted the current hermeneutical discussion.

Many philosophers and literary critics (including Nietzsche, Kermode, and Derrida) have assumed that texts must be either totally perspicuous or totally indeterminate. Kermode, for example, sets up the contrast between "insiders" and "outsiders," between "spiritual" and "carnal" readings, between pellucid and obscure narratives, in order to show that inside and spiritual interpretations are finally illusory. They can be powerful illusions, particularly when buttressed by the authority of institutions, but they are for all their influence still illusions. We are all finally outsiders. Thus Kermode does not really transcend his own dichotomy but finally absorbs one term of his contrasting pair into the other. So also Nietzsche, at least in *The Gay Science*, poses the alternatives of a stable God-oriented world or a dizzy free fall into the darkness. Finally, Derrida and his followers appear to offer a similar dichotomy in their contrast between the presence and centeredness of the ontotheological tradition and their own focus on absence and difference. In every case these thinkers seem to be victims of what Richard Bernstein has called the Cartesian anxiety, that "grand and seductive Either/Or. *Either* there is some support for our being, a fixed foundation for our knowledge, *or* we cannot escape the forces of darkness that envelop us with madness, with intellectual and moral chaos."[9] With varying degrees of fervor these postmodern thinkers are urging us to come to terms with the madness and chaos that are our inevitable fate.

But madness is inevitable only if illumination is unachievable. And illumination is unachievable only if it is construed as a perfect light that dispels all darkness and banishes all shadows. Admittedly, modern philosophers and theologians have often seen their task as one of seeking the ultimate source of knowledge that enlightens all understanding. The eighteenth-century *philosophes* called their movement the Enlightenment, because they were confident that reason was the beacon that would lead them into all truth. Modern theologians have relied heavily upon images of light and vision in order to express God's illuminating self-disclosure in revelation. These philosophers and theologians have conceived the goal of inquiry to be the discovery of an unshakable, incorrigible foundation for knowledge.[10] For them, the true foundation for knowledge needs no external illumination but glows with the light of self-illumination. They have believed that only such a sui generis source of enlightenment can serve as the basis for human assurance and security.[11]

As the contemporary philosophical discussion has shown, this epistemological foundationalism is conceptually incoherent.[12] Ironically, the deconstructionists, who have been among the most vigorous critics of the foundational tradition, remain wedded to the essential assumptions of that tradition when they seek to describe the consequences of their criticism. Madness, darkness, and chaos follow inevitably only if there can be nothing except that or perfect illumination. In rejecting the "either" of Descartes's search for clarity and distinctness, they seize the "or" of Cartesian anxiety. Kermode, for example, seems to assume that because literary texts yield multiple interpretations they are "endlessly disappointing" and "unfollowable." Interpretive diversity does not necessarily imply hermeneutical relativism. Nor does the fact of such diversity decide the question of whether texts yield followable worlds.

In arguing that biblical narratives illumine a followable world, I am not denying that there are other plausible readings of the narratives, including readings that stress primarily the obscurity and indeterminacy of the texts. The fact that multiple interpretations are possible does not decide the issue of whether any one interpretation is more plausible than others. Nor does the phenomenon of narrative obscurity preclude the existence of criteria by which we can decide upon preferable readings. What interpretive diversity does determine is that such questions cannot be settled abstractly or theoretically, that is, in isolation from actual interpretations of the text. Only when we take a detailed look at rival readings of a narrative can we be in a position to judge between them. Whether a narrative portrays a followable world cannot be decided on the basis of any theory of narrativity. Interpreters must risk interpretations and readers must patiently hear and evaluate their exegeses before deciding whether a plausible world has been presented and whether such a world is inhabitable. "Followability" is a predicate of particular narratives, not of one's theory about all possible narratives.

Erich Auerbach, in his monumental study of realism in Western literature, *Mimesis*, notes two qualities of biblical, and particularly Hebrew biblical, narrative. Such stories are "mysterious and 'fraught with background' ";[13] they heighten suspense by describing terrible events in spare and unadorned prose. Because characters' thoughts and feelings are rarely expressed, they remain layered and entangled. The narratives' meaning remains latent in the depiction, and demands from the reader an act of interpretation. These are, of course, the same qualities that Kermode attributes to all narratives and that he suggests account for the indeterminateness of all stories. In biblical narrative, however, Auerbach argues, latent meanings are combined with a second distinctive quality, a "tyrannical" claim to truth. "The world of the Scripture stories is not satisfied with claiming to be a historically true reality—it insists that it is the only real world, is destined for autocracy. . . . Far from seeking, like Homer, merely to make us forget our own reality for a few hours, it seeks to overcome our reality: we are to fit our own life into its world, feel ourselves to be elements in its structure of universal history."[14] Those two elements, Auerbach asserts, create a tension that reaches its breaking point in the modern era, when the acknowledgment of the Bible's literary qualities increasingly entails a denial of its claim to truth. Obscure narratives with latent meanings cannot, the modern wisdom goes, claim absolute authority over our attempts at interpretation. Thus emerges the dichotomy that Kermode so clearly sets before us.

The witness of diverse voices speaking against the possibility of an authoritative reading of a text, particularly a biblical text, is certainly impressive. But I want to suggest that despite the apparent persuasiveness of the arguments that Kermode, Auerbach, and others have presented, we do not have to accede either to interpretive relativism or to the political and moral relativism such a position might entail. Nor must we accept the bleak vision that narratives yield only obscure tales and unfollowable worlds. The very literary qualities that Auerbach notes serve not to undermine but to *define* the Bible's authority. Scripture, I will argue, presents a complicated but finally coherent narrative that invites the reader to consider the world there depicted as the one true reality. Scripture's claim to truth comes not in the form of tyrannical dogmatic assertion but in the form of an invitation—or better, a promise. The text's authority lies not in its ability to coerce or compel but in its ability to persuade and convince the reader that the promise it presents is trustworthy. Like all such pledges the Bible's storied promise can be accepted or denied; the promiser can be accepted as trustworthy or rejected as deceptive. Whether or not the reader chooses to follow, the world depicted in this narrative is surely followable. And that among other things makes the biblical story a most promising tale.[15]

LITERARY ANALYSIS OF
BIBLICAL NARRATIVE

In his path-breaking book *The Eclipse of Biblical Narrative*,[16] Hans Frei noted that post-Reformation interpreters of the Bible failed to see the theological significance of the "realistic or history-like" features of biblical narrative, because they lacked an "appropriate analytical or interpretive procedure" for identifying and employing those features. In *The Identity of Jesus Christ*, Frei pioneered the use of intention-action models in order to analyze the realistic aspects of the Gospels' story about Jesus. This "experiment in Christology" constituted the first step in the development of the required "analytical procedure" for the interpretation of realistic biblical narrative. Several other theologians and philosophers of religion have attempted to refine and extend Frei's work,[17] even though Frei himself seems to have moved in other directions.[18]

The most important work, in addition to Frei's, on the literary analysis of biblical narrative is Robert Alter's *The Art of Biblical Narrative*. Alter has developed a method of analysis that gives careful attention to the intricate literary patterns of narration, characterization, and techniques of repetition which constitute the biblical texts' literary unity. By attending to both the microscopic and macroscopic aspects of the texts Alter helps us draw nearer to the goal of stating clear textual warrants for the description of an overarching biblical narrative.

> Attention to such features leads not to a more "imaginative" reading of biblical narrative but to a more precise one; and since all these features are linked to discernible details in the Hebrew text, the literary approach is actually a good deal *less* conjectural than the historical scholarship that asks of a verse whether it contains possible Akkadian loanwords, whether it reflects Sumerian kinship practices, whether it may have been corrupted by scribal error.[19]

Precisely in discovering the *literary* art of the biblical narrative the interpreter begins to approach the elusive goal of discerning rational controls for the interpretation of ancient texts.

One of the most important contributions of Alter's work is to show that the latent and indeterminate quality of biblical narrative does not (*pace* Auerbach) call into question the Bible's authoritative claim but rather provides the essential clue for understanding the true nature of that claim.

> [A]n essential aim of the innovative technique of fiction worked out by the ancient Hebrew writers was to produce a certain indeterminacy of meaning, especially in regard to motive, moral character, and psychology. . . . Meaning, perhaps for the first time in narrative literature, was conceived as a *process*, requiring continual revision—both in the ordinary sense and in the etymological sense of seeing-again—continual suspension of judgment, weighing of multiple possibilities, brooding over gaps in the information provided. . . . The implicit theology of the

Hebrew Bible dictates a complex moral and psychological realism in biblical narrative because God's purposes are always entrammeled in history, dependent on the acts of individual men and women for their continuing realization. To scrutinize biblical personages as fictional characters is to see them more sharply in the multifaceted, contradictory aspects of their human individuality, which is the biblical God's chosen medium for His experiment with Israel and history.[20]

The world cast up by the Bible's realistic narratives is nuanced and complicated. Like all good stories, biblical narratives are filled with the unexpected, the sudden turn of plot, the coincidence—what Frank Kermode has called "peripeteia."[21] God's intentions and actions are rarely described and almost never depicted. Instead we are invited to view God's intentions in the actions of human agents, particularly in the actions of the people of Israel and of the man Jesus. Those actions are themselves deeply ambiguous. Abraham's faithfulness to the God of promise is tested by a heinous demand that he sacrifice his son. Isaac's blessing is passed on to the son who will become the namesake of God's people (Jacob/Israel) through an act of deception. Israel's liberator from slavery is a murderer, and their greatest king is a murderer and adulterer. Yet in and through these ambiguous human actions God is said to be acting. In the New Testament, God is depicted as acting through the agency of Jesus of Nazareth. Yet the Gospel writers show Jesus as uncertain about his own relation to God's reign, as reluctant to exercise his divine authority, as engaging in such unmessianic activities as sharing table fellowship with sinners. The climax of the narrative that purportedly depicts God's ultimate triumph is a story of the betrayal, rejection, and death of Jesus. The meaning of these stories is indeed latent and appears to call forth an act of extraordinary interpretation from the reader.

The stories do indeed call forth a remarkable act from the reader: Christians call it faith. But faith is neither blind nor irrational. It is an act of intellectual and personal commitment based upon a coherent reading of the biblical narratives. Faith is not the necessary or inevitable response to the texts, nor is the interpretation upon which the commitment of faith is based the only possible way of reading the stories. Faith not only accepts narrative obscurity, it presupposes that the meaning of the narratives is latent within their rich and nuanced depictions. But in responding with faith, the reader recognizes a followable world within the texts and accepts an invitation to enter that world. In so responding, the faithful reader becomes a disciple who acknowledges that the chief character in the stories (and the one who issues the invitation to faith and discipleship) is God. Such acceptance may appear to be a futile act based upon an implausible claim, particularly since God is rarely depicted in the stories and almost never engages the reader in direct address. I want to argue instead that the claim is ironic but true. Precisely in upsetting our expectations about how a god ought to be revealed, the stories introduce readers to Yahweh, God of promise who has raised Jesus from the dead.

Two brief examples must suffice to illustrate the way illumination emerges from obscurity in biblical narrative. The Hebrew Bible offers two apparently contradictory accounts of David's accession to kingship.[22] In the first (1 Samuel 16) God is clearly in control of events, summoning Samuel at the outset of the chapter to go to the household of Jesse the Bethlehemite, "for I have provided for myself a king among his sons" (16:1). Samuel proceeds to Bethlehem but is not told which of the sons he is to anoint king. Indeed, as he encounters Eliab, the oldest and strongest of Jesse's sons, Samuel assumes that he must be the chosen one of God. But God addresses Samuel and explains the difference between appearance and reality. "For Yahweh sees not as man sees; man looks on the outward appearance, but Yahweh looks on the heart" (16:7). Having learned his lesson, Samuel rejects the first seven sons, until finally Jesse sends for the youngest, David, who "is keeping the sheep" (16:11). Yahweh specifically directs Samuel to anoint David, "and the Spirit of Yahweh came mightily upon David from that day forward" (16:13). At the same time "the Spirit of Yahweh departed from Saul, and an evil spirit from Yahweh tormented him" (16:14). David is then appointed Saul's armor bearer, but his effective role is a reflection of the fact that he bears the Spirit of Yahweh. "And whenever the evil spirit from God was upon Saul, David took the lyre and played it with his hand; so Saul was refreshed, and was well, and the evil spirit departed from him" (16:23).

The second telling of the David story (1 Samuel 17:1—2 Samuel 5:5) contradicts the first in many details and is notable for the virtual absence of God from the narrative. In this long and detailed account we have a rich example of "realistic narrative." The story "adopts a style that draws us at once into the thick of historical experience."[23] David is portrayed as an epic hero who through courageous exploits earns his recognition as king. He slays Goliath and wins the accolades of all Israel. He marries Saul's daughter and develops a deep friendship with Saul's son, precisely as the king turns against David and seeks to kill him. David flees from Saul's wrath, and the two enemies have a series of dramatic encounters during which each spares the life of the other. Finally Saul is defeated in battle by the Philistines, and both Saul and Jonathan are killed. God's role in bringing these events to fruition is never mentioned in the lengthy narrative cycle. At the end of twenty long and exciting chapters, after the murder of Saul's son Ishbosheth, David is finally anointed king by the tribes assembled at Hebron. Though David has apparently "earned" this honor by his valiant action, the tribes remind David (and the reader) of God's hidden but active presence in the events. "In times past, when Saul was king over us, it was you that led out and brought in Israel; and Yahweh said to you, 'You shall be shepherd of my people Israel, and you shall be prince over Israel' " (2 Sam. 5:2).

The reference to Yahweh seems almost gratuitous unless the reader sees the previous twenty chapters in the context of the first telling of the story, in 1 Samuel 16. By juxtaposing these two apparently contradictory stories the "writer" is able to give witness to the complicated reality of a world in which historical agents are the vehicles for God's action. Through his role as chief character in this realistic story, David simultaneously enacts his own intentions and those of God.[24] Though in form and content the latter narrative is far more subtle and detailed, it reinforces the simple truth of the first story— that Israel's destiny is controlled by Yahweh's action. Both forms of narration are necessary to depict Yahweh's identity as a God who brings order from chaos both through his magisterial word and through his careful forming of human shape from the soil. God is not so much absent from as hidden within the biblical narrative. "God's promise to fulfill a design in history" is enacted in "the brawling chaos of historical experience."[25] The world illumined by the biblical narrative has all the complexity and untidiness of historical reality, but it is for precisely that reason an inhabitable world.

The Gospel of Matthew is characterized by a similar pattern of identification through hiddenness. Except in a few key events (e.g., Jesus' baptism and transfiguration) God is not a primary actor in Matthew's narrative; rather, God remains hidden within the actions of Jesus, who takes center stage in the Gospel drama. God's hiddenness is, however, an essential element of the New Testament message, for as readers discover the true identity of Jesus, they recognize that through this narrative God is inviting them to enter into a life of faith and discipleship.

The Gospel writer manipulates various techniques of emplotment and characterization in order to display the relation between Jesus and those who respond to his ministry, crucifixion, and death. As the Gospel's plot develops toward its climax in Jesus' crucifixion and resurrection, the reader is slowly drawn into the story through identification with those who respond to the unfolding of Jesus' identity. Precisely as Jesus' identity becomes fully manifested within the concluding events of the narrative, the flow of the action turns outward toward the reader, who is invited to become a character in the ongoing story. The author provides no final closure to the narrative, its unfinished quality allowing for continuation of the story in the life of the reader.

In the Gospel's earliest chapters Jesus is identified solely by reference to his mission. He is Son of God (a title accorded to Israel's kings), who has the unique role of saving "his people from their sins" (1:21). Matthew avoids all techniques of verisimilitude in these early chapters in order to identify Jesus simply as the fulfiller of Israel's promises, the one who enacts the saving intentions of the Father. The reader is thus presented with a stylized, almost symbolic figure, the Son of God, who is clearly linked to Israel and Israel's God. But of the personal, individual identity of Jesus, the reader knows virtually nothing.

In the middle chapters of the Gospel, Matthew begins the gradual depiction of Jesus' personal identity. As this section of the narrative unfolds, however, Jesus' relation to God becomes ambiguous. Precisely as Jesus begins to act as an agent in his own right, his relation to God's intentions becomes unclear. How can this "carpenter's son" be "the Christ, the son of the living God"? Matthew signals this ambiguity by displaying a wide range of responses to Jesus' teaching and healing ministry.

In chapter 9, a paralytic is brought to Jesus, "and when Jesus saw their faith, he said to the paralytic, 'Take heart, my son; your sins are forgiven' " (9:2). The scribes who overhear these words are shocked at the apparent act of blasphemy (9:4). The other onlookers who observe the miracle of healing are startled but feel an ambivalent response. "When the crowds saw it, they were afraid, and they glorified God, who had given such authority to men" (9:8).

The three reactions are typical of the responses to Jesus' ambiguous ministry. The scribes and other leaders have a growing sense of outrage at what they presume to be Jesus' blasphemous behavior. They recognize that he is exercising the authority granted only to the Son of God but cannot accept that he is the true inheritor of the promises to Israel. "With them is indeed fulfilled the prophecy of Isaiah which says: 'You shall indeed hear but never understand, and you shall indeed see but never perceive' " (13:14). The crowds continually marvel at Jesus and identify him as healer, teacher, the carpenter's son, and one who has authority, but never as Son of God. The identification of Jesus with the saving mission of the Son of God is made by only a few marginal characters in the Gospel narrative: a leper (8:2), a Roman centurion (8:10), the Gadarene demoniacs (8:29), a paralytic (9:2), a hemorrhaging woman (9:22), two blind men (9:29), a Canaanite woman (15:28), the woman in the house of Simon the leper (26:13), and the centurion at the foot of the cross (27:54). These outcasts and sinners alone respond with faith to Jesus' ministry.

The disciples play a particularly ambiguous role throughout the Gospel narrative. In 8:18–22, Matthew skillfully pairs the inquiry of a "scribe" concerning discipleship with that of a "disciple." Both speakers are shown to have a false or incomplete understanding of the demands of Jesus' call. In the story immediately following (8:23–27), Jesus calls the disciples men of little faith when they show fear in the midst of a storm. Their response to Jesus' act of calming the tempest anticipates the reaction of the crowds in the succeeding chapter: "What sort of man is this, that even winds and sea obey him?" (8:27). The disciples, like the scribes and the crowds, neither respond to Jesus' ministry with an act of faith nor recognize him as Son of God.

Even after Jesus grants the Twelve "authority over unclean spirits" (10:1) and shares with them "the secrets of the kingdom of heaven" (13:11), they still do not grasp the full significance of their call to discipleship. In chapter 14, Matthew constructs a second storm story, in which Peter seeks to respond to Jesus' call but fails "when he saw the wind" (14:30). Once again Jesus calls his would-be disciple a man of little faith (14:31). In the following chapter Matthew contrasts Peter's behavior to that of a persistent Canaanite woman whom the disciples seek to send away: "O woman, great is your faith!" (15:28).

It is significant that the theme of "little faith" is struck once more in the story of the confusion concerning bread (16:5–12), a vignette Matthew juxtaposes to his account of Peter's confession (16:13–20). In the latter story all the conflicting responses to Jesus' identity come together in the person of Peter. Peter becomes the first disciple to confess that Jesus is Son of God (16:16) but then immediately objects to Jesus' foretelling his suffering, death, and resurrection (16:23). For failing to understand that Jesus' Sonship and his followers' discipleship entail the cross, Peter, the blessed confessor, is condemned as a Satanic hindrance to Jesus' mission (16:23).

At this point in the narrative the reader can see the variety of responses that Jesus' ministry elicits. Confusion, wonder, offense, and faith are all possible not only for the characters in the story but also for the reader of the text. But in the midst of the ambiguity and uncertainty, one coherent pattern has emerged. To identify Jesus as Son of God, that is, to recognize Jesus as an agent enacting God's saving intentions, is to identify with those who live on the margins of society. And to follow Jesus' invitation to faith and discipleship is to embark on a journey of self-denial, crossbearing, and death. The text may be coherent and the world followable, but the path illumined by this text is hard, narrow, and fraught with danger. The demands of discipleship are far more daunting than the problems associated with hermeneutical obscurity!

The Gospel's concluding section brings the various themes together in a remarkable realistic narrative that summons the reader to enter

the world of the text. Jesus' passion is inaugurated in the home of an
outcast, Simon the leper. There an unnamed woman anoints Jesus
with ointment in preparation for burial (26:12). The disciples are
"indignant" at the waste of ointment, but Jesus offers an extraordinary reply: "Truly, I say to you, wherever this gospel is preached in
the whole world, what she has done will be told in memory of her"
(26:13). This intriguing story provides the initial frame for the entire
passion story, a story that ends with Jesus' body being hurriedly
placed in the tomb of Joseph of Arimathea, apparently without
proper preparation. Matthew, however, in contrast to Luke, does not
have the women who approach the grave on the day after the
Sabbath bear spices. Mary Magdalene and the other Mary come
simply "to see the sepulchre" (28:1), because the unknown woman
had already prepared Jesus for burial. At this early point in the
passion story the unknown woman, alone among Jesus' followers,
recognizes the destiny awaiting this Son of God. She thus provides a
contrasting witness to that of Peter, who confesses Jesus' Sonship
with his mouth but cannot bear the suffering consequences of that
confession.

Indeed, throughout the passion narrative the *women* remain the
silent followers of the crucified Messiah. They are the only witnesses
to the crucifixion (27:55–56). Mary Magdalene and the "other
Mary" go along to the sepulcher, hear the announcement of the
angel, and then become the first witnesses of the risen Christ (28:9).
Matthew describes their unequivocal reaction to Jesus' appearance:
"And they came up and took hold of his feet and worshiped him." By
contrast the male disciples function more to disrupt than to enhance
Jesus' mission. They fall asleep in Gethsemane; one of them betrays
him; another denies he even knows him; all of them forsake him and
flee at the moment of his arrest. None of them is numbered among
those who witness the crucifixion. Consequently the Son of God is
forced to face his final destiny alone. In the final gripping scenes of
the passion story Matthew ironically places the confession of Jesus'
identity as Son of God in the mouths of those who seek to destroy
him: Caiaphas (26:63), the taunting crowds (27:39, 43), and the
Roman centurion (27:54). Though they do not recognize what they
have said, they acknowledge that the true Son of God must be a
crucified Messiah.

Matthew brings his Gospel to a close with a story that shifts the flow of the narrative into the world of the reader:

> Now the eleven disciples went to Galilee, to the mountain to which Jesus had directed them. And when they saw him they worshiped him; but some doubted. And Jesus came and said to them, "All authority in heaven and on earth has been given to me. Go therefore and make disciples of all nations, baptizing them in the name of the Father and of the Son and of the Holy Spirit, teaching them to observe all that I have commanded you; and lo, I am with you always, to the close of the age." (28:16–20)

This beautifully crafted scene, which juxtaposes Jesus' promise to the doubting response of his disciples, functions to carry the world of the Gospel narrative into that of the reader. Matthew devises no dramatic confession of faith to conclude his story, nor does he introduce an explicit narrator to proclaim the Gospel's message. Rather, he uses Jesus' final act of promising to extend the Gospel's promise "to the whole world." Jesus, whose identity is depicted in the Gospel's narrative, now becomes the agent of promise as the story becomes a proclamation addressed to the reader. It is as if in the final episode Jesus directs his gaze for the first time outside the frame of the story and issues his promise directly to the reading audience. Thus the reader is invited to respond to the promise by entering the world of the text and joining with those on the mountain who worship Jesus.

Matthew creates "narrative space" for his readers within the Gospel story by reminding them that the fellowship of the disciples has been reduced in number. Only eleven of those originally called to follow still remain, and some of them continue to doubt. In addition, some not originally numbered among the Twelve have taken on the responsibilities of discipleship. The women alone continue to follow Jesus during the events of the passion and are the recipients of the angel's proclamation of his resurrection. Joseph of Arimathea, though not previously identified as one of the Twelve, is called a disciple of Jesus when he asks for the body. Thus the opportunity remains for the reader to join the company of disciples by responding in faith and undertaking the journey of discipleship.

By refusing to provide premature closure for his story, Matthew allows the narrative discourse to flow from the text to the reader. The reader who responds in faith is incorporated into the world of the

narrative, and the story continues through the community created by
the narrated promise. Precisely as the narrative provides definitive
identification of Jesus as Son of God, it also extends an invitation to
those who read the story. To recognize Jesus as Son of God is to join
those who worship Jesus on the mountain and to undertake the
arduous journey of faith and discipleship.

FAITH AND THE FOLLOWABLE WORLD
OF THE GOSPEL

Do these biblical stories present a coherent narrative that illumines
a followable world? I have tried to show that the stories are coherent,
and that they function to invite the reader into the world of the tale.
Whether the world we are invited to enter is inhabitable is not a
question that admits of a general answer. That the reader may refuse
to accept the story as God's personal promise of salvation is a possibility with which the text itself reckons. Moreover, the event that
establishes both God's identity and the narrative's promise is Jesus'
resurrection. To acknowledge the narrative as God's promise is to
confess that Jesus, the crucified, now lives. That confession requires
an act of faith that contradicts ordinary experience concerning the
finality of death. The Gospel narrative can be God's promise if, and
only if, he has raised Jesus from the dead. The Gospel's claim to truth
thus demands acceptance of a deeply paradoxical claim that lies at the
heart of the narrative's meaning.

A reader who takes the biblical narrative as God's personal promise
has performed an intelligible act based on a coherent reading of the
text. *How* the reader comes to such a decision is a complex matter not
easily subject to either hermeneutical or theological analysis. The act
of coming to believe is a person-specific act with both reasons and
causes related to the person's individual history. Theology ought not
seek to devise an explanatory theory for the subjective conditions for
the possibility of faith, for any such theory obscures both the diversity
and the mystery of human response to the gospel. To acknowledge
the biblical narrative as God's promise is to believe that the crucified
Jesus lives. Theology can explain neither why nor how persons come
to believe such a paradoxical claim. Theology can only show that the
sense of the biblical text does imply that assertion. If a reader hears

the biblical narrative as God's promise, theology can indicate that such a response is warranted given the content, force, and context of scripture. But the ultimate explanation of the mysterious movement from unbelief to faith lies beyond theology's descriptive competence. Whether the gospel's followable world leads to its promised end, we cannot know with certainty now, for "we see through a glass darkly." Whether this promising tale leads us through that door into a world of light we can know only if and when "we see face to face." For now we have only faith and discipleship and the identity of one who bids us come and follow. And for some, that is enough.

NOTES

1. Franz Kafka, *The Trial* (New York: Vintage Books, 1956), 267–69.
2. Frank Kermode, *The Genesis of Secrecy: On the Interpretation of Narrative* (Cambridge: Harvard Univ. Press, 1979).
3. Ibid., 28.
4. Ibid., 45.
5. Ibid., 145.
6. Hans Frei uses the arguments of the deconstructionists to challenge the hermeneutical tradition, in "The 'Literal Reading' of Biblical Narrative in the Christian Tradition: Does It Stretch or Will It Break?" in *The Bible and the Narrative Tradition,* ed. Frank McConnell (New York: Oxford Univ. Press, 1986), 36–77.
7. Friedrich Nietzsche, *The Gay Science,* in *The Portable Nietzsche,* trans. and ed. Walter Kaufmann (New York: Viking Press, 1954), 95–96.
8. Those who accept Nietzsche's position are led to an assertion of human autonomy that ultimately contradicts the Christian belief in human dependence upon God's grace. See, e.g., the constructivist position of Richard Rorty, *Consequences of Pragmatism: Essays, 1972–1980* (Minneapolis: Univ. of Minnesota Press, 1982): "When the secret police come, when the torturers violate the innocent, there is nothing to be said to them of the form 'There is something within you which you are betraying. Though you embody the practices of a totalitarian society which will endure forever, there is something beyond those practices which condemns you.' . . . There is nothing deep down inside us except what we have put there ourselves, no criterion that we have not created in the course of creating a practice, no standard of rationality that is not an appeal to such a criterion, no rigorous argumentation that is not obedience to our own conventions" (p. xlii).
9. Richard Bernstein, *Beyond Objectivism and Relativism: Science, Hermeneutics, and Praxis* (Philadelphia: Univ. of Pennsylvania Press, 1983), 18.
10. Richard Rorty has shown that the notion of "foundations of knowl-

edge" follows quite naturally from the use of visual epistemological meta-phors. If we think of knowledge as a privileged relation to the objects that propositions are about, "we will want to get behind reasons to causes, beyond argument to compulsion from the object known, to a situation in which argument would be not just silly but impossible, for anyone gripped by the object in the required way will be *unable* to doubt or to see an alternative. To reach that point is to reach the foundations of knowledge" (*Philosophy and the Mirror of Nature* [Princeton: Princeton Univ. Press, 1979], 159).

11. The existential importance of the search for the foundations of knowl-edge is evident not only in Nietzsche but also in the father of the foundational strategy, René Descartes. In describing his reaction to his exercise in methodic doubt, Descartes writes in the Second Meditation, "I feel as though I were suddenly thrown into deep water, being so disconcerted that I can neither plant my feet on the bottom nor swim to the surface" (*Discourse on Method and Meditations* [Indianapolis: Library of Liberal Arts, 1960], 81).

12. Among the best discussions of philosophical foundationalism are William P. Alston, "Two Types of Foundationalism," *Journal of Philosophy* 73 (1976): 165–85; Wilfrid Sellars, "Empiricism and the Philosophy of Mind," in *Science, Perception, and Reality* (New York: Humanities Press; London: Routledge & Kegan Paul, 1963), 127–96; Richard Rorty, "Intuition," in *Encyclopedia of Philosophy* (New York: Macmillan Co., 1967), 3:204–11; and idem, *Philosophy and the Mirror of Nature.* For discussions of foundationalism and religious belief, see Alvin Plantinga, "Is Belief in God Rational?" in *Rationality and Religious Belief,* ed. C. F. Delaney (Notre Dame, Ind.: Univ. of Notre Dame Press, 1979), 7–27; Jeffrey Stout, *The Flight from Authority; Religion, Morality, and the Quest for Autonomy* (Notre Dame, Ind.: Univ. of Notre Dame Press, 1981); and Nicholas Wolterstorff, *Reason within the Bounds of Religion* (Grand Rapids: Wm. B. Eerdmans, 1976). The two most thorough discussions of foundationalism and theology are Francis Fiorenza, *Founda-tional Theology* (New York: Crossroad, 1985), esp. 285–310; and Ronald F. Thiemann, *Revelation and Theology: The Gospel as Narrated Promise* (Notre Dame, Ind.: Univ. of Notre Dame Press, 1985), esp. 1–91.

13. Erich Auerbach, *Mimesis: The Representation of Reality in Western Liter-ature* (Princeton: Princeton Univ. Press, 1953), 12.

14. Ibid., 15.

15. I will use the expression "biblical story" even though I have not produced the exegetical arguments to justify that rather sweeping term. In this article, I offer only two illustrations of the Bible's narrative art as support for my argument that scripture portrays a followable world. For a more detailed exegetical justification of my argument, see my *Revelation and The-ology,* 112–56. In order to justify my case more fully, I would need to show that the themes I identify in these biblical narratives are reflected more broadly throughout the canon. I believe that the case can be made, but I have not yet undertaken that more complex exegetical task. For now the David

cycle and the Gospel of Matthew constitute the core of what I expect to be an expanding "working canon." For my use of that phrase, see David H. Kelsey, *The Uses of Scripture in Recent Theology* (Philadelphia: Fortress Press, 1975), 100–108.

16. Hans W. Frei, *The Eclipse of Biblical Narrative: A Study in Eighteenth and Nineteenth Century Hermeneutics* (New Haven: Yale Univ. Press, 1974).

17. In addition to the works already cited, see Thomas F. Tracy, *God, Action, and Embodiment* (Grand Rapids: Wm. B. Eerdmans, 1984).

18. See Frei, " 'Literal Reading' of Biblical Narrative." In this essay Frei argues that the *sensus literalis* is most appropriately understood as the way the text has commonly been used in the community. This understanding of the "literal sense" moves Frei away from the close textual analysis his earlier work seemed to call for.

19. Robert Alter, *The Art of Biblical Narrative* (New York: Basic Books, 1981), 21; Alter's emphasis. It is important to recognize that Alter does not offer literary analysis as an *alternative* to historical scholarship. Rather, he sees literary analysis as incorporating the insights of historical-critical investigation. On these points, see chap. 1.

20. Ibid., 12; Alter's emphasis.

21. Frank Kermode, *The Sense of an Ending: Studies in the Theory of Fiction* (New York: Oxford Univ. Press, 1967), 18.

22. See Alter, *Art of Biblical Narrative*, 147–54.

23. Ibid., 151.

24. One is reminded of Joseph's comment to his brothers in Gen. 50:20: "As for you, you meant evil against me, but God meant it for good."

25. Alter, *Art of Biblical Narrative*, 154. In this passage, Alter moves a bit too swiftly from realistic narrative to historical reality. His argument is intended to claim that through the use of the techniques of realistic narrative the biblical writers were able to depict a world fit to the "untidiness" of historical reality.

3

Scriptural authority and theological construction: the limitations of narrative interpretation

Maurice Wiles

The question is not whether scripture has authority for Christians. That it has is an analytic truth. Inherent in the designation of certain writings as scripture is an affirmation of their authoritative status.[1] The question is what kind of authority can rightly be ascribed to them. For authority can take many forms, and more than a few of those forms cannot properly be attributed to the Christian scriptures.

If we are to throw any light on this well-worn problem, it will be useful to place the issue in a broad historical perspective. The motives that gave rise to the initial emergence of an authoritative Christian scripture were, no doubt, mixed. The story can be presented as a quenching of the Spirit, a way of protecting the church from the kind of disconcerting prophetic challenge with which Jesus himself had faced the Judaism of his day. With Christopher Evans we may feel an urge to speak of the "curse of the canon."[2] But that would be at most a very partial presentation of the story—if a useful corrective to some uncritical versions of it. For the emergence of the Christian scriptures was the outcome also of a laudable concern to ensure that the faith not be led astray by the siren voices of contemporary cults or theosophies but remain true to its roots in the person of Jesus and the initial teaching of the apostles. But once the scripture was established as an indispensable authority in

42

relation to faith, the nature and extent of that authority did not cease to develop. All authorities have a tendency to overreach themselves. We know that to be widely true of people in authority; and since it is people who operate institutional forms of authority, it is true of them also. So there was a rapid expansion of the range of issues on which scripture was expected to speak. The history of early biblical exegesis shows scripture being asked to give precise answers to questions with which it was hopelessly ill suited to deal. The result was an overexegesis, which, since the answers it was being expected to produce had to come from somewhere, inevitably took the form of eisegesis. So although scripture provided the *form* of authority, the *substance* came more and more from the ecclesiastical powers who determined the tradition of how scripture was to be understood. The Reformation sought to rescue scripture from this subservience to ecclesiastical authority, and did so primarily by an appeal to its literal sense. But however effective such a move may have been in its immediate objective of challenging established ecclesiastical tradition, it had its own difficulties to contend with. It was not a very successful court of appeal in debate with Socinians or later Unitarians.[3] But the extent of its shortcomings came to light only more gradually, in the course of the attempt to come to terms with the rise of biblical criticism, described with masterly insight by Hans Frei in *The Eclipse of Biblical Narrative*.

It is not my purpose here, nor do I have the competence, to undertake detailed discussion of that complex story. But some very general points need to be made in the light of it as we approach the question of how we ought to understand the authority of scripture today. There has never been a golden age when scripture has functioned in an unproblematic manner in the life of the church. There have always been attendant difficulties. So if we find the issue beset with difficulty, we are not in that respect in a totally different position from our forebears in the faith. On the other hand, critical study of the Bible has enabled us to see things about the nature of the scriptural texts which were not so evident before and whose general truth cannot seriously be questioned. The new insights are of many kinds: the rootedness of the texts in the particular sociocultural understanding of their times; the variety of theological standpoints represented by the various scriptural authors; the differing degrees of historical accuracy characteristic of different scriptural writings. The shifts of understanding so baldly summarized here are extensive and cannot fail to affect the way in which the writings can function as authoritative scripture. We may not be in a *totally* different position from our forebears in the faith, but we are in a *significantly* different position. Neither theology nor the church more generally has yet taken the full measure of that significant difference. They have not come fully to terms with the new situation in which they find themselves. They still expect scripture to fulfill essentially the same role in the life of the church that it has fulfilled in the past, establishing the church's doctrine and providing firm guidance for its practical life. But the critical stance accepted by the great majority of scholars does not fit easily with that expectation. Where such a critical approach is broadly accepted in the church, it would seem that scholarly authorities must now control the way scripture is to be understood, as the ecclesiastical authorities used to do, and those scholarly authorities are in important respects less well oriented to mediate scripture in a form that will serve the deeper needs of men and women. It is not surprising that there are calls for a new reformation to free the scriptures once again, this time from the papacy of the scholar.[4]

Biblical scholars do not want to keep the scriptures to themselves. It would hardly be in their professional interest to do so. And more important, most of them embarked upon their field of study because of the religious value they apprehended in scripture as it was functioning in the life of the church. Various strategies have been designed specifically to address the problem of how scripture, critically understood, can continue to serve the needs of the church. In that aim, movements often contrasted as "radical" and "conservative" can be seen to be at one. Thus it was the aim of both Bultmann's program of demythologization and the "biblical theology" movement to present the heart of the scriptural message in a form appropriate for contemporary belief and action. Each approach has serious limitations that have been rehearsed often enough to need no further repetition here. What is more significant for our purpose is the way in which the two approaches sought to deal with the problem posed by the critical exegesis of the Bible, on the one hand, and the church's expectation of an authoritative role to be fulfilled by scripture, on the other. Certainly there was no repudiation of the critical approach as such.

But there was an attempt to find a form of it that would enable the Bible to continue to fulfill something very like its traditional role in the life of the church. Thus it was the understanding of scripture rather than its role in the life of the church that was the prime candidate for modification.

That way of approaching the task still dominates the theological scene. Today there are those who look to "narrative interpretation" to achieve the goal that has eluded earlier attempts. Critical study of the Bible, it is rightly claimed, has been conducted too exclusively in terms of *historical* criticism. Not all the scriptural writings are historical in character, except in the trivial sense that they all come from the past. But they are all *writings*, varied forms of literature. Any insights from literary criticism are therefore to be welcomed as likely to redress the balance and correct the lopsidedness resulting from over-emphasis on historical criticism. A more balanced approach, it may be hoped, will have the potential to overcome the present impasse, without requiring any repudiation of the valid insights of earlier critical work.

Narrative interpretation is a particularly attractive form of literary assessment for the biblical scholar, because it concentrates on a category of literature that stands close to historical writing. In particular it is readily applicable to the Gospels, which, if not "history" in a strict sense (as we are constantly reminded they are not), are certainly, in Frei's phrase, "history-like."[5] There is no question about the value of such an approach to certain scriptural writings that are of a clearly narrative form. But narrative interpretation is being pressed into far wider service at the present time. "Narrative," says Ronald Thiemann, "highlights both a predominant literary category within the Bible and an appropriate theological category for interpreting the canon as a whole."[6] The wider role must indeed be claimed for narrative if the approach is to make a significant contribution to our more general problem. And that is certainly what Thiemann looks to it to provide. "The turn to narrative," he asserts a little later, "is one way of providing an alternative to that predominant modern tradition" which affirms "the primacy of anthropology in modern theology."[7] But can narrative properly fulfull this larger task?

Thiemann is by no means alone in looking to it to do so. Thus Charles Wood speaks of how the "overall narrative character of the canon . . . suggests that the canon might plausibly be construed as a story which has God as its 'author.' "[8] And George Lindbeck answers his own question "What is the literary genre of the Bible as a whole in its canonical unity?" by claiming that the diverse materials contained within it "are all embraced, it would seem, in an overarching story that has the specific literary features of realistic narrative"; he then goes on to describe the "primary function of the canonical narrative" as " 'to render a character . . . , offer an identity description of an agent,' namely God."[9] To treat scripture in this way is not something that can easily be done without going back on the genuine insights that critical study has engendered. All the authors I have cited are well aware of the difficulties involved but believe that they can in fact be overcome. In my view the difficulties are more damaging than the authors believe.

It needs to be said at the outset that there is no necessary unity to the contents of the canon apart from the fact that they are the documents to which the church has chosen to ascribe an authoritative status as scripture. The process of that choice was a gradual one lasting more than two centuries, with different concerns predominating at different times. It has certainly been claimed from early times that the scriptural writings do constitute a unity, but whether they really do is an entirely different matter. Wood is very conscious of this and speaks of the hermeneutical use of the canon as grounded in a "decision" to "read scripture *as if it were a whole,* and as if the author of the whole were God."[10] On the face of it, the double "as if" suggests a twofold arbitrariness. In the past when the divine authorship of scripture was affirmed without any qualifying "as if," it could serve as a justification for reading scripture as a whole, however difficult the task itself might prove to be. Wood's use of the "as if" may save him from having to produce an account of divine inspiration to give specific substance to the concept of divine authorship, but it also prevents him from using the claimed divine authority in an explanatory role in relation to the reading of scripture as if it were a whole. The quasi-divine authorship is a part of the description of what we decide to do, not a reason for the decision. As Thiemann points out, some attempt is made to rescue the act of decision from sheer arbitrariness by claiming that this way of reading scripture is to read it in its "literal sense," where literal sense is understood as that "sense whose discernment has become second nature to members of the community."[11] But two problems assail such a claim. In the first place, it is questionable how close Wood's narrative reading of the canon under the influence of modern literary theory really is to the way it was read in precritical times.[12] But even setting that difficulty aside, the claim does not help very much toward getting rid of the arbitrariness of the decision. For it amounts simply to saying that it is a decision to go on regarding scripture as it has been regarded in the past, whatever new insights about its nature may have arisen in the meantime.

Having once made the decision that scripture is to be read as a unity, there is still a choice to be made about the nature of that unity. "Narrative," as Thiemann puts it, "is one of a number of possible images around which the diverse materials of the canon can be organized."[13] The choice is not a straightforward one. There are many elements within the canon, such as the wisdom literature, which do not easily fall within such a category. Moreover, even within the more explicitly narrative material that certainly bulks large within the scriptural corpus, there is, as Thiemann rightly points out, the further problem of the "irreducible diversity of the integral narratives" that are found there.[14] Nevertheless, if a choice of category has to be made, the choice of narrative is not unreasonable. Narratives or stories can be wide ranging and allow for various subplots within an ordered whole. But when the concept of narrative is applied as broadly as it is in its application to the canon as a whole, it is questionable whether it is right to claim of it at that level, as Lindbeck does, that it "has the specific literary features of realistic narrative." The term when applied to the whole of scripture has been stretched beyond the point at which such precise description is appropriate.

But more significant is the difficulty of determining how this varied literature is to be read as one story. Lindbeck speaks of the "canonical narrative" as if, once the possibility of speaking in such terms has been raised, the substance of the story is clear. Almost any combination of things can be read as one story, given sufficient ingenuity— just as the later findings of science *could* be incorporated into a Ptolemaic understanding of the universe, given sufficient epicycles, special cases, etc. But where twists of fortune and shifts of character in some proffered narration become excessive, we would say to anyone who still wanted to call it one story, that in that case it was a very bad story. Is there a sufficiently coherent canonical narrative to provide us with an "identity description" of God?

We can approach the problem by way of what may appear at first to be a more straightforward case. The Gospels, we have already acknowledged, are more clearly examples of narrative than is scripture as a whole, and may properly be said to provide us with an "identity description" of Jesus. Or does one need to say "identity descriptions"? Ought we to speak of the story of Jesus or the stories of Jesus?[15] It depends on the context within which we are speaking and the degree of specificity with which we hope to give our identity description. For certain purposes and at certain levels of detail, the differences between the identity descriptions provided by Matthew, Mark, Luke, and John are highly significant. But for other purposes, we can legitimately speak of the story of Jesus in the singular. Certainly the church has tried to do so, though not without strain, and in its christological definitions has sought to offer an identity description of Jesus that unifies that offered by John with those which derive from the other three evangelists. If the difficulties inherent in the narrative interpretation of the Gospels in relation to the figure of Jesus are significant, are they not likely to be much greater in any attempt to read the canonical narrative as offering us an identity description of God? Of the many problems entailed by such an undertaking, one merits special mention. If we take seriously, as we should, the apocalyptic emphases in the New Testament, the most natural way of reading the canon as a narrative account of the agency of God involves seeing the story as leading up to an imminent denouement—which did not happen in anything like the way suggested. Does that fact affect the story itself? Or is it to be regarded as outside and therefore irrelevant to, the canonical narrative and its authoritative identity description of God?

What we have to acknowledge is that, even if the concept of reading the Bible as one story is allowed, it is not at all clear what that one story is. The approach may be a useful antidote to fundamentalist and similar ways of understanding the authority of scripture. But it does not make a significant contribution of its own. Nicholas Lash writes in a way that might suggest that it does: "As the history of the meaning of the text continues, we can and must tell the story differently. But we do so under constraint: what we may *not* do, if it is this text which we are to continue to perform, is to tell a different story."[16] But that is to restate the problem, not to provide an answer to it. Admittedly Lash has his own account of what constitutes the story and how its essential character is to be determined; it is the "answer (expressed in the text)" to the "question to which the text originally sought to provide an answer." But whether there was one such question and, if so, what it was are themselves questions to which a host of different answers might reasonably be offered. And there is no way of assessing the various possible answers that does not pay careful attention to the work of the critical scholar. The insistence on the need to tell the same story does nothing to rescue the scriptures from the alleged tyranny of the scholar—though it may fruitfully suggest that the scholar needs to be better trained in a wider range of disciplines.

For the writers whose works I have principally been discussing, what is involved in reading the Bible as one story is seen somewhat differently. It is a way of reading scripture to be clearly distinguished from understanding it as historical source.[17] It has its own grounding, whether that is located (as by Wood) in the sense of scripture "which has become second nature to the members of the community" or (as by Thiemann) in the sense of God's prevenience as it prevailed in an intellectual and cultural atmosphere prior to our own (which he regards "as an indispensable background belief within the logic of Christian faith").[18] Such procedures succeed in insulating this way of reading scripture from the acids of recent and contemporary criticism, without having to deny the validity of that criticism within its own restricted sphere. Indeed, the approach can be developed in a way that insures against the likelihood of almost any change of understanding whatsoever. Since Lindbeck regards the traditional trinitarian and christological dogmas as grammatical rules determining correct Christian usage, and since those dogmas are immensely influential in determining how the biblical story is read, even the possibility of any significant change of reading is ruled out in principle.[19] The outcome is a retreat into the ghetto of a world created rather than illuminated by the scriptural text—indeed created by a particular way of reading the text.

I have ventured, in an article in honor of Professor Frei, to react

somewhat sharply to the writings of three men all of whose work
bears explicit and implicit testimony to his influence upon them. But
Frei, as I know to my great benefit, would be the last person to regard
theological disagreement as an act of disrespect or a betrayal of
friendship. My reaction has been sharp because it seems to me that
when narrative is used as the key concept in an attempted rehabilita-
tion of the role of scripture in the church, the result can be dan-
gerously misleading. That is not to deny the magnitude or urgency of
the problem these writers are tackling with courage, nor the possibility that narrative interpretation may have a useful role to play in
the attempt to find some answer to that problem. It is incumbent
therefore on the one who makes such criticisms to offer suggestions
about how one might best address the problem. This is the more
pressing since one of the reasons for Lindbeck's advocacy of a
"postliberal" theology is precisely the failure of liberal theologians to
deal effectively with the issue.[20]

I suggested earlier that the main strategy has been to look for some
particular form of critical study that will enable scripture to continue
to play a virtually unchanged role in the life of the church. But it may
be that we would do better to look for a modification of the role
expected of scripture in the church than to search for a more con-
genial style of criticism.[21] The old adage speaks of "the church to
teach, the Bible to prove." It is this directly probative employment of
the Bible that needs to be renounced. It is indefensible, and we ought
to be grateful to the critical studies that have released us from its
burden and not seek to be "entangled again with the yoke of bondage" (Gal. 5:1). For the view of the Bible as having directly probative
force is not only untenable but distracting. As John Barton puts it in a
perceptive article, there are important "positive aspects of the Bible
which are lost sight of as soon as debate begins to circle around the
small and sterile issue of whether 'biblical teaching' is *binding*.[22] But
does this amount to an abandonment of the idea of the Bible as
authoritative at all—and therefore, since I argued that the notion of
authority is implicit in the notion of scripture, the abandonment of
the Bible as scripture?[23]

"Authority," as we have earlier said, can take many forms, and the
word has a wide range of connotation. But its popular understanding
is closely limited to the binding or probative role that we are calling

into question. Thus it may well be that although the concept is still lawful, the term has become inexpedient. No contributor to *The Myth of God Incarnate*[24] can be unaware of such a phenomenon in relation to our theological vocabulary. Indeed, the abandonment of the use of the word "authority" in this context has already been canvassed in the church.[25] If we do succeed in extricating ourselves, not only in theory but in feeling, from the sense of scripture as *binding*, and assist ourselves in this difficult task by forgoing the use of the term "authority," what will be the implications for the life of the church? And what are the uses of scripture that will emerge as important, not on the basis of preassigned roles that it is required to fulfill, but in the light of the kind of resource it is actually proving itself to be?

The first result of learning to see scripture as an indispensable resource rather than as a binding authority will be to help us perceive it better. It is well known how extensively presuppositions and prior expectations can affect what is perceived. The conviction that what we are seeking to perceive has binding authority over us is particularly likely to distort our vision. Freed from that presumption, the church will be better able to hear what the scriptural authors were saying and thus to understand the nature of its own origins. The little glimpses of reality that this will make possible will not always be easy to bear. But in the long run such understanding can only help the church to be truer to its own given character.

More specifically, it will make it easier for the church to acknowledge the varied nature of the stories to be found in the scriptural record, without immediately going on to clip the wings of their invigorating variety in the interest of an already assumed unity. I referred earlier to the way in which the stories of Jesus have come, with the help of agreed christological doctrine, to be read as one story. But the grammatical rules for reading the Christian story (as Lindbeck regards them) have served the cause of institutional control at least as much as the cause of religious truth. For it is not only the diversity of stories that we have to recognize but the degree to which unresolved conflicts and controversies lie at the heart of so many of the writings that make up the New Testament.[26] And having come to a fuller recognition of that, we will be the more ready to acknowledge the continuing presence of diversity and conflict in the later church, not simply as evidence of a sadly fallen later age but as a characteristic of how things are, for good as well as for ill. Thus Stephen Sykes has recently argued in the light of such an understanding of the New Testament that Christianity is an "essentially contested concept" and that "Christian identity is . . . not a state but a process; a process, moreover, which entails the restlessness of a dialectic, impelled by criticism."[27] For if the truth by which we are to live is not authoritatively given in the past but continually to be discovered in the present, such a process of discovery is bound to involve experimentation, with attendant error and conflict.

Theology, indeed, has always been a more creative enterprise than it has been keen to admit. It has sought, sometimes consciously but more often unconsciously, to conceal its originality by presenting its new vision as a restoration, or at least a reinterpretation, of the past. This is a common enough ploy in social and political life, but it has been exacerbated by belief in an authoritatively binding scripture to a degree that has involved serious and unhealthy misperception of what has in fact been going on. Yet a religion of the Spirit ought not be afraid of creative novelty, even though appeal to the Spirit cannot legitimately be made to justify any particular instance of creativity.[28]

In the last three paragraphs I have tried to sketch a revised context of expectation that might make possible ways of using scripture which would be both religiously constructive and true to critical insights. What form might such uses take?

In the article from which I have already quoted, John Barton lists three positive aspects of the Bible that, far from depending on its being regarded as a binding authority, are likely to function better in the absence of any such attitude. The Bible is (1) the "primary . . . evidence for the events that lie at the source of Christian faith," (2) a "collection of theological reflections from the classic periods in which Jewish and Christian faith was forming," and (3) a "body of literature whose power to inform the lives of those who read it is amply attested in many ages."[29] In all three respects the importance of the Bible for Christian faith and life is obvious. To pursue the Bible's implications in each of these ways is to deepen one's understanding of this fundamental Christian resource. And since what emerges from such reflection is not to be regarded as directly binding on the Christian, the tension between faith and critical study is less severe.

The transforming power of literature works in any event by its appeal to the imagination and its widening of our sense of the possible rather than by any form of binding teaching. But in the other two respects the revised role being proposed for scripture within the church is more significant. The fact that the earliest theological reflection is rooted in cultural and religious assumptions that we may not share (about, e.g., divine intervention or apocalyptic expectation) becomes less problematic. For that theological reflection is not something we have to take over for ourselves, even in some reinterpreted guise, but is rather something to be used as a resource for our own theological exploration and construction. Similarly, the fact that our historical inquiries leave (and in the nature of the case seem likely always to leave) a large measure of uncertainty about the nature of the founding events of the faith also becomes less problematic. For the precise form of those events is not the heart of the matter. Indeed, the contemporary stress on the narrative character of much biblical writing is not simply a trimming of our sails to the prevailing winds but is in line with the nature of the scriptural sources themselves. Much of the Old Testament, as well as of the Gospels, is historylike rather than historical, not simply in that it has a narrative structure but also in that, while relating to real historical events, it is prepared to redescribe the events with a remarkable freedom born not of any revised historical knowledge but of the revised requirements of the changing experience of faith. Scripture itself can hardly therefore be appealed to as a witness against a similar freedom on the part of those who use it as a resource for their faith.

Nevertheless, objections certainly will be raised against the approach I suggest, and four potential difficulties demand consideration:

1. The uses that I have been describing, it may be argued, do not do justice to the distinctiveness of the canon. In each category—historical evidence, early theological reflection, and transformative literary power—there are other writings that can be called upon, as indeed they are, just as or even more appropriately than some of the writings included in the scriptural canon. That fact must simply be accepted. There are no objective criteria that can justify our treating the scriptural writings as if they were distinctive; to treat them in that way is only possible on the basis of an "as if."[30] The particular canon we have received is a matter of contingent fact. But the recognition that

its precise contours do not correspond to any set of determinable criteria should not lead us to suggest the abandonment or the modification of the canon as such. The existence of a universally acknowledged set of writings is of proven value, a value that would be freed of its attendant disadvantages if the writings were freed of the claim to binding authority. Two illustrations of that value will suffice. In the first place, the existence of an agreed canon helps to provide a common sensibility for the Christian community as a whole; the canon is compact enough to serve that role and also varied enough to relate as a basic resource of faith to the very wide range of human needs. Second, the canon's distinctive status enables it to stand apart in its historic singularity from the changing patterns of Christian belief, and so to serve as a potential source of prophetic correction over against the ever-present danger of Christians' being carried along uncritically by the beguiling streams of contemporary thought.[31]

2. The approach I have adopted, it may be argued, does nothing to rescue scripture from the tyranny of the scholar and restore it to its rightful place in the ordinary life of the church. Instead it increases the scholar's power by ascribing to him or her not only special skills in relation to interpretation but an innovative function in the form of theological construction also. Certainly the contribution of the scholar remains important. One could hardly expect otherwise, for what the scholar does is only a more concentrated form of what is involved in any reflective reading of scripture—and it cannot be the church's goal to exclude that. But the language of "tyranny" is out of place. For in the revised account that I am offering, neither scripture nor theology is being afforded any prescriptive role to which the term "tyranny" might be suited. Scripture and theology are both important contributors to the never-ceasing process of discovering the most appropriate forms of Christian belief and practice. But that is a process in which neither has an exclusive role or any right of veto. For it is a process in which all Christians, out of their varied experience of the life of faith, have a contribution to make.

3. A further result of this approach is that it will no longer be possible for the church to pronounce on some issues of traditional Christian doctrine in a way that it has seemed important to the church in the past to be able to do. That too must be accepted. Similar limits have been accepted many times in the past. A mythological

understanding of the story of the Fall in Genesis has made it impossible to affirm a doctrine of original sin which will any longer function as an explanation of the presence of evil in God's world.[32] So the understanding of scripture outlined here makes it impossible to speak of the virginal conception or the bodily resurrection of Christ in the definite way that has been thought requisite in the past. But we ought not think as if there were a fixed agenda of topics on which Christian doctrine has to pronounce or die. Christian doctrine is the process of making Christian sense of what the evidence of scripture and experience makes available to us. Doctrine exists for the sake of the church, not the church for the sake of doctrine.[33]

4. Finally, it may be objected that the church will be left with no clear message to proclaim or to live by. Doctrine, it may be said, has been turned into so elusive a phenomenon that it would serve better as the basis for an academic seminar than for a life of faith. But the older approach has always had to face the difficulty of the link between the *fides quae* and the *fides qua*, between the doctrinal content of belief and its effective integration into the life of faith. And on that score our approach may actually have a positive contribution to make. For if the theological task itself, the determination of what can properly be believed, is something that has continually to be discovered in the light of changing experience, then the integration of that belief with life is not a second, distinct activity but an integral part of the process of discovery. The insights of a narrative theology point in the same direction. For the narrative structure of much in the scriptural resource of faith is appropriate to the calling of Christians to enact the story of their lives in the light of it. And the sacramental practice of Baptism and Eucharist is well adapted to that goal.

The account I have given of the role that scripture should play in the church is similar to that in which James Barr speaks of a " 'soft' idea of authority,"[34] and to David Tracy's description of scripture as a religious classic.[35] In spite of the fact that my account corresponds pretty closely to widespread practice, I have described it as something likely to be spoken against. That is not altogether surprising if Christianity is itself an "essentially contested concept."[36] But there are also the latent guilt feelings that one ought to be ascribing to scripture a "hard" rather than a "soft" authority. It is those guilt feelings that I hope to exorcise, so that with fewer anxious backward glances the

church can concentrate on the positive potential of the uses appropriate to the present and the future. In particular I have argued that
narrative interpretation has a valuable contribution to make to that
process, but that if allowed too dominant a role within theology it can
have a contrary effect.

NOTES

1. See David H. Kelsey, *The Uses of Scripture in Recent Theology* (Philadelphia: Fortress Press, 1975), 89.

2. See Christopher Evans, *Is "Holy Scripture" Christian? and Other Questions*
(London: SCM Press, 1971), 1–36. The phrase "the curse of the canon" is
appropriately part of the oral tradition of Evans's teaching, not committed to
writing!

3. See, e.g., the judgment of Leonard Hodgson in relation to the unitarian
controversies in Britain in the 17th and 18th cents., that *"on the basis of
argument which both sides held in common,* the unitarians had the better case.
They could counter their opponents' biblical exegesis with interpretations
equally, if not more, convincing" (Leonard Hodgson, *The Doctrine of the Trinity*
[London: Nisbet & Co., 1943], 223; Hodgson's emphasis).

4. See Colin E. Gunton, *Enlightenment and Alienation: An Essay Towards a
Trinitarian Theology* (Grand Rapids: Wm. B. Eerdmans, 1985), 111.

5. For this term, see Hans W. Frei, *The Eclipse of Biblical Narrative: A Study
in Eighteenth and Nineteenth Century Hermeneutics* (New Haven: Yale Univ.
Press, 1974), 11–12.

6. Ronald F. Thiemann, *Revelation and Theology: The Gospel as Narrated
Promise* (Notre Dame, Ind.: Univ. of Notre Dame Press, 1985), 83.

7. Ibid., 85.

8. Charles M. Wood, *The Formation of Christian Understanding: An Essay in
Theological Hermeneutics* (Philadelphia: Westminster Press, 1981), 100.

9. George A. Lindbeck, *The Nature of Doctrine: Religion and Theology in a
Postliberal Age* (Philadelphia: Westminster Press, 1984), 120–21 (citing Kelsey, *Uses of Scripture,* 48).

10. Wood, *Formation of Christian Understanding,* 70; Wood's emphasis.

11. Thiemann, *Revelation and Theology,* 65–66 (citing Wood, *Formation of
Christian Understanding,* 43).

12. For a different assessment of what was implied by earlier claims that
scripture was a God-given unity, see John Barton, *Oracles of God: Perceptions of
Ancient Prophecy in Israel* (London: Darton, Longman & Todd, 1986), 149–50.

13. Thiemann, *Revelation and Theology,* 86.

14. Ibid.

15. See Leslie Houlden, "Trying to Be a New Testament Theologian," in

Alternative Approaches to New Testament Study, ed. A. E. Harvey (London: SPCK, 1985), 139.

16. Nicholas Lash, "Performing the Scriptures," in *Theology on the Way to Emmaus* (London: SCM Press, 1986), 44. Despite the title of the article, the actual discussion is exclusively in terms of the New Testament.

17. See Wood, *Formation of Christian Understanding* 72, 89.

18. For the first approach, see the passages cited in n. 11 above; for the second, see Thiemann, *Revelation and Theology*, 5, 75–78.

19. See Lindbeck, *Nature of Doctrine*, 92–96, 104–8.

20. The subtitle of Lindbeck's book *The Nature of Doctrine* is *Religion and Theology in a Postliberal Age*.

21. See pp. 44–45 above. See also J. L. Houlden, *Connections: The Integration of Theology and Faith* (London: SCM Press, 1986), 35–37.

22. John Barton, "The Place of the Bible in Moral Debate," *Theology* 88 (1985): 207; Barton's emphasis.

23. Cf. the title of an article by Krister Stendahl: "The Bible as a Classic and the Bible as Holy Scripture" (*Journal of Biblical Literature* 103 [1984]: 3–10).

24. John Hick, ed., *The Myth of God Incarnate* (Philadelphia: Westminster Press, 1978).

25. See James Barr, *The Bible in the Modern World* (New York: Harper & Row, 1973), 25. The whole section (pp. 23–30) is a useful survey of the various uses of "authority" in relation to the Bible.

26. See John Fenton, "Controversy in the New Testament," in *Studia Biblica 1978*, 3 vols., ed. E. A. Livingstone, Journal for the Study of the Old Testament Supplement Series 11 (Sheffield, England: JSOT Press, 1979–80), 3: 97–100, with its judgment that there are only "three books of the New Testament in the production of which, as far as one can see, controversy between Christians played no part" (p. 106).

27. Stephen Sykes, *The Identity of Christianity: Theologians and the Essence of Christianity from Schleiermacher to Barth* (Philadelphia: Fortress Press, 1984), 285. For the New Testament, see chap. 1; for Sykes's use of W. B. Gallie's "essentially contested concept," see pp. 251–56.

28. See Maurice Wiles, "In What Context Does It Make Sense to Say 'God Acts in History'?" in *Witness and Existence*, ed. Philip E. Devenish and George L. Goodwin (Chicago: Univ. of Chicago Press, forthcoming).

29. See n. 19 above.

30. Cf. Wood's use of that phrase, discussed on pp. 46–47, above.

31. The themes adumbrated in this paragraph are more fully discussed in my essay "The Uses of 'Holy Scripture,'" in *What about the New Testament? Essays in Honour of Christopher Evans*, ed. Morna Hooker and Colin Hickling (London: SCM Press, 1975), 155–64.

32. See Maurice F. Wiles, *God's Action in the World* (London: SCM Press, 1986), 43–44.

33. See Houlden, *Connections,* 35–37.

34. See Barr, *The Bible in the Modern World,* 27.

35. See David Tracy, *The Analogical Imagination: Christian Theology and the Culture of Pluralism* (New York: Crossroad, 1981), chaps. 3–5.

36. See n. 27 above.

4

Theology and the plain sense

Kathryn E. Tanner

As a Christian theologian, Hans Frei has championed the primacy of the "plain sense" of scripture, understood as the narrative depiction of the identity of Jesus Christ. Beginning with *The Eclipse of Biblical Narrative*, Frei has sought the conditions for an appreciation of that sort of reading. In his most recent work he suggests that this appreciation is promoted best not through any general account of texts and their interpretation (literary or philosophical) but through an approach to the Christian use of scripture similar to that of an eclectic, nonreductionist social scientist.[1] Theologians who approach scripture with the contextualist bent of interpretive social scientists rather than with a philosopher's penchant for generalities are the ones most likely to read it in the traditional way that Frei advocates.[2] By making this connection between a social-science approach to scripture and an appreciation of scripture's plain sense, Frei's concern for the future of a certain way of reading scripture becomes a more general concern about the future of theology. Here his work dovetails with that of George Lindbeck, who in *The Nature of Doctrine* attempts both to suggest the usefulness of a social-science approach in addressing theological issues and to argue for a form of theology congruent with it.

Should an approach like that of a social scientist help bring a Christian understanding of the plain sense of scripture into view, the positive task becomes, for Frei, to describe "how and in what specific kind of context a certain kind of reading functions."[3] The general enterprise of explaining what that sort of reading is about turns into the narrowly circumscribed agenda of specifying how such a form of reading works within specifically Christian sociolinguistic contexts. Taking up the task that Frei sets, my essay begins to sketch a function of appeals to the plain sense of scripture within Christian communities.[4] The intent is to show how appeals to a plain sense of scripture work to distinguish those communities—to shape or structure a distinctive convention of Christian practice. Specifically, I shall suggest that the plain sense of scripture works in a Christian context to form a tradition that is self-critical, pluralistic, and viable across a wide range of geographical differences and historical changes of circumstance. The argument will proceed by way of a theological inquiry that more closely resembles sociological or anthropological investigation of communal practices than it does traditional philosophy prior to Ludwig Wittgenstein, Michel Foucault, Jacques Derrida, and Richard Rorty. By pushing to an extreme the association between theology and social science, I hope to contribute to two lines of conversation that Frei's work opens up: one concerns the importance of the Christian understanding of the plain sense of scripture for a Christian form of life; the other concerns the potential benefits and risks of a theological procedure whose closest analogue is some form of social science.

THE PLAIN SENSE AS A FUNCTION
OF COMMUNITY PRACTICE

Before beginning the actual argument, we need to discuss more thoroughly the general question of what it might mean to focus on the *function* of the notion of a plain sense in the course of a theological investigation that is almost sociological in nature: what, more exactly, is the character of the theological enterprise engaged in here, and what is at stake in trying to give a functional account of the plain sense?

Theology, on the kind of approach taken here, is a part of the self-description of the Christian community.[5] Theology is the precipitate of the Christian community's turn on itself in moments of self-reflection. It has for its object the communal practices of an ongoing tradition of Christian adherents; its subject matter, in other words, is the Christian religion as that is constituted by distinctive habits of action, belief, and attitude.

To the extent that communal practices are the theologian's subject matter, he or she may consider Christianity much the way a sociologist or anthropologist might—as a kind of sociocultural frame within which individuals are socialized; as a communal structure that shapes the experience, beliefs, expectations, and behaviors of individuals as participants. Specific beliefs, actions, and attitudes are understood in terms of the place they hold within a wider network of community practices. Communal practice as a whole is the touchstone, therefore, in unpacking the significance of particulars: a holistic bias requires any account of particulars to be given within an overall description of the ways things customarily proceed and hang together (or not) within a community. The theologian, unlike the sociologist or anthropologist, undertakes this sort of description as a member of the community investigated. The project of describing community practice is set by the religious community under discussion and not by a scientific community separate from it. The theologian engaged in such a project is simply filling a place that opens up within the sociocultural practice of a religious community complex enough to include reflexive pursuits: talk, action, attitudes about itself.

On this account of theological investigation, should a particular notion (like "God") or belief (like "God is good") come up for discussion insofar as it figures in communal practice, the interpretive strategy of the theologian is not first to isolate such a belief or notion for identification of its meaning or reference, experiential expressiveness, rational justification, or evidential support—the traditional preoccupations of philosophers. Rather, the theologian accounts for the belief or notion by situating it in the framework of communal practice and considering its function or use within the form of life whose construction it is. Within the course of this procedure, epistemological questions may arise (though clearly they need not) to the extent that preoccupations with meaning, reference, and so on, are actually a part of the use of a belief or notion in its communal context. In any case, the interpretive approach to a particular involves determining its site within the discursive field of other communal conventions, its position within the rest of what goes to make up a specific form of life. Even when epistemological matters come up intracontextually, the theologian's approach is itself fundamentally "a-semantic": reasons end (and begin), in other words, with the consideration of behavioral habits (broadly construed), with "This is what we do." Whatever the actual function a particular turns out to have in context, the interpretive procedure of the theologian involves locating that particular within a basically a-semantic weave of conventions and practices. As a result, what used to be known as philosophical theology has its place taken by a sociological sort of theology; or better, the traditional concerns of philosophical theology, should they be relevant in a Christian context, are encompassed by the theological analogue of a sociological procedure.

If one uses this sort of theological approach to discuss the Christian notion of scripture's having a plain sense, one arrives first of all at a very formal, functional definition of "plain sense" comparable, I believe, to those given for "scripture" and "canon" by David Kelsey.[6] According to Kelsey, as I read him, to say that a text is a part of either scripture or a sacred canon is not to ascribe a property to the text: in neither case is it to make an informative remark about the character of the text itself. It is rather to say something about the way the text functions in the religious community; it is to say something about the way the text is used, about what is *done with* the text. To call a text scripture is to say, in a Christian context, that the text is to be used (in some fashion or other) to shape, nurture, and reform the continuing self-identity of the church.[7] To classify a number of texts under the rubric of "canon" is to say that "*just these* writings are sufficient" for those purposes.[8] Similarly, the plain sense of scripture is not a property of those texts that happen to function as scripture for the Christian community. One does not specify the meaning of the notion, therefore, by any philosophical discussion of hermeneutic circumstances or epistemological preconditions for the appropriation of texts in general—discussion that might tempt one to try to identify the plain sense per se with, for example, "what the text simply says," the "text's own immanent sense," the "text's sense when the expositor is a purely passive or transparent recorder of objective meaning," or the "text's sense without the imposition of extratextual categories." The plain sense is instead viewed as a function of communal use: it is the obvious or direct sense of the text according to a *usus loquendi* established by the community in question.[9] Most generally, the plain sense is that sense of the text "normally acknowledged as basic [by the community], regardless of whatever other constructions might also properly be put upon the text . . . , [that] sense whose discernment has become second nature to the members of the community."[10] The plain sense is a consensus reading, interpretation having distilled into conventional opinion when a certain approach to texts has come to be a community's unselfconscious habit. As the established sense of a text within a community that makes that text its ongoing concern, it is the traditional sense of a text. As the immediately apparent sense, produced by a habit of reading in which the members of a community engage without thinking about it, the plain sense is the standard sense of a text. It provides a normative reading, that is, in at least some minimal degree: all other senses, as both new and nonobvious senses, require some additional warrant. In sum, the plain sense is the "familiar, the traditional and hence authoritative meaning" of a text within a community whose conventions for the reading of it have therefore already become relatively sedimented.[11]

The plain sense of a *scriptural* text in specific would consequently be what a participant in the community automatically or naturally takes a text to be saying on its face insofar as he or she has been socialized in a community's conventions for reading that text as scripture. As the sense of a text functioning as scripture, the plain sense is the sense of the text that establishes group identity: Christians are those who assume that sense as basic in their use of the text to shape and reform their lives as Christians. Because it is scripture's, the plain sense, in the process of serving as a standard sense vis-à-vis other interpretive or applied senses, works as a standard for the community's continuing self-identity. The plain sense, as the traditional distillate of communal practice, becomes the norm governing the ongoing practice of using such a text to shape, nurture, and reform community life: the product of traditional practice norms its further operation.

What are the general consequences of approaching the notion of a plain sense in this quasi-sociological way? We have already pointed out that the plain sense of a text is not considered here as if it were anything "in itself," apart from an interpretive practice of using texts. As a result there is no longer any *absolute* distinction between the text's "proper" sense and the contributions of an interpretive tradition. The plain sense is itself a product of an interpretive tradition; the distinction between what is and is not the plain sense of a text becomes, therefore, a relative distinction between different sorts of communal uses of a text. Because the plain sense of a text is a functional reality—a function of a community's practice of appealing to a text—it is also a function of all the rest of the interpretive conventions constituting such a practice. Assuming that the language of Michel Foucault is clarifying, we could make this point by saying that the plain sense is a discursive object that emerges only out of the relations that hold among interconstituent elements of a particular practice. What this amounts to in the case of Christian appeals to a plain sense of scripture will be a subject for discussion in the next section. Combining the two points just made, we can say with Jacques Derrida that "the literal [*propre*] meaning does not exist [strictly], its 'appearance' is a necessary function—and must be analyzed as such—in the system of differences. . . . The literal meaning . . . should be *situated* as a function responding to [a] relative necessity, within a system that encompasses it."[12]

Since it is a function of a particular practice and, more specifically, of the conventions such a practice comprises, the plain sense on our approach is clearly not a given of history to be looked for in any and all contexts. The plain sense of a text has not always existed along with that text; one cannot assume its constant availability in the attempt to trace its recognition and changing forms over differences of time and place. With Foucault we can say that "there can be no question of interpreting discourse [about a plain sense] with a view to writing a history of the referent [of that term]."[13] We do not consider the plain sense as something anterior to the interpretive practices that make it an object for discussion. We therefore do not presume the notion's universality and look for its operation in any and all discursive practices making reference to written material. Asking what a community makes of the plain sense of a text may not always be a pertinent question to ask. Analysis of a discursive practice on that basis is proper only in case the specific practice under consideration works in fact by appealing to such a notion.

On our approach it becomes an empirical question, then, whether or not appeals to a plain sense are an integral part of the use of written material in the community of special interest to us—the Christian community. If that happens to be the case (we assume it is for Christianity in this essay), notice finally that how the plain sense is materially specified by communal practice is also left a matter for empirical determination. The functional definition of the plain sense given above follows analytically from the nature of the approach we are taking. It is a purely formal definition that does not itself prejudge the material character of the plain sense as that is variously established in fact by different communities or by the same community at different times or in different circumstances. Our approach simply says *to look for* the plain sense as a function of communal practice— that is what is captured by our definition and what is unpacked tautologically in the previous statements that explicate that definition. The approach does not tell you beforehand *what* you will find when you look. The approach does not itself comprise, then, a theory or analysis of what the plain sense of a text consists in; if anything, it is a refusal even to address such a question apart from the concrete investigation of particular practices in which the notion functions. To say, as we did, that communal consensus on the use of texts is what establishes their plain sense is therefore not to say that consensus is what carries weight when the plain sense of a text is specified in the course of community practice. What participants in a practice are talking about when what they are talking about is identified by them as the plain sense of a text is not necessarily their own agreement. When participants in a practice of appealing to texts talk about the plain sense, they need not (and perhaps usually do not) *mean* by that the sense that commands general agreement. They may mean in- stead—for example, in the Christian community—"the sense the author intended," "the verbal or grammatical sense," "the sense for the writer's public," "the sense that God intends," "the sense a text has when included in the canon," "the sense Church authorities designate"; they may materially identify the plain sense of a text so specified with proposals for belief, a historical account of events, prescriptions for action, promises of salvation, narrative depictions of divine identity, etc.[14] In all these cases one can still say, however, that the plain sense is what is established by communal consensus; the plain sense cannot be identified in any of these ways without a communal consensus to take the text in that way. Communal habits of appealing to texts are what give rise to talk about a plain sense, even when such a consensus in practice is not itself what is talked about.

Notice that this sort of difference between a formal functional definition of the plain sense and its material specifications within particular practices does not drive a wedge between theological investigation and the practice of the Christian community: the theologian is not, because of that difference, operating outside the Christian community and offering an alternative account of the plain sense from that presumed in the community's actual practice of making appeals to texts. The theologian is doing nothing more than incorporating the very notion of the plain sense specified by the Christian community within an explicit account of Christian communal behaviors. Ordinarily when engaged in a practice of appealing to texts around which there is general agreement, no mention is made of that fact: theology is just the same practice become self-reflective.[15]

HOW THE NOTION OF THE PLAIN SENSE SHAPES CHRISTIAN PRACTICE

Nothing so far in our account of the plain sense would suggest that the notion is a crucial component in sociocultural complexes that are specifically self-critical, pluralistic, and viable across historical and geographical variations of circumstance. The functional approach to the notion we have just presented might in fact suggest the contrary. The approach itself assumes communal practices already set up and running; it does not go behind or beyond them to anything more basic from which they derive or to which they might be accountable. Without appeals to anything outside them, traditional practices seem to be granted a kind of inviolable givenness by our approach. Our holistic interpretive strategy might suggest, furthermore, a kind of built-in advocacy of conformity to established collective practices. Our initial functional definition of the plain sense in specific would seem only to highlight the self-enclosure of traditional practices according to our approach: what a text itself directly says becomes whatever the community makes of it. Since the plain sense of a text is already its traditional sense within some community of discourse, there seems to remain no sense of the text itself to which one might appeal against the prevailing opinion of a community's conventional reading. The text apparently becomes the captive of a sociocultural context whose interpretive habits enjoy an uncontested and potentially quite rigid monopoly over the determination of sense.

What we have said generally about our approach and about the initial functional definition of plain sense which follows from it should counter to some extent these sorts of charges. Our purported failure to discuss discursive practices in relation to either external grounds or external norms in all likelihood *undercuts* the sort of naturelike indispensability that communal habits may otherwise appear to have in virtue of those very relations. Communal habits, on our approach, are just communal habits. In a similar fashion, focusing on particulars as functions of wider communal contexts undermines as a matter of course the "absolute" character that might otherwise be ascribed to those particulars should their status as productions of certain human practices remain unnoted. To charge that the approach itself constitutes a policy of conservatism, and that the functional definition of plain sense confirms that fact by promoting the inviolability of a rigid and potentially coercive uniformity of social convention, is to mistake an approach for a theory and a functional definition for a concrete analysis of communal practice. By confusing in that way a formal approach and definition with a particular substantive position, such charges presume that what we have claimed to be left open for empirical investigation is already established: the specific character of the Christian conventions within which the notion of the plain sense operates. If the Christian tradition of appealing to texts has the self-critical, pluralistic, and flexible character we contend, our analysis of that tradition will effectively demonstrate the fallacy behind these charges. It is to a concrete analysis of Christian interpretive conventions, then, that we now turn.

The task is twofold. First, it involves positioning the plain sense in relation to other interpretive conventions making up a Christian discursive practice. Second, it involves specifying the material character of the plain sense of scripture for Christian communities. In both cases, the practical force of the plain sense for community life is made clearer by our referring to possible discursive alternatives, by our looking, that is, at the plain sense as one option among other logical possibilities with differing practical effects. (In the notes I will be associating these other possibilities with the textual practices of historical communities. The reader will be referred to historical works that provide evidence, I believe, in support of these claims.)

The plain sense, I am arguing, is first of all a function of, and precondition for, a distinction between "expository" and "applied" senses. As such, it is a function of, and precondition for, a difference between "text" and "interpretation." The notion of a plain sense, in other words, gives rise to these other discursive elements; and they to it. The plain sense bound up with this set of mutually constitutive elements goes to form a particular kind of discursive practice; it is not a universal or constant in all practices of appealing to written materials, as the following discussion makes clear.

Should appeals to written materials be a community's concern, it is possible that the writings will be reworked in the course of community use. What the community makes of written materials in that case comes to be a part of them. The materials may be effectively rewritten and in that way physically displaced, thus exhibiting the sort of fluidity that we in our culture associate more readily with oral retellings. Or the wording of this material may be retained unaltered: there may be communal rules for use prohibiting deletions or verbal substitutions. What is made of the material will then enter within it instead by way of editorial interpolations, or the recombination of passages, or their repositioning within new contexts of additional written material.[16]

In cases like these, the community's ongoing use of written material does not appear as an interpretive activity: the community's discursive practices do not effect a distinction between text and interpretation.[17] What the text says and what the community makes of it at any particular time are also not differentiated. The very sense of written material is continually reestablished in the process of its reception by the contemporary community.[18] Written material and its obvious sense mirror, therefore, changes in the circumstances of communal life.

When a community begins to talk about the plain sense of written material of concern to it, contemporary reception of that material is no longer being incorporated within it. Written materials begin to take on that character of invariability typical of writings included in a "canon": communal conventions prohibit the reworking and pre-scribe the closure of written materials so designated. The way written material has been traditionally read and understood is identified with "what the text itself says," and that plain sense is set in tension with the text's further reception in the ongoing life of the community. Written material for the first time becomes a text with the closure which that implies, a well-defined entity not to be confused with the interpretive activity of the community making use of it.[19] The com-munity's use of a text in present circumstances emerges in this way as a self-consciously interpretive activity, as a subsequent and distinct working with, or application of, an established sense identified with the text's own. Because "interpretation" is being distinguished from "text," a text's wording and form are protected from further rework-ing: interpretation changes while the text remains as it is. The text and its direct sense no longer change in step, therefore, with changes in community life.

This relative independence from changes in community life allows a text and its plain sense to exercise a critical force over contemporary interpretive practice. Such a critical force is exercised in fact to the extent that the text and its obvious sense are privileged or au-thoritative for that practice. The privileging of the text and its plain sense is a discursive option opened up once distinctions are made between text and interpretation and between "expository" and "ap-plied" senses; taking that option renders a practice of interpretation self-critical.

When a text of concern to a community is designated scripture, that text and its plain sense have indeed some authority and they have it for the ongoing life of the community per se. We have already had occasion to mention that, as scripture, a text and its obvious sense function authoritatively: the self-understanding of community members, their group identity, is formed by appealing to that text with that basic sense. Questions of how to express community iden-tity under changing circumstances become, therefore, questions of what to make of that text with that plain sense under these new conditions. Questions of faithfulness to one's communal identity become questions of textual interpretation, broadly construed. The

ongoing practice of shaping behaviors, attitudes, and beliefs in a
religious way *is* an interpretive practice in that sense. The critical force
that a text and its plain sense gain in virtue of their authority as
scripture is therefore a critical force exercised generally over contemporary forms of communal life.

Variations are possible, however, in the degree and scope of the
authority granted to texts working as scripture. The critical force of
the scriptural text and its plain sense will vary accordingly. In the first
place, the authority of a scriptural text and its plain sense may be
limited to strictly cultic practices. The text may still function as
scripture, and appeals to its direct sense may still be what establish
group identity, but scriptural authority may just not extend to the
changing circumstances of a community's wider political, economic,
and social life.[20] The critical force of the text and its plain sense for
contemporary practice will be similarly restricted, since a great part of
community life does not stand in any relation of interpretation or
application to scriptural texts and their plain sense. In a second case,
texts may function as scripture for community life as a whole, but
their authority for contemporary practice may be undermined by
appeals to something independent of them—for example, a secret or
subsequent oral communication.[21] Communities operating along
these lines tend to be radically revisionary of previous traditions
whose group identity is formed by appeals to those same texts. They
tend to be unselfcritical advocates of their own proposals for reform,
however: scriptural texts and their plain sense no longer possess any
critical leverage vis-à-vis innovations in community practice supported by appeals to esoteric or novel oral communications of an
equivalent or greater status.[22]

In a third case, appeals may be made to a parallel oral tradition that
is public and thought to intersect with scriptural texts at their origin.[23] Such appeals do not particularly undermine the scriptural
function of texts: the living of communal identity according to a
public oral tradition is assumed to dovetail with what could be made
of texts functioning as scripture. This convergence does not, however,
have to be *shown*, and therefore the ongoing life of the community
need not involve an active process of textual interpretation. Any
tension between the plain sense of a scriptural text and the contem-

porary practice of the community is relaxed. The critical force of the plain sense for community practice is thereby undercut.

In a fourth case, appeals to scripture may be relevant to the whole of community life, and contemporary communal practice may be actively interpretive: questions of how to live one's communal identity in changing circumstances must be addressed as questions about what to make of certain texts. The plain sense of the text may not be privileged, however, over further interpretive or applied senses. Senses which are admittedly the result of subsequent interpretive activity will be considered latent aspects of the text itself—not *additions*, or *new* readings for changed circumstances, but disclosures, uncoverings, of the text's own "deeper" or "hidden" senses.[24] These senses are as much what the text itself says, then, as the plain or obvious sense. They accordingly share in the authority of the text as scripture; and, as interpretations appropriate to changed circumstances, they supersede the authority of its plain sense for ongoing communal life. Because the plain sense is not privileged, what the text says automatically harmonizes with what it is taken to say at any particular time. The plain sense of scriptural texts thereby loses its critical purchase over contemporary custom: contemporary custom supported by appeals to hidden senses of scripture becomes as binding as scripture itself for community life at a particular time.

Interpretation is engaged in self-consciously in this fourth case, but text and interpretation are of equivalent status. Interpretation does not infiltrate the very scriptural texts it concerns, but distinct works that are explicitly interpretive come to be included along with those texts in an enlarged scriptural corpus.[25] Because of the scriptural status of its own interpretive enterprise, the attempt to live one's communal identity in changed circumstances creates for itself its own legitimation.

Let us assume (since we have no space to argue) that Christian communities maintain the priority and unrestricted relevance of the plain sense of scripture and do not relax in any of the above ways the resulting tension between the obvious sense of a scriptural text and its use in changing circumstances. We can conclude from the above analysis that the plain sense in that case works with considerable force to promote a tradition that is critical of its own changing forms.

Nothing we have said suggests that the Christian tradition is equally self-critical about established interpretive practices that have sedimented into the form of the plain sense. Moreover, nothing seems to prevent the plain sense of scriptural texts from exercising a repressive, hegemonic influence over the ongoing life of Christian communities, contemporary appeals to scripture being constricted through that influence into narrow channels of previous use.

A tradition self-critical of its own specifications of the plain sense will arise, however, when the network of conventions that the plain sense helps to constitute turns back on that notion and complicates its function. The distinction between "what the text itself says" and further "interpretive" or "applied" senses comes to infiltrate the very discussion of the plain sense, to produce a more radical differentiation of text and interpretation. The text and its plain sense are now distinguished from, and privileged with respect to, the specifications of that sense by the community. Any account of the plain sense distinct from the text itself becomes an interpretation over which the text has critical purchase.

This happens because part of the functional import of privileging the plain sense is the denial of a semantic equivalence between text and interpretation: interpretive accounts, in other words, cannot capture without remainder what the text conveys, and therefore none of them can take its place. Specifications of the plain sense in the form of paraphrase or distinct works of exposition must themselves, on that account, fall under the rubric of interpretation. Attempts to set forth a text's plain sense cannot claim, therefore, the privilege of the plain sense for their results. The general consequence of such a radical distinction between text and interpretation is an authoritative plain sense that is unavailable in any form distinct from the text itself. The plain sense of the text becomes an independently unspecifiable locus of meaning, something that transcends any and all attempts to reformulate it. As such it functions critically even with respect to consensus readings of a text; it works to evacuate the pretensions of communal discourse generally.

Two aspects of Christian practice converge to prevent the Christian privileging of the plain sense of scripture from promoting a rigid uniformity in community life: (1) the practice of canonizing a body of texts that work as scripture; (2) the practice of classifying the plain sense of those texts under the rubric "narrative." However the plain sense is categorized, to claim that just these texts—without revisions or additions—suffice in all times and places for the formation and regulation of community life is to force a certain degree of interpretive license in the use of them. I know that the canon, this limited body of unrevisable texts, is of crucial relevance to my life now as a Christian whatever my particular circumstances: a practice like this that makes a finite number of texts cover every eventuality of life will no doubt falter without some display of exegetical ingenuity.[26] The demand for the universal relevance of a fixed body of texts will eventually compel creative efforts to find in texts more significance for one's life as a community member than is initially apparent there—than is apparent, that is, from previously established uses. The demand compels a free use of those texts and their plain sense even when, as in the Christian case, the plain sense retains priority.[27]

The degree and scope of exegetical ingenuity necessary for a body of texts to function effectively as a canon depend upon the categorization of the plain sense of those texts. These variations in exegetical ingenuity determine in turn the practical effect on community life of requiring universal relevance of canonical texts. The plain sense may be identified with some classification of a directly catechetical nature—for example, with cultic regulations or general teachings about beliefs and behaviors. In such cases, no exegetical ingenuity is required to determine a form of life in conformity with those texts: it should be materially specified in advance, substantively derivable, from catechetically identified plain senses. The repetition of the same would constitute the ideal of such a plain sense's universal prescriptiveness. In the case where the plain sense is identified with general teachings, particularities of situation are to be subsumed under the general, viewed as mere specifications of general principles. The more particularities of circumstance such teachings readily encompass, the more colorless they are in their generality. In the case where the plain sense is identified with specific cultic regulations, universality of application ideally requires the same laws to be followed in any and all circumstances; differences of time and place are either irrelevant or destructive of the form of life to be instituted. Problems of application that prompt exegetical ingenuity arise in both cases only in the

degree that circumstances stray from the requirements of the sort of
community life the plain sense makes evident.

When the plain sense of canonical texts is identified as a narrative—the sense of canonical texts focused in particular in the Christian case around the narrative depiction of a God made man—the
very use of these texts to shape and nurture community life becomes
open-ended.[28] The plain sense in the form of a narrative does not
itself specify communal practice—the elements of belief, attitude, and
behavior that make one Christian—in the way a catechetical plain
sense would: those elements are not materially derivable in any
straightforward way from the peculiar interaction of character and
circumstance, for instance, that renders the identity of Jesus Christ.
How the particularities that make up the story of a unique life are to
be used to form a practice of Christian behaviors and beliefs is not at
all clear. A creative display of exegetical ingenuity is necessary, then,
to answer even the most basic question of establishing Christian
identity through appeals to canonical texts. Exegetical ingenuity is
not limited, as it was in the case of catechetical plain senses, to
questions of how to live under new conditions a form of life already
clearly established through the plain sense of scripture. As a structural feature of Christian practice, the convention of identifying the
plain sense of scripture with a narrative leaves open—better, forces
open—the material specifications of a distinctively Christian way of
life. The formation of a Christian character is always set as a task, in
other words, by such a structural indeterminacy in Christian conventions of appealing to texts. Problems of showing the universal relevance of canonical texts for Christian life never become, therefore,
problems of *applying* a preestablished notion of group identity in new
or changing circumstances: the problems are always ones once again
of active reformulation of that identity. The ideal of universal prescriptiveness for the plain sense of canonical texts consequently cannot
amount to a repetition of the same; the universal relevance of the
plain sense will not be worked out ideally in the form of a boundless
monotony in community practice. Faithfulness to a Christian form of
life is not exhausted by conformity to Christian cultic regulations or
by simple specifications of general Christian principles to fit particular
circumstances: it involves the constructive process of continually
reinitiating a Christian self-understanding by imaginatively reposi-

tioning the particulars of one's own life within a story. The storied plain sense of scripture will not specify the substance of a Christian form of life, but that is its power: it takes up and reshapes whatever has been produced without it, however diverse or variable.[29] It is this revisionary rather than constitutive function of appeals to a narrative plain sense of scripture that promotes a Christian community inclusive of difference and unperturbed by change.

What has been said goes some way, I hope, toward showing the discursive conditions for a tradition of appealing to texts that is inherently self-critical, pluralistic, and flexible. These conditions have been specified not by any general hermeneutic or epistemological treatment of the relation between text and interpreter but by an analysis of what follows from a particular convention in community practice as that becomes clear against the background of logically possible alternatives. I have offered a typology of potential communal uses of written materials and an argument about their various practical effects. On that basis we concluded that a discursive convention that privileges the plain sense fosters a community critical of its own contemporary practice. Radicalizing the same conventions produces in the Christian case the notion of a plain sense that transcends community practices of appealing to texts generally: this notion of a plain sense irreducible to the community's specifications of it makes criticism of even sedimented Christian practices possible. Christian conventions of canonizing a body of texts and identifying their plain sense with a narrative are what keep the use of scriptural texts from producing a monolithic Christian practice and what grant that tradition its enormous powers of assimilation. These suggestive results concerning the practical force of the notion of the plain sense of scripture for Christian life testify to the potential fruitfulness of theological investigation in a sociological mode.

NOTES

1. See Hans W. Frei, "The 'Literal Reading' of Biblical Narrative in the Christian Tradition: Does It Stretch or Will It Break?" in *The Bible and the Narrative Tradition*, ed. Frank McConnell (New York: Oxford Univ. Press, 1986), 36–77.

2. Hans W. Frei, The Shaffer Lectures, Yale Divinity School, 1983 (mimeographed).

3. Frei, "'Literal Reading' of Biblical Narrative," 62.

4. Although the agenda is Frei's, I of course assume full responsibility for the way it is carried out in this paper.

5. See George A. Lindbeck, *The Nature of Doctrine: Religion and Theology in a Postliberal Age* (Philadelphia: Westminster Press, 1984), for this notion of theology. No exclusive claims are being made here; theology works in many different ways.

6. See David H. Kelsey, *The Uses of Scripture in Recent Theology* (Philadelphia: Fortress Press, 1975), chap. 5.

7. Ibid., 90ff., 207ff.

8. Ibid., 105.

9. Charles M. Wood, *The Formation of Christian Understanding: An Essay in Theological Hermeneutics* (Philadelphia: Westminster Press, 1981), 40ff., 116ff.

10. Ibid., 43.

11. Raphael Loewe, "The 'Plain' Meaning of Scripture in Early Jewish Exegesis," in *Papers of the Institute of Jewish Studies, London,* ed. J. G. Weiss (Jerusalem: Magnes Press, 1964), 1:181.

12. Jacques Derrida, *Of Grammatology* (Baltimore: Johns Hopkins Univ. Press, 1976), 89; my interpolations.

13. Michel Foucault, *The Archaeology of Knowledge* (New York: Harper & Row, 1972), 61; my interpolations.

14. For historical variations like these in the "plain" or "literal" sense of scripture within Christian communities, see James Samuel Preus, *From Shadow to Promise: Old Testament Interpretation from Augustine to the Young Luther* (Cambridge: Belknap Press of Harvard Univ. Press, 1969); Brevard S. Childs, "The Sensus Literalis of Scripture: An Ancient and Modern Problem," in *Beiträge zur alttestamentlichen Theologie: Festschrift für Walther Zimmerli zum 70. Geburtstag,* ed. Herbert Donner, Robert Hanhart, and Rudolf Smend (Göttingen: Vandenhoeck & Ruprecht, 1977); and Hans W. Frei, *The Eclipse of Biblical Narrative: A Study in Eighteenth and Nineteenth Century Hermeneutics* (New Haven: Yale Univ. Press, 1974). To avoid the narrow identification of "literal sense" with particular sorts of readings (e.g., verbal or grammatical ones), I use the term "plain sense" to talk about the obvious or direct sense of the text for the Christian community.

15. In this and the preceding paragraph, I am following closely, for my own purposes, remarks about the consequences of a Wittgensteinian approach to rationality made by Sabina Lovibond in her *Realism and Imagination in Ethics* (Minneapolis: Univ. of Minnesota Press, 1983); see secs. 35, 37, 48.

16. For discussions of precanonical intrabiblical interpretation and exegesis, see Michael Fishbane, "Torah and Tradition," in *Tradition and Theology in the Old Testament,* ed. Douglas Knight (Philadelphia: Fortress Press, 1977);

and idem, "Inner Biblical Exegesis: Types and Strategies of Interpretation in Ancient Israel," in *Midrash and Literature*, ed. G. Hartman and S. Budick (New Haven: Yale Univ. Press, 1986).

17. I am assuming for purposes of argument in this paragraph and the next that a community's use of written materials is all of a piece. Practices of the sort discussed below, in which "text" is distinguished from "interpretation," might, however, be selectively at work. If that were to happen, a self-conscious occlusion of interpretive activity would likely be involved in cases of the sort discussed now, where what is made of written materials comes to be part of them: a distinction between text and interpretation would already be available in the wider discursive practices of the community.

18. "Apocalyptic" rewrites of received material provide especially clear instances of this: no distinction is made between "exposition" and "application." See Daniel Patte, *Early Jewish Hermeneutic in Palestine* (Missoula, Mont.: Scholars Press, 1975), chap. 8.

19. Although we happen to be talking here of written texts, notice that on this definition texts need not be written.

20. The scriptural tradition of the Sadducees may have taken this form. See J. Z. Lauterbach, *Rabbinic Essays* (Cincinnati: Hebrew Union College Press, 1951).

21. The early Christian church was a weakly scriptural practice of this sort in the use of the writings it came to call the Old Testament; the Montanists and some gnostic groups provide examples of the same sort of weakly scriptural use of New Testament writings. See Hans von Campenhausen, *The Formation of the Christian Bible*, trans. J. A. Baker (Philadelphia: Fortress Press, 1972).

22. Cf. Patte, *Early Jewish Hermeneutic*, on sectarian Judaism. A critical dynamic between text and ongoing interpretation in community life will be set up again should those oral communications themselves come to be treated as texts and no further oral communications of a comparable authority be admitted. This happened in the Christian case.

23. A historical case is the oral tradition of rabbinic Judaism, which is said to have been given along with the written Torah to Moses at Sinai; oral traditions may have this status in Christian communities, particularly before the close of the canon (see von Campenhausen, *Formation of the Christian Bible*), and subsequently in intracommunal disputes as a counter to reform movements appealing to scriptural texts (see Heiko A. Oberman on traditions 1 and 2 in *The Harvest of Medieval Theology: Gabriel Biel and Late Medieval Nominalism* [Cambridge: Harvard Univ. Press, 1963], 365–75).

24. See, e.g., Judah Goldin, "Of Change and Adaptation in Judaism," *History of Religions* 4 (1965): 269–94; and Susan Handelman, *Slayers of Moses* (Albany: State Univ. of New York Press, 1982), chap. 2. This practice is legitimated by an account of revelation as a process that includes the interpretive activity of the religious community; see Gerschom Scholem, "Revela-

tion and Tradition as Religious Categories in Judaism," in *The Messianic Idea in Judaism* (New York: Schocken Books, 1971).

25. Thus in rabbinic Judaism midrashes of the written Torah are themselves considered Torah; oral Torah, however, unlike written Torah, expands with continuing interpretive practice.

26. See Jonathan Z. Smith, "Sacred Persistence: Towards a Redescription of Canon," in *Imagining Religion: From Babylon to Jonestown* (Chicago: Univ. of Chicago Press, 1982), 36–52.

27. See Frei, "'Literal Reading' of Biblical Narrative," 39–41, on the priority of the literal sense in allegorical, figural, and spiritual readings of scripture in Christian communities.

28. With this claim I do not mean to rule out (1) the possibility of the same effect's being produced by some other, nonnarrative identification of the plain sense, or (2) the importance in this connection of the sort of narrative identified as scripture's plain sense. Another level of analysis, setting out possible narrative types, would be required to explore the second point.

29. See George A. Lindbeck, "Barth and Textuality," *Theology Today* 43 (1986): 361–76. for a discussion of what this sort of shaping function amounts to.

5

"The bible
as . . . ":
fictional
narrative and
scriptural truth

Garrett Green

The recent popularity of the concept of narrative among theologians has done more to disguise than to illumine one of the most sensitive issues of modern religious thought. Put rather baldly, the question is this: Granted that storytelling is basic to religion generally, and more specifically that biblical narrative is crucial to Christian faith, are the stories true?

The single book most responsible for the new theological prominence of narrative is undoubtedly Hans Frei's *Eclipse of Biblical Narrative.* By examining how and why the scriptural story faded from view in modern thought, Frei has aroused new interest in the theological significance of narrative. Of particular importance for both constructive theology and biblical studies is the distinction that Frei draws between literal meaning and historical reference. Precritical Christian thinkers did not really make the distinction; they generally read the stories literally and simply assumed that the events took place as described. Modern thinkers, on the other hand, have learned to question the historicity of the narratives, at the same time confusing literal sense and historical reference. From one end of the theological spectrum to the other, virtually all have assumed that taking the stories literally means affirming their historical veracity. For the supernaturalists or fundamentalists the identification of literal and historical has meant defending the ostensive historical truth of the texts. Theological liberals, on the other hand, also assume the identity of literal meaning and historical reference, but they have sought to detach the meaning of the texts from their literal-historical sense. In other words, the liberal alternative has been to abandon the literal reading of the Bible in order to preserve its religious value. Especially noteworthy is the tacit agreement of both sides that reading the texts literally is the same thing as taking them to be historically accurate reports. Stated in Frei's terminology, nearly everyone has assumed that acknowledging the "history-like" quality of biblical narratives means affirming their "historical likelihood."[1] By common consent a "biblical *literalist*" is one who affirms the *historical* reliability of narrative texts in scripture.

One reason for the popularity of the concept of narrative is that it brackets the question of truth: accurate historical reports and the purest fictions are both narratives. Attention to narrative thus gives theologians some breathing room by allowing the literal sense of the text to come into focus without its becoming immediately confused with historical questions. At the same time, of course, attention to narrative offers theologians a chance to duck awkward questions about the *truth* of the stories. But having rediscovered the long-eclipsed narrative heart of the Bible, theologians may postpone but cannot evade forever the issue of narrative truth.

Van Harvey has given expression to the dilemma of modern theologians by describing the "pathos of the modern mind" as a crisis in the "morality of knowledge."[2] Modern theologians have been torn between their desire to affirm the truth of the biblical texts and their commitment to critical historical judgment. Harvey characterizes Protestant theology since the end of the nineteenth century as a "series of salvage operations, attempts to show how one can still believe in Jesus Christ and not violate an ideal of intellectual integrity."[3] But Frei's contention that there has been a long-standing confusion between the literal and the historical suggests that this "pathos" may be rooted in a misunderstanding. Might it be possible after all to affirm the literal narrative as theologically normative without thereby compromising one's critical integrity?

To test this possibility, I propose to take a hard look at the non-historical or fictive elements of the biblical narrative, which have been largely ignored by modern theologians, and to examine the relation of fiction and truth. Finally, I want to suggest an approach by which postcritical theologians might recover the ability to read the Bible literally without either betraying their historical-critical consciences or abandoning the doctrine of scriptural authority.

THE PROBLEM OF FICTION
IN MODERN RELIGION

The usual modern term for a narrative text having no claim to truth is "fiction." Modern biblical interpretation, by combining historical critical method with the identification of literal sense and historical reference, has seemed to consign large portions of the Bible to fiction. The dominant thrust of apologetics since the European Enlightenment has thus been directed toward rescuing the Bible from fictional status. Conservative attempts to effect the rescue by proving the historical accuracy of the narratives have done little to convince any but the already-committed and have probably contributed to the erosion of the Bible's plausibility for other modern readers. Liberal apologists, likewise accepting the identification of meaning and reference, have sought to show that biblical narratives "really" have a nonhistorical (e.g., ideal, mythical, or existential) meaning. But in that case the literal sense of the texts (since it is not factual) can only be assumed to be fictional, and therefore untrue. Now that the identity of literal and historical reading has been called into question, however, the whole matter of what it means to call a text fictional appears in a new light. Three theologians, among them Frei himself, have made explicit comments about fiction that may help us to see better what is at stake.[4]

Lonnie D. Kliever presents an arresting case for the "fictive" nature of all religion in the contemporary world.[5] The modern spirit, according to Kliever's analysis, has survived assaults like those of technological change and secularism, but it has also given birth to the twin forces of relativism and pluralism, which contain the seeds of its own destruction. Drawing on the ideas of Ernest Gellner,[6] Kliever seeks to show the "essentially reductive and fictive character of all modern religiosity."[7] Unlike more familiar dismissals of religious truth claims by critics whose philosophical assumptions are positivistic, this critique takes for granted that we live "in a world where all thinking proceeds by normative paradigms and all knowledge consists of symbolic constructions."[8] In view of this relativistic epistemology, it is surprising that Kliever (in his most interesting thesis) concludes that religion has lost its plausibility not only as a set of literal truth claims but also as a persuasive symbolic world. "The modern debunking of literal religion," he claims, "extends to symbolic religion as well. Neither can establish a real world beyond the symbolic imaginings and posturings of those not predisposed to believe already."[9] The reason, according to Gellner's thesis, is that the two "selectors" of empiricism and materialism function as the "final arbiters of reality claims" in modern culture, thus systematically filtering out the plausibility of competing paradigms and symbol systems.[10] Kliever does not shy from the inevitable conclusion. Since the "cold, heartless, impersonal universe is the real world," he reasons, the only function left to religion is "largely diversionary and decorative."[11] Against the backdrop of this powerfully negative vision, his final positive appeal for a "religiosity of, by, and for the fictive imagination"[12] rings hollow indeed.

By contrast with Kliever's nihilistic tour de force in behalf of the fictive imagination, Frei's almost incidental remarks about the fictional quality of the Synoptic passion-resurrection narratives appear rather unsystematic and surprisingly cheerful. "We are actually in a fortunate position," he tells us, "that so much of what we know about Jesus . . . is more nearly fictional than historical in narration."[13] The reason for our good fortune is apparently the fiction writer's "direct or inside knowledge of his subjects," in contrast to that of the historian or biographer. But Frei's use of the fact-fiction duality turns out to be a subtle one (as suggested by the "more nearly" in the passage just cited). He does not call the story fictional; rather, he acknowledges that someone who finds the account implausible will necessarily regard it as a "kind of hyperfiction."[14] His own claim is that the narrative is "fiction-*like*," that it "is at once intensely serious and historical in intent and fictional in form. . . . "[15] This odd convergence of intent and form lies, I believe, at the heart of Frei's christological hermeneutic in *The Identity of Jesus Christ;* it is part of a thesis that could almost be called an ontological argument for the presence of Jesus Christ. Put succinctly, Frei claims that in the unique case of Jesus, "we may not think his presence and identity apart from each other," that in the Gospel accounts, "the being and identity of Jesus in the resurrection are such that his nonresurrection becomes inconceivable."[16] Like Anselm in his famous argument, Frei affirms that in this unique case "commitment in faith and assent by the mind constrained by the imagination are one and the same."[17] We are compelled—by what or by whom Frei does not say—to take an apparently fictional story as the gospel truth.

THE CASE AGAINST
FICTIONAL REDUCTIONISM

One way to defend the truth claims implicit in the fictional, or fictionlike, narratives of the Bible against the reductionism of critics like Kliever is to take the offensive against their uncritical use of the duality of fact and fiction. There is, for instance, an inexplicable gap between Kliever's epistemological relativism—the claim that all our knowledge depends on irreducible paradigms and cultural selectors—and his reductionist assumption that religion makes no persuasive cognitive claims because it deals in fictions, defined as "unreal and impossible cases."[18] Not only is there considerable cause to suspect that when Kliever speaks of what "we" moderns think, he is excluding the vast majority of human beings, but his argument also fails to entertain the possibility (implicit in his epistemology) that "we" may be wrong, that our empirical and materialist selectors may be filtering out essential data. His very definition of fiction, borrowed from the Neo-Kantian philosopher of "as if," Hans Vaihinger, reflects the decidedly nonrelativist epistemology of an earlier age that was quite sure which world was "real" (the one described by the sciences) and how we could obtain knowledge of it (by using the "scientific method").

Here the comments of a third theologian are suggestive. In a recent article on the meaning and significance of "fictions" in the Old Testament, Manfred Oeming acknowledges the unhistorical status of much biblical material, without drawing reductionist conclusions. Like Frei, Oeming eschews the ususal modern criterion that the "theologically valuable" portions of the Bible are necessarily the same as the "historically reliable" ones.[19] He wishes to accept the "'fictive' character of the texts," at the same time acknowledging their "important and irreplaceable" function.[20] He defines "fiction" as a "kind of narrative presentation that relates what is historically inaccurate [*historisch Unzutreffendes*] but that is still related to history in that it intends to disclose a truth in the past that does not become apparent in mere description."[21] In order to distinguish this usage from Vaihinger's fictionalism, Oeming insists on quotation marks around "fiction." Claiming that the "essential intention of a 'fiction' may lie precisely in disclosing the true situation in the first place," Oeming argues that "the 'fictive' can . . . have *counterfictive and not counterfactual character.*"[22] He points to the necessary selectivity of the historian as an example of the unavoidability of shaping events in the course of narrating them historically.

Oeming is saying in effect that just as it is undeniably the case that one can lie with the facts, so there are occasions where one can tell the truth with fiction. Indeed, if Frei's account of the gospel narratives is correct, we would have to say that for Christians there are truths— or at least one very important truth—that can *only* be told as fictions. It would appear, at any rate, that Kliever's attempt to use the fact-fiction duality as an absolute is inconsistent with his own assumptions about the pluralism and relativism of modern culture. To assume that because modern people are aware of the gap between the "cognitive imagination and the religious imagination," their "religion is largely diversionary and decorative"[23] is to make the same kind of error as would be made in assuming that the nuclear physicist who knows that atoms are not "really" miniature solar systems is not serious in using atomic theory to understand the nature of matter. As odd as it may appear to some, an increasing number of religious believers seem to be aware of the "fictive" nature of the stories they tell though they continue really to *mean it* when they say that they are telling the truth. Are such people simply being stubbornly inconsistent? The analogy with the sciences suggests that one should be very cautious about making such charges. Many honest and intelligent people—especially in an age of pluralism and relativism—do and say a variety of things that cannot be reduced to a single consistent context (not even that of "empiricism and materialism").

One reason for this behavior is precisely their awareness that this *is* a pluralistic and relativistic world. What is appropriate or meaningful for one endeavor need not have a systematic relationship (i.e., share a common larger context) with appropriate and meaningful behavior of a different kind. Think, for example, of Wittgenstein's discussion of the "dawning of an aspect."[24] His well-known (but poorly understood) example of the simple figure that can be seen either as a duck or as a rabbit (see figure), far from being an anomaly, focuses our attention on a common feature of all experience—that everything we

WITTGENSTEIN'S DUCK-RABBIT

perceive or know depends on our grasping a particular *pattern* by which diverse parts present themselves as a whole. We do not construct the world piecemeal by assembling discrete elements into organized wholes; rather, having a world *means* seeing according to a pattern, having a vision of how things hang together as the precondition for recognizing the parts *as* parts in the first place. Whether the statement "That is a duck" is fact or fiction depends on various factors of context, relationships, and intent. "What I perceive in the dawning of an aspect," says Wittgenstein, "is not a property of the object, but an internal relation between it and other objects."[25] The pattern of such internal relations is what constitutes the object as a particular whole (duck or rabbit in this case). Here the two patterns are incompatible and incommensurable, but such matters must be determined on a case-by-case basis, since the "descriptions of the alternating aspects are of a different kind in each case." The seeing of aspects therefore "demands imagination" and depends on the "mastery of a technique."[26]

The polemical case against the fictional reduction of religious narratives can be summarized by saying that the distinction between fact and fiction has itself come to be viewed as highly pluralistic and relativistic. Scientists and philosophers of science in the late twentieth century have become considerably less sanguine and more pragmatic about making claims to know reality. Although simplistic contrasts between science and religion continue to exert influence today, especially among nonspecialists in both fields, it is becoming increasingly evident that the perceived opposition rests on positivist assumptions that are no longer defensible, and that the parallels between natural scientific and religious thought are more striking and potentially more fruitful than their divergences. In particular, mutually irreducible and incommensurable paradigms, highly resistant to falsification, now appear to play essential and analogous roles in shaping the imaginations of both the research scientist and the religious believer.[27]

Such considerations ought to make us wary of those who are oversure about which symbolic worlds are real and which are fictive. But apologetics is always a two-edged sword: out of their zeal to defend religion against its detractors, those who employ such arguments run the risk of immunizing it against all possible criticism, thereby rendering impotent religious claims to be making genuine assertions about reality. Theologians who like to quote Wittgenstein have frequently been labeled fideists by critics who charge that describing religion in terms of incommensurable "language games" or "paradigms" is really an illegitimate apologetic ploy designed to render all religious truth claims immune to criticism. This is a serious charge, and one to which some theological programs are clearly vulnerable. In order to show that fideism is not inevitable, and how it can be avoided, it will be helpful to introduce a subtle but decisive distinction.

THE PHILOSOPHY OF "AS IF" AND
THE HEURISTICS OF "AS"

In discussions of fiction in religion, one often encounters the name of Hans Vaihinger, who may be regarded as the first thinker to formulate an explicit theory of fiction and apply it to religion. Vaihinger, who called his work *The Philosophy of "As If,"* was part of the late nineteenth-century movement to reappropriate Kantian philosophy after the demise of Idealism. His subtitle indicates the program he sought to carry out over several decades: *A System of the Theoretical, Practical, and Religious Fictions of Mankind.* He tells us that he chose his title because he was convinced "that 'As if,' i.e. appearance, the consciously-false, plays an enormous part in science, in world-philosophies and in life."[28] Especially in the fields of ethics, aesthetics, and religion, he argues, "we operate intentionally with consciously false ideas, or rather judgments," whose "secret life" he sought to lay bare. Vaihinger was convinced that the fullest articulation of the "as if" philosophy had been undertaken by Kant, though he had sometimes expressed himself with unfortunate ambiguity. An example of Vaihinger's reading of Kant is his paraphrase of Kant's interpretation of the virgin birth of Jesus: "The 'Idea' of the virgin conception is another expedient religious fiction, a beautiful, suggestive and useful myth!"[29] It would make Kant's real intention plainer, he argues, to replace the concept of the "objectively, practically real idea" with what Vaihinger calls the "equivalent but clearer expression, *expedient fiction.*"[30]

Whether or not Vaihinger's reading of Kant's philosophy of religion is the correct one is not the issue at hand. For whatever Kant may have intended, his way of dividing up consciousness into a "theoretical" realm of empirically based science and a "practical," nonscientific realm of ethics, aesthetics, and religion has been enormously influential in the religious thought of the past two centuries. And Vaihinger is surely not alone in drawing the conclusion that religion, for better or for worse, is a wholly practical matter inhabiting an "as if" world of symbol, myth, and fiction. It is important to note that this group comprises not only skeptics and unbelievers but also a number of thinkers who (like Vaihinger and Kliever) value religion and see in fictionalism a viable apologetic strategy in the modern world.

But the fictionalist case is doubly flawed. On the one hand, as we have already seen, its philosophical underpinnings have been eroded by the pragmatic and antifoundationalist critiques of recent philosophy, especially the philosophy of science. The naively realistic view of scientific theories as direct descriptions of reality ("fact") has given way to positions that frankly acknowledge the symbolic and relative nature of basic scientific concepts. In an instructive parallel to debates about fiction in religion, philosophers of science now argue whether theoretical models and paradigms should be considered "useful fictions" or whether they are representations of reality.[31] At least one philosopher, Richard Braithwaite, has argued explicitly for fictionalism in both science and religion.[32] From the religious side as well, there are good grounds for rejecting the fictionalist case. To claim that Christian believers, for example, act *as if* they live in a world created by God and redeemed by Jesus Christ is precisely to beg the crucial question. Surely most Christians, both pre- and postcritical, understand themselves to be making assertions about reality, about the way things are, whether or not they can supply a second-order theory to justify that intent. They may be right or wrong in what they assert about reality, but it misrepresents their intent to describe them as producing fictions, "useful" or otherwise.

In place of the flawed fictionalism of "as if," I want to propose a subtle but important shift of connective: not "as if" but "as" is the key to the logic of religious belief. What characterizes religion is not understanding the world *as if* . . . but rather understanding it *as* . . . The fact-fiction duality tries to distinguish between "is" and "is not": whatever *is* the case merits the designation "fact"; what *is not* so is called "fiction." The move to "as if" may soften the negative implications of "is not," suggesting that fictions have useful functions to fulfill, but the underlying dichotomy remains unchanged: to live in the world *as if* it were the creation of a beneficent God entails that in fact it *is not*—whatever the usefulness of maintaining the fiction. Such is not the case, however, if we substitute "as" for "as if." When Calvin, for example, admonishes us to see the world *as* the theater of God's glory, he means that it really *is*. Why not, then, say "is" instead of "as"?

One of the more inconspicuous but intriguing signs of the emerging pluralism of the modern age has been the growing prominence of the word "as," especially in the titles of serious works of nonfiction.[33] The writer who looks at something *as* something else is signaling awareness of other, different ways of viewing the same object. Such a writer is ordinarily commending his own way of seeing, though not always (e.g., his intent may be playful, fantastic, or satirical). The grammar of "as," one could say, is not ontological but analogical. The point of using "as" is heuristic: not to affirm that something is or is not the case but rather to draw attention to one possibility among others by proposing an analogy. If a viewer of Wittgenstein's famous example reports that he sees the figure as a rabbit, he communicates two things to us simultaneously: (1) the pattern or gestalt currently governing his perception of the figure, and (2) his awareness of alternative possibilities. He is implicitly appealing to a comparison by using the word "rabbit," which proposes that this figure is *like* an already familiar model. (A viewer who was unaware of alternative possibilities would report that it *is* a rabbit, not that it can be seen *as* one.) The ontological indeterminacy of "as" can be made apparent by everyday examples. A critic might reasonably write, for example, "This novel can be read as a parable of moral choice, but such a reading distorts the book's deeper meaning." This judgment acknowledges the possibility of a particular way of construing the whole, at the same time denying its validity. One can imagine two kinds of rebuttals. Critic A could agree that the book can be read as a parable while maintaining that this is the correct reading; critic B, on the other hand, might disagree with both on the grounds that the book cannot plausibly be read as a parable of moral choice.

Seeing something as something else is an ability, a "faculty" in the classical sense of the word. Its most appropriate name is imagination, defined as the analogical faculty, the ability to see one thing as another. Kant called "is" the copula of judgment; we can call "as" the copula of imagination. In this quite technical sense, imagination is common to the natural scientist, the poet, and the religious believer. Living in the modern world makes demands on imagination in a way that traditional worlds did not, because it forces us to be continually aware of multiple options, of a myriad of sometimes competing, sometimes compatible ways of seeing. With the help of this concept of imagination as the "as" faculty, we can give conceptual precision to Paul Ricoeur's suggestive distinction between a "first" and a "second naiveté."[34] The first inhabits the world of "is," blissfully unaware of other possibilities. The second lives in a world of "as," construing reality according to a particular vision in full awareness of other options. Imagination is integral to both, for the only way to have a world is to imagine it. But the first imagines implicitly ("knows") while the second imagines explicitly—not as if, but as. This account of modern pluralism avoids the fictional reductionism of Kliever and Gellner not by returning to an epistemological absolute but by a

more consistent relativism. Whether it can help us with the question
of the truth of religious narratives remains to be considered.

Modern writers about the Bible have been especially prolific in the
production of "as" titles. An earlier generation of educators tried to
read the "Bible as literature," while most biblical scholars were preoccupied with the "Bible as history." More recently, in a particularly
significant trend, treatments of canon and biblical authority have
begun to appear in this form. Krister Stendahl, for example, has
written "The Bible as a Classic and the Bible as Holy Scripture," and
Brevard Childs has followed his *Introduction to the Old Testament as
Scripture* with *The New Testament as Canon.*[35] This development is
significant theologically, because it signals a move beyond the typically modern terms of argument about the Bible, which has taken
place according to the logic of "is" and "is not," or of "fact" and
"fiction." The defenders of orthodoxy have argued that the Bible is
divinely inspired scripture; their opponents have responded that it is
not because it is a historically conditioned human document. The
newer approach proposes that the Bible be read *as* scripture—which
acknowledges the possibility, and perhaps the legitimacy, of other
ways of construing the same texts. Since the beginnings of modernity,
theologians have made the circuit from the implicit assumption that
the Bible *is* scripture to the explicit reading of the Bible *as* scripture.

What becomes of the question of narrative truth in this heady
atmosphere of epistemological relativism and hermeneutical pluralism? Let me state briefly several implications that I see.

1. The fictional status of many biblical stories is not to be denied
but relativized. Fact-fiction is a dichotomy more appropriate to some
kinds of textual interpretation than to others. In particular, it has to
do with questions of historical reliability; and insofar as biblical texts
make historical statements, it may be legitimately employed, with the
result that the Bible will be shown to contain "fiction" *(historisch
Unzutreffendes,* in Oeming's phrase) along with fact. At the same time
it must be acknowledged that the long-standing modern preoccupation with historical questions, and the confusion of these questions
with the literal meaning, has "eclipsed" other ways of reading biblical
texts—and precisely those ways that are most important theologically. It is appropriate to call certain texts "fictive" (Oeming) or

fictionlike (Frei), with the proviso that the question of their truth is not thereby prejudged.

2. The literal sense of scripture can be reclaimed as the theologically normative reading.[36] The "plain sense" of biblical stories is not their historical reference but their narrative meaning. Quite simply, the meaning of the texts is the story they tell—"fictive" elements and all! Because, with Frei's help, the difference between the literal meaning of the text and its historically ostensive sense is now clear, it is possible to affirm the truth of the text without self-contradiction or intellectual dishonesty. The pathos of the theologians, at least in Van Harvey's sense, has more to do with hermeneutical confusion than critical integrity. The truly "pathetic" behavior of modern theologians has been their headlong retreat from the plain sense of scripture in the mistaken belief that "modernity" required the sacrifice. By leaving questions of historicity to the historians (along with the fact-fiction dichotomy that is part of it), theology may hope to achieve a "second naiveté" that has passed through the fires of historical critical reductionism and learned once again to tell the story on its own terms. Our challenge is to become "literalists of the second naiveté"— readers whose critical awareness of the fictionlike quality of the text does not prevent them from affirming the truth of the story it tells.

3. Fideism is not entailed by this position. The hallmark of what has been dubbed Wittgensteinian fideism[37] is the attempt to immunize theological assertions against hostile criticism by treating the assertions as aspects of particular, self-referential "language games," world views, or paradigms. Its operative assumption is that, since there are no viable epistemological absolutes, all languages must be treated in their own terms and it makes no sense to call one "truer" than another. The error of the position is not its relativism but its unwarranted assumption that choices among language games are arbitrary. But all paradigms are not created equal, as even a cursory look at the natural sciences ought to make clear. The view that they are is often justified by a careless appeal to the work of Thomas S. Kuhn.[38] But his point about the role of paradigms in the sciences is not that paradigm switches are arbitrary and therefore irrational but rather that they are logically holistic; they cannot be made piecemeal since they involve changes in the basic ordering pattern itself. Again,

the simple visual model is a useful analogy. The fact that a viewer cannot move in stages from seeing the duck aspect to seeing the rabbit aspect does not mean that he has no good reasons for moving from one aspect to the other, but means rather that gestalt switches involve all-or-nothing alternatives. People are in fact influenced by arguments—in religion as well as science—to move from one paradigm commitment to another. And retrospectively they are often able to adduce compelling reasons for having done so. That such a position involves a fiduciary element—a commitment to one way of seeing among others—does not entail that it is fideistic. Religious faith commitments, like scientific paradigms, are not exempt from criticism; but their holistic grammar requires that for such criticism to be effective it must be addressed to the position as a whole. A paradigm is refuted only by appeal to a more persuasive paradigm. The Bible, read literally and used scripturally, makes that kind of appeal.

4. The Bible thus appeals to the imagination of its readers. It invites them to see the world differently—to see it *as* something different from the kind of world that it otherwise appears to be. Occasionally the appeal from one world to another is explicit in the texts themselves—for example, in the Johannine opposition between "this world" and the kingdom of God. But the Christian use of these texts as scripture continually implies such an appeal by its very nature. A recent liturgical innovation in some churches makes it explicit: scripture readings are prefaced by an admonition to the congregation to "listen for the Word of God!" Listening-for is the aural correlative of seeing-as; it acknowledges the possibility of perceiving more than one unifying pattern or gestalt in the spoken words. Thus Frei's comment about the resurrection narrative turns out to be characteristic of the Christian use of the Bible generally: "Commitment in faith and assent by the mind constrained by the imagination are one and the same." What makes the Bible scripture for the believer is precisely that "constraint," the inescapable conviction that, in hearing the story *as* the Word of God, it truly *is* the Word of God. The appearance of fideism is rooted in this surprising move from "as" to "is." Seen from outside the world of the narrative itself— in methodological terms, from the standpoint of religious studies— the "as" governs: Christians (virtually by definition) are those who

hear the Bible *as* the Word of God and who accordingly see the world *as* the "theater of God's glory." Imagining the world in terms of the biblical story, they find themselves persuaded that the story is true; others, no doubt, will hear it differently—as a piece of hyperfiction, perhaps. Seen from within that imagined world, on the other hand— in methodological terms, from the standpoint of theology—the "is" governs: the Bible *is* the Word of God, because it speaks with the authority of the Holy Spirit, who is, of course, a central actor in that very story.

A THEOLOGICAL EPILOGUE

The distinction just made between the standpoints of religious studies and of theology is a reminder that these remarks have so far been confined to the former standpoint, outside the storied world of the Bible. Their aim has been a strictly second-order one: to make some sense of the odd things religious people do with fictionlike texts, and particularly what Christians do with the Bible. In conclusion I would like very briefly to indicate how the question of biblical narrative and fiction looks from the other side, through the spectacles of scripture itself—in a word, theologically.

As my text I take a well-known passage from St. Paul:

> . . . God chose what is weak in the world to shame the strong, . . . even things that are not, to bring to nothing things that are, so that no human being might boast in the presence of God. (1 Cor. 1:27–29)

Quite apart from the pluralism of the modern age, there are good reasons for Christians to experience a tension between the biblical narrative of God's creation, reconciliation, and redemption of the world and the everyday reality of living in that world. The Gospel story, told in the present age (in the *regnum gratiae*, as our orthodox forebears called it), will necessarily appear in significant respects "fictive," unrealistic. But that, according to the same story, is how it should be, since Christ's kingdom is "not of this world." For a narrative about another world is—by definition—a fiction. Christians, in other words, quite on their own and apart from any pathos engendered by the post-Enlightenment world, have always found themselves needing to say at the same time that the scriptural story is true and that it is fictionlike, not descriptive of present experience.[39] How can they do justice to both? Not by allegorizing the story, as the Reformers made clear, and not by speaking merely "as if" it were true, but rather by insisting that God's truth can *only* be told (in this world) as a narrative—and precisely as *this* narrative. "The kingdom of God is like . . . "—not simply in the parables of Jesus where it is explicit but throughout the whole sweep of the story from creation to consummation.

Seeing "in a glass darkly" (*ainigmatos*, "enigmatically," is the key term in 1 Cor. 13:12) is the mode proper to the *regnum gratiae*. This age is the time for groaning in travail, for singing hymns of praise— and for telling stories about the great king who gave a banquet, the widow who lost her coin, the divine Logos who entered the womb of a young woman to be born in a stable, die as a criminal, and rise triumphant over sin and death. The important point to be emphasized, to theologians especially, is that this story, however enigmatic, is the true story, the only story Christians have to tell, and that it has no unstoried form. If it sometimes seems so incredible as to strain the imagination and offend the reason, the wise theologian will attempt no defense beyond a reminder (paraphrasing 1 Cor. 1:25) that the fictions of God are truer than the facts of men.

NOTES

I am grateful to Charles M. Wood for his criticisms and suggestions in response to an earlier draft of this essay.

1. Hans W. Frei, *The Eclipse of Biblical Narrative: A Study in Eighteenth and Nineteenth Century Hermeneutics* (New Haven: Yale Univ. Press, 1974), 11–12.

2. Van Austin Harvey, *The Historian and the Believer: The Morality of Historical Knowledge and Christian Belief* (New York: Macmillan Co., 1966), 103.

3. Ibid., 104.

4. For an informative variety of viewpoints on the meaning of "the fictive," by contemporary theologians, philosophers, and literary critics, see Dieter Henrich and Wolfgang Iser, eds., *Funktionen des Fiktiven*, Poetik und Hermeneutik 10 (Munich: Wilhelm Fink Verlag, 1983).

5. Lonnie D. Kliever, "Polysymbolism and Modern Religiosity," *Journal of Religion* 59 (1979): 169–94.

6. See Ernest Gellner, *Legitimation of Belief* (London: Cambridge Univ. Press, 1974); Kliever summarizes Gellner's arguments and gives specific references.

7. Kliever, "Polysymbolism," 182.

8. Ibid., 187.

9. Ibid., 185.

10. Ibid., 187.

11. Ibid., 190, 191.

12. Ibid., 194.

13. Hans W. Frei, *The Identity of Jesus Christ: The Hermeneutical Bases of Dogmatic Theology* (Philadelphia: Fortress Press, 1975), 144.

14. Ibid., 143. Gary Comstock's misreading of Frei's position, in "Truth or Meaning: Ricoeur versus Frei on Biblical Narrative," *Journal of Religion* 66 (1986):117–40, is rooted in his failure to grasp the distinction, so basic to Frei, between textual meaning and historical reference. Comstock thus attributes to Frei two "general interpretive principles"—namely, that the "meaning of a realistic narrative is autonomous" and that the "narratives of the Bible are self-referential" (pp. 122–23). Comstock concludes that Frei is a "pure narrativist"—in short, a fideist, who is "content to except narratives from rigorous debate about truth conditions." By confusing meaning and reference, Comstock misses the point of the first "principle" and is simply wrong in attributing the second to Frei. That the *meaning* of a narrative text is "autonomous" implies nothing at all about its *truth;* nor does it bear on the question of the text's reference. Many biblical narratives *do* refer beyond themselves—as Frei's treatment of the Gospels makes clear—but this reference is not to be identified with the *meaning* of the text.

15. Ibid., 145; my emphasis.

16. Ibid., 14, 145.

17. Ibid., 146.

18. Kliever, "Polysymbolism," 189.

19. Manfred Oeming, "Bedeutung und Funktionen von 'Fiktionen' in der alttestamentlichen Geschichtsschreibung," *Evangelische Theologie* 44 (1984): 255.

20. Ibid., 258.

21. Ibid., 262.

22. Ibid., 263; Oeming's emphasis.

23. Kliever, "Polysymbolism," 191–92.

24. Ludwig Wittgenstein, *Philosophical Investigations,* 2nd ed., trans. G.E.M. Anscombe (New York: Macmillan Co., 1958), 193ff.

25. Ibid., 212.

26. Ibid., 207–8.

27. For an elaboration of this point, see my article "On Seeing the Unseen: Imagination in Science and Religion," *Zygon* 16 (1981): 15–28; and the literature cited there.

28. H[ans] Vaihinger, *The Philosophy of "As If": A System of the Theoretical, Practical, and Religious Fictions of Mankind,* 2nd ed., trans. C. K. Ogden (New

York: Harcourt, Brace & Co., 1935; reprint, Boston: Routledge & Kegan Paul, 1965), xli.

29. Ibid., 298–99.

30. Ibid., 308; Vaihinger's emphasis.

31. See Ian G. Barbour, *Myths, Models, and Paradigms: A Comparative Study in Science and Religion* (New York: Harper & Row, 1974), chap. 3. The early chaps. of this book contain useful surveys of recent currents in the philosophy of science and their implications for philosophy of religion.

32. Ibid., 50–51, 57–58; Barbour gives references to Braithwaite's works.

33. I am indebted to a remark several years ago by Professor Michael Welker of Tübingen University, which first drew my attention to the frequency of "as" titles in modern works. Investigation of this hunch could be a fruitful research topic for a historian of modern culture; a model for such study is Wilfred Cantwell Smith's tracing of the term "religion" in the titles of modern books in *The Meaning and End of Religion* (New York: Harper & Row, 1978), 32–48, esp. 219–20 n. 63.

34. Paul Ricoeur, "The Symbol Gives Rise to Thought," in *The Symbolism of Evil*, trans. Emerson Buchanan (New York: Harper & Row, 1967), 347–57.

35. Krister Stendahl, "The Bible as a Classic and the Bible as Holy Scripture," *Journal of Biblical Literature* 103 (1984): 3–10; Brevard S. Childs, *Introduction to the Old Testament as Scripture* (Philadelphia: Fortress Press, 1979); and idem, *The New Testament as Canon: An Introduction* (Philadelphia: Fortress Press, 1984).

36. In addition to Frei's *Eclipse of Biblical Narrative*, see his recent essay "The 'Literal Reading' of Biblical Narrative in the Christian Tradition: Does It Stretch or Will It Break?" in *The Bible and the Narrative Tradition*, ed. Frank McConnell (New York: Oxford Univ. Press, 1986), 36–77. For a useful historical survey reaching back to ancient and medieval Jewish and Christian exegesis, see Brevard S. Childs, "The Sensus Literalis of Scripture: An Ancient and Modern Problem," in *Beiträge zur alttestamentlichen Theologie: Festschrift für Walther Zimmerli zum 70. Geburtstag*, ed. Herbert Donner, Robert Hanhart, and Rudolf Smend (Göttingen: Vandenhoeck & Reprecht, 1977), 80–93.

37. The term was coined by Kai Nielsen in his essay "Wittgensteinian Fideism," *Philosophy* 42 (1967): 191–209.

38. See Thomas S. Kuhn, *The Structure of Scientific Revolutions*, 2d ed. (Chicago: Univ. of Chicago Press, 1970).

39. Theologians who want to make "common human experience" one of the *sources* for theology miss the significance of this essential tension between biblical narrative and human experience. See, e.g., David Tracy, *Blessed Rage for Order: The New Pluralism in Theology* (New York: Seabury Press, 1975), 43–45.

6

The spatial dimensions of narrative truthtelling

Stephen Crites

For the best of reasons, Hans Frei has exhibited a certain chariness toward arguments about the truth or falsity of theological claims. In the background has doubtless lurked a Barthian suspicion that such argumentation has been conducted on the basis of philosophical, historical, and psychological premises so alien to the biblical foundations of theology that the claims have been eviscerated in the very process of defending them. But this general suspicion was refined in Frei's most ambitious historical study to date, *The Eclipse of Biblical Narrative*, by his attention to the narrative form of the Bible generally and of the Gospels in particular. From his deep-going study of hermeneutical debates from the seventeenth through the early nineteenth century, Frei concludes that the "realistic narrative reading of biblical stories, the gospels in particular, went into eclipse throughout the period."[1] The issue, much debated during that period and since, concerning the truth of these stories, has eclipsed the more vital hermeneutical issue of what they mean in the narrative form in which they are written.

In establishing this thesis, at a time otherwise marked by thick theological claims and thin theological scholarship, a scholar has shown what scholarship can do: it can expose the axioms of generations of theologians, still taken for granted in our theological education, by showing that our assumptions about biblical interpretation have a definite and highly problematic history. With respect to biblical hermeneutics, Frei has confronted us with the largely forgotten history of our own minds, returning us to fundamental questions that had seemed long settled. In a different but no less significant sense than Freud intended, a work of scholarship has made the unconscious conscious. The meaning of biblical narrative, not only what but *how* the Bible means, has been subordinated to various kinds of putative truth: to its historical truth, given a conception of history independent of scripture itself; to its utility in furnishing moral lessons; to the policy and polity of various churches; to the metaphysical aspirations of speculative theology; to the search for a usable history; and to a host of other concerns praiseworthy in themselves but resulting collectively in the total eclipse of the meaning of biblical narrative.

On Frei's showing, this issue is essentially formal. Distinguishing between general and special hermeneutics, Frei suggests with characteristic caution that

> it is at least possible that in regard to realistic narrative literature, the function of general hermeneutics should be formal rather than material; it should be confined to identifying a piece of literature as belonging to that particular genre rather than some other, rather than claim to interpret its meaning or subject matter.[2]

How it means, that is, is a question of genre. Interpreting specifically *what* it means is the task of special hermeneutics: "Whether it is found in the Bible or elsewhere," Frei suggests, ". . . every narrative of the sort in which story and meaning are closely related may have its own special hermeneutics."[3] First and foremost, however, attention must be paid to the fact that it is a story, which can only "mean" in a narrative way. Frei criticizes the mythological school of Strauss, for instance, along with earlier allegorical and naturalistic interpreters, because

> they confused the claim to the close, intimate relation between the sense of a story and its narrative shape with the claim to the identity between sense of story and reliability or unreliability of its reports.
>
> This was hardly surprising, for the literary parallel between history writing and history-like writing is perfectly clear: in each case narrative form and meaning are inseparable, precisely because in both cases

meaning is in large part a function of the interaction of character and circumstances. It is not going too far to say that the story is the meaning or, alternatively, that the meaning emerges from the story form, rather than being merely illustrated by it, as would be the case in allegory and in a different way, in myth.[4]

To accuse Frei of formalism would be like throwing Br'er Rabbit into the briar patch. How a story means is, on his showing, a function of its specific narrative structure, quite independently of whether it is historical or historylike, fact or fiction, not to speak of its moralizing or legitimizing uses.

Still, granted this vital hermeneutical point, Frei might perhaps agree that at least some stories may be truthtelling, in just this strictly formal sense. Truthtelling, as it functions in stories, is not a matter of whether the story refers to a specific state of affairs historically. A story can deceive even if it refers to well-established facts, and it can be truthtelling even if it does not. Nor is the truthtelling merely or necessarily in the intentions of the narrator. The most sincere story-teller can unintentionally lie, and the most notorious liars can tell true stories in spite of themselves. Nor does the truthtelling consist in plumbing some mythic or metaphysical depth "behind" the story. If, say, the Gospels are truthtelling stories, their truth is integral to the stories they tell.

Stories create an intricate temporality and a no less intricate narrative space. Much has been said about their temporality, which is certainly relevant to their truthtelling. But I want to address the following remarks to their spatial dimension, for that is the other way of bringing out how stories may be truthtelling in a sense relevant to the life of the spirit. For storytelling is one of the primary means by which we human beings establish a homology between our own inner space and the multidimensional space outside and between, above and below, us in which we are psychically as well as physically located.

I think I already see Professor Frei beginning to frown. It seems that we are going to move beyond the "text" of the story after all. But the story is precisely the locus of the homology between inner and outer in which truthtelling consists. The story is, in its very form, a spiritual production, which is to say that it is a dialectical achievement, a creation of form that actively overcomes the alienation between inner and outer. But there may be more frowns to come!

I am uneasy about referring to inner space by such terms as "mind" or "soul" or "consciousness," though they are often handy. Such terms seem to connote self-enclosure. The word "spirit" has some embarrassing connotations too—spirit is hardly the sort of thing folk on the cutting edge talk about—but I prefer the word because it implies an intersubjective, shared inner space and also implies a circuit or metaphoric consonance between inner and outer. Spirit is the movement that circulates freely in the actual world and at the same time hollows out an inner space, homologous with the actual world, in the bodily life of human being. It hollows out this inner space through such artful devices as word and image, rhythm, sound, and story. To speak of such a hollowing-out is already, of course, a metaphor. No physical cavity appears, comparable to the gastro-intestinal tract, and efforts to locate this inner space variously in head, heart, or bowels simply reify it. No, spirit is a thing of metaphor through and through, not in the sense of being a mere figure of speech but in the sense of being a movement that transports things from one space to another. The Greek term for a moving van is *metaphoros,* and spirit is just such a vehicle, furnishing its own space, like a graduate student making the rounds of the thrift shops, from its rummagings in the world. In languages as unrelated as Latin and Hebrew, and in many others, the word for spirit refers at once to the wind outside and the animating breath within, and also to that inwardness that is sometimes said to make a human being akin to a god or an angel.

But leaving gods and angels suspended for a while, as befits them, we find lodged in this inner space memories of things that once existed in the public space of our visual field, including the still-vivid presence of people we knew long ago and the familiar furniture of a childhood home, which to the child seemed eternally fixed and secure. Memory rescues people and places from the relentless flux of the public world and preserves them in another specious eternity. In dreams and imaginings this inner space seems to extend itself visually again, setting in motion the places and persons long since passed from the scene. But in this same inner space—spirit-formed and spirit-indwelt—are lodged not only remembered images but possibilities, some ideal and some fantastical or horrific, expressing our darkest fears and brightest yearnings, and mathematical structures, string quartets, designs for buildings like none yet seen, coming into the inner space of reflection, as we say, out of thin air. In inner space the mundane images once pressed on the senses mingle and combine with the transmundane possibilities never seen on land or sea, and when the building gets built or the quartet gets played the circuit between inner space and public space is complete and extended to the inner space of others, the hearers of the quartet, the occupants of the building; and this circuiting among spaces is the very life of metaphor, and of the spirit.

Storytelling is a spiritual activity in this sense, intersubjective and circuiting metaphorically between the shared inner space and public space. Stories are told and retold, gathering resonance in the retelling and creating an inner bond among tellers and hearers. Stories are community-creating. Narrative space comprises not only the shared inner space of people who know some of the same stories but also the space that is constituted by the action of the narrative, which unfolds in that shared space. As a spiritual creation in this double sense it reflects the spirit's excursions in the actual world.

Assuming some such homology between inner and outer, between narrative space and the actual space of a manifest world, let us sort out some of the broad spatial dimensions that register in truthtelling stories.

THE HORIZONTAL PLANE
OF SOCIAL SPACE

The middle region of narrative space that supports all the other dimensions is the horizontal, the horizon in which the eyes of human beings meet and their words pass in conversation. Our most mundane stories, such as soap operas, take place entirely in this horizon. They are too thin to be truthtelling. But all stories must sooner or later, implicitly or explicitly, transect this social plane. Whether the narrator undertakes to depict episodes in the lives of historically existing persons or fabricates a deliberate fiction, the narrative space of his story must in some respects be homologous with the topography of the social horizon. Even the Babylonian creation myth set in an age antedating the very world inhabited by teller and hearers, the *Enûma Elish*, opens with the primeval parents, Tiamât and Apsû, spawning a host of young gods and then becoming irritated with the noise and commotion they make. (Reading this story in my office, across from a fraternity house with stereos ablast, I am in perfect sympathy with their annoyance. Where have we gone wrong, Tiamât?) Since stories are told, after all, within the social horizon where teller and hearer meet, even a story set in the most unearthly region must betray identifiable features of that horizon. The story told and the storytelling must share a common narrative space. Stories with psychological depth constantly take soundings beneath the horizontal plane, in the inner space of the characters, and yet this depth would not be objectifiable in a psychological novel without being exteriorized in the horizontal action and dialogue. All stories must in some such manner register in social space.

This social horizon, in more traditional or archaic societies, had a definite center and circumference. Mircea Eliade has taught students of religion to speak of the social horizon of traditional societies as a "sacred" space, in Eliade's somewhat domesticated sense of the term.[5] It was formed by an identifiable, closed community of people who shared a common bond of language, custom, religious practice, and institutional structure. Sacred space was homey. It was also exclusive. It was concentrically organized around some definite geographic point, a holy mountain, a temple, a huge tree, which centered not only the community but the entire world as the community knew it. This *axis mundi* was the hub around which the world turned, and it often figured in creation myths as the center of power, divinely charged, from which all other reality was derived. And it tended to project perpendicularly from the horizontal plane of the social space it organized. In the community collected around it people knew where they were, geographically and socially. A clearly defined social role provided the primary sense of personal identity for the traditional man or woman. Each person internalized the sacred space in which the community dwelt, spiritually oriented by its divinely charged center, the center of personality being in consonance with the cosmic axis at the center of the community. The language of the community was the language of his or her thoughts, its mores were internalized as the morals of each person, and the daily round of life orbited around its center. The sacred space of the community, in short, formed the homologous inner space of each member.

I have spoken of the traditional community and its sacred space in the past tense, but the midwestern village in which I grew up in the 1930s was more or less like that, and of course the pattern survives in many other cultures and vestigially among us as well.

Social space is always to some extent parochial. The stories we understand best concern the people who are closest to us, in a family or ethnic or geographical sense, and many of the stories we hear are told to us by people who bear the same proximity. That is particularly true for the inhabitants of traditional sacred space. They are no doubt aware of a larger space beyond, just as the New Yorker knows there is a world beyond Hoboken, and the Bostonian assumes there must be something west of Waltham. But in the concentrically organized life of sacred space the world grows ruder and more confused the farther one moves from the center, and out beyond the last perimeter is wilderness, godless and profane. It is out of bounds, both geographically and morally, its inhabitants strange, its ways forbidden. Of course there is a narrative genre, of which the *Odyssey* is our classic, that revels in this strangeness and celebrates the bravery of the hero who copes with it. It is important, however, that he return home to tell the tale. It is a very different sort of story, a horror, really, if he is destroyed out there. Otherness, alterity (let us be fashionable), is tolerable in a traditional society only if one finds one's way back to the sacred space. Traditional communities consign the "others" to negative identity. The Greek divides all humankind into Greeks and barbarians, with the whole world beyond sacred Hellas falling into the second class. Their strange tongues sound like bar-bar-bar to the Greek ear, and they are lawless and wild. Revulsion toward these out-of-bounds folk reinforces one's moral identity as a Greek. Exile among the barbarians is a punishment for criminals, and one of the most fitting, since by criminal behavior they have already broken the code that makes them Greeks, have already violated the sacred space, and so are already barbarians at heart. The traditional Jew divides the inhabitants of the world into Jew and goyim, along similar lines, and the traditional Christian referred to all others as heathen. The word "cherokee" simply means "human being" in the Cherokee language, and then there are all those others.

Despite this concomitant exclusivism, the ethnic identity of traditional societies is graceful and musical, a free-flowing metaphorical
circuit that links the shared life of the community in sacred space to
the inner space of each of its members. The same stories, the same
thoughts, the same musicality of style, join the individual to the
community, together with its land and its gods.

The narrative space characteristic of the modern sensibility, like the
social space in which we moderns dwell, is more pluralistic, less
homogeneous, less centered but less exclusive, indefinitely extended
and arguably less intimate. An older European city is still collected by
the spire of its cathedral, but in the newer urban developments on
both sides of the Atlantic such spires are overshadowed by buildings
that are simply piled high, towers of Babel dedicated to more worldly
pursuits. No doubt the World Trade Center is a world axis of sorts, but
its force is centrifugal rather than centripetal, radiating expansively
toward an economic empire rather than collecting a community. Any
axis mundi has a rather phallic appearance, by the psychoanalytic
definition of a phallus as anything that is longer than it is wide, and
there is doubtless a great deal of erotic energy concentrated around
such centering perpendicularities. If the newer cities have a center it is
likely to be a cluster of priapically tall buildings that provide office
space for business interests. The character of any community's center
is apt to give a clue to the locus and focus of its libidinal energies if not
to the nature of its gods and goddesses. Where sheer urban sprawl has
replaced any centered human habitation, the secularization of space
is complete. No angel has been sighted in the city of Los Angeles for
some generations, and only the most antic providence is evident to
the naked eye in Providence, R.I. The randomly distributed convention hotels that tower around many of our cities provide no *axis
mundi,* but they do point skyward, erotically charged enough to stir
the blood of the conventioneers and to raise their eyes from the
otherwise sterile horizontal plane of the desacralized city to a ver-
ticality awesomely erect, though too glassy and proud for love.

The narrative space of stories told in such a city will likewise be
hospitable to strangers out on the town. This narrative space will be
far less concentrically or hierarchically organized than that of more
traditional stories, and the characters that pass through it as strangers
or nodding acquaintances will likewise exhibit no integrally centered

personalities. They will be active in their pursuit of many objects, including one another, but they will not be concerned much about their souls, because they will not have any. That is not as fatal a condition as more traditional folk may think, reading novels about them or seeing them on film or television. The stories in which they appear are, after all, also works of the spirit in which a homology is achieved between the inner life of tellers and hearers and the public world they inhabit, even if the stories that pass among them violate the Aristotelian standards of character as well as plot. This homology is a necessary but not sufficient condition of truthtelling. If this homology were lacking, if for instance the characters in the stories exhibited moral qualities in which tellers and hearers could not honestly recognize themselves, the stories would be false. Whether, on the other hand, these stories are truthtelling will depend on other conditions as well.

Of course the world is not divided simply between traditional folk inhabiting sacred space and desacralized and deracinated moderns. Most people nowadays probably exist somewhere on a continuum extending between these extremes, and storytellers and hearers are not necessarily at the same point on the continuum. In other words, the situation between contemporary novelists, screenwriters, or playwrights and their audience is not unlike the situation in which people are reading and hearing stories that come down to them from the past. We must, if we are to understand the contemporary situation, avoid the lure of a historicism that locks people into their historical moment, and also a sacred-secular typology that locks them into one or the other of these categories. The narrative space in which storytellers and hearers meet is far more capacious than traditional sacred space, and also more capacious than stereotypical modernity, for it extends over vast stretches of historical time and vast cultural differences alike. This delightfully confused situation has important implications for the prospects of truthtelling.

THE CELESTIAL CANOPY OF
GODS AND ANGELS

The holy mountain, the spire, the Maypole, the sacred oak, the Hilton Towers, all point to the sky, introjecting a vertical axis into the horizontal plane of social space. It is not inevitable that the eyes of the entire community should follow that pointing finger to the heavens, but some eyes do, even today. It would be incautious, furthermore— an example of the dogmatic historicism we have already deplored— to regard the prodigious energies exhibited by the contemporary religious imagination as merely a vestigial survival of bygone times. As always, the religious imagination populates the heavens with a host of divine and angelic figures, lively and vivid, including even a reappearance of goddesses. Many of these figures carry on much the way people in the community do and generally have a human form, even a gender. To that extent the heavenly space to which the point- ing vertical axis directs the religious eros seems the upper story of the horizontal social plane below, encompassing it like a celestial um- brella. Yet at least beyond the first tier of such bright spirits there exist divinities that cannot be considered merely gods of the tribe. They are the high gods, the high goddesses, or the high God or Goddess: though if the high deity exists in solitary splendor there is usually a compensating proliferation of holy angels in the lower tiers. The religious imagination cannot live with transcendence alone, in large part precisely because the exigencies of storytelling require personal agents with whom to deal.

Now the deities of the sky, who may or may not resemble human beings, and even the holy angels, must differ from us in at least one respect: not being earthbound, they have no bodies. They are ethe- real, as airy as the region they inhabit, gravity defying. In this respect they are like our inner space, where thoughts and images fly free and stories pass among us. They are weightless, not needing to proceed over the earth at the burdensome and plodding pace of our bodies. I think of Paris and I am there—though, alas, only in my thoughts. Angels, similarly, are said to be able to appear instantaneously any- where at will. They do not have to fly, nor is it a matter merely of great speed. Even a ray of light must pass through every inch of the way, but angels have only to will their destination, though it is a debated question among angelologists whether an angel can appear in two places at once. The heavens the angels inhabit, again like our inner space, are immeasurable and free of topographic impediments. The angelic ether is pure transparency.

So there is a consonance between our inner space and the angelic transparency, reminiscent of the affinity of inner and outer that we found in social space. Let us not be too quick to decide whether this consonance is of our own making. The affinity with social space was not of our making, though it certainly was imaginative, a metaphorical circuit between inner and outer. If we say that the angelic transparency is imaginative, we again merely identify the medium in which we conceive it. But it does not follow that the bright spirits we imagine are only imaginary. To imagine is a spiritual act, a transportation of metaphors, nor is it implausible to suppose that the imagination itself is a spiritual medium formed in us by the bright spirits to provide the tabernaculum for their appearance, indeed to suppose that the inner space in which the imagination moves in such angelic fashion is hollowed out by the spirit in consonance with the heavenly ether in which the angels dwell.

Dante, though deeply devoted to the social space of his native Florence, was one of our great poetic explorers of the celestial canopy, his spirit ascending among the bright spirits on high in order to bring us one of the tallest of tales. Following in broad outlines an ancient cosmogony, he conceived the earth as a solid sphere surrounded by concentric spheres of pure ether. These ethereal spheres made up the paradise of the blessed saints and angels, through which the poet and Beatrice, his muse, proceeded after he had rid himself of the weight of sin ascending the mount of purgatory. Weightless, he proceeded by his own natural movement, like an angel or a thought or the very story he tells, through the heavens, drawn by the divine light that encircles the entire system of spheres and extends into infinity. For the high God, unlike the blessed saints and angels, bears no human form. Located as a point of pure light, the God's radiance fills infinite space, like the sun which, as in Plato, is the visible image of the divine. The earth, then, is a solid sphere suspended in the infinite heavenly ether.

But what of the inner space of the poet himself, this most visual of poets in whose imagination this vast celestial scheme is reflected? In a sense his inner space can be said to contain this vast outer space, though of course he is also contained in it, and would doubtless protest that all he could contain was its faint image. At any rate I again suggest that inner space and this celestial space are homologous, the inner the mirror of the celestial. But, of course, mirror images are also opposites: In heavenly space the solid material of earth is a sphere at the core of the ethereal spheres extending from it concentrically into the divine light. In the poet, on the contrary, his body, solid as earth, is as it were the enclosing perimeter, the ethereal spheres moving inward toward spiritual light at the core, toward a point of light that is the image of the infinite light. So his ascension from the earth through the heavenly spheres is homologous with the turn inward, ever more profoundly plumbing the depths of that inner space, reaching toward the core. The way up is the way down.

I have used Dante as an example not because he is unique, though in his mastery he obviously is, but because he is so typical of a spirit in flight along the vertical axis. With Dante, as a supremely visual poet, the metaphorical movement between heaven and earth is transparently clear, with vivid visual image transmuted into narrative. I also find it attractive that he remains so passionate a Florentine, the sacred space of his motherland augmented but never supplanted in his inner space by the skyward excursions of the spirit. With him inner space is fully three-dimensional, the horizontal plane and the vertical axis forming a perfect sphere; the vertical is not a mere line leading away from the soil on which he grew.

THE SUPERCELESTIAL SUBLIME

Now it is characteristic of the horizontal plane of social space to have natural limits. Even if it opens up, as it has done in the modern period, beyond the ethnically defined enclosures of sacred space, we know that it curves in on itself. The flat-earth people to the contrary, it constitutes a sphere, a universal social sphere. No such natural limits confine the vertical pointing of the sublime perpendicular. If it stops with the divinely populated region of the heavens, it does so because the homologous inner space of the storytelling community cannot accommodate a depopulated region, not because the vertical axis itself has reached a necessary stopping point.

Pascal was forced to peer out into the great emptiness opened up by the new astronomy. An early modern, a mathematician who grasped the import of the boundless space that came into view with the overthrow of the geocentric view of the universe, Pascal was also a contemplative theologian who understood the theological significance of this displacement. For him the great spires of Europe no longer pointed merely to the populated regions of the heavenly canopy but they pointed into a beyond more empty and limitless than the traditional cosmologists had ever contemplated. He not only looked up into this dark space but listened, and was aghast at its deathly silence: "The eternal silence of these infinite spaces fills me with dread."[6] No divine word from on high, no music of the spheres. Yet there was no denying or refusing this silent emptiness. To accommodate it, a new region of inner space has opened up for many moderns since Pascal, homologous with this boundless outer space. The spirit that ventured abroad into the height of this awful sublimity returned to hollow out an infinite depth of emptiness inside frail flesh itself.

I do not mean to imply that the emptiness in outer and inner space is purely a modern development. In the East it is at least as old as Buddhism, and even in the West there were ardent spirits gathered round the *axis mundi* in whom the eros of the boundless took deep root, contemplatives and farseers of every stripe, whose love of the old stories of the gods and angels took on an ironical coloration in the shadow of the empty vastness. In a homologous development in inner space they reached toward a depth in the self in which, paradoxically, it ceased to be a self at all. The suspicion of rabbis and clerics toward these wild heaven stormers and self-abnegators was well founded, for in the depths of their spirits a cold wind blew, a sublimity that made of the old stories and of self-identity alike a kind of divine jest. Even Plato sensed it, as evidenced by the very horror with which he recoiled from the thought of the boundless. The craftsmanly god of Plato's *Timaeus*, the *demiourgos*, was careful to construct a world bounded on every side and well ordered within, as was the world moved by the Prime Mover of Aristotle and Saint Thomas, for whom an infinite regress of causes was a horror to the intellect. This love of limit and order, the other side of their horror of the boundless, formed the great philosophical tradition of the West, which incidentally protected the homey world and divine, angelic, and human agents loved by the West's great storytellers and theological tall-tale spinners.

But in the modern period the eros for the boundless was no longer to be denied, for it had taken root in the spirit's own inner space. For the spirit searches out the deep things of God, even to this homogeneous emptiness where *altitudo* and *profundo* are one and the same, and this same spirit, completing its metaphoric circuit, lodges the no-self at the base of the self. The spirit that cries out of the depths, *de profundis*, to the height of heaven, now recognizes that this height and depth are the same, the boundless of outer space and inner space alike. It has long been a commonplace of Western thought that we frail mortals, who know that we must die, already carry our mortality about with us in the depths of our spirits. But this worm within is also the image of the all-devouring serpent without, this emptiness. In this boundless space, within and without, in which no bird sings and no angel, we hear only the doleful tolling of our mortality. For in this boundlessness, as Plato knew, there is no life, the many-splendored colors of nature fall dark, and the storytelling voice falls silent. Our eros for the boundless recoils on us, becomes a deep-lying pathos within.

For we who have developed this fearful inner amplitude, we mesmerized stargazers and gazers into the empty space beyond, we space travelers—we have contemplated this empty sublimity for so long that our own inwardness threatens to lose all shape and limit. Of course farsightedness, in one sense of the term, is a good thing, the capacity to look beyond the immediate scene and quick advantages. But in the optometric sense of the term, farsightedness can also be a nuisance, as the near at hand blurs into indeterminate mud and the head spins in vertiginous dizziness. Augustine, mourning for the death of his friend, saw only death wherever he looked.[7] The farseer despairs of what is near at hand in the daily round of social space, and he with ears for the ominous silence alone disdains the familiar rattle and bang of the world. The pathos of the boundless strikes us half dumb, we farseers and deep thinkers. We speak in a barbarous tongue, the stammer of reason, that only the initiates can understand. In this stammer of reason no story can be told.

An antidote for this affliction, I find, is a wholesome dose of narrative. After attending a conference of learned fellow stammerers I find myself reaching desperately for my storybooks, sacred and profane, like a returning astronaut or deep-sea diver, to reacclimate myself to the regions in which life goes on. For stories take place in those middle regions between the emptiness beyond and the emptiness within. Still, for us who bear this cold acosmic emptiness like a nitrogen bubble in our inner space, there can be no truth in a story that is not edged by this chill.[8]

THE EARTHLY GROUND

There is one final dimension that must be mentioned in our analysis of the spatial conditions of narrative truthtelling, though it defies adequate description within the spatial constraints of the present essay. If there is a space between us, and another above us, and yet another beyond, there must finally be a space below into which the spirit may conduct its usual soundings. This space below is the soil of Earth our mother, from which we sprang and to which we shall return, and with which meanwhile we are biologically, chemically linked by ties beyond our numbering. For we are entirely of earth and earthly. The inner space we have attempted variously to identify is not really separable from our earthliness at all. It is no cavity in our body, no vacuum sealed off from its physical enclosure; it is not, in the dualistic sense of the term, a soul. It is an aspect of the living body itself, a realized possibility of organic life generally. Because we are earthly organisms our vital subsistence depends on forces much larger than our conscious purposes can accommodate. We hunger, for instance, and because of the total dependence on earthly nutrients that this hunger expresses we are no more than extended digestive tracts—to be sure, with some embellishments, such as brains and hands, but the embellishments, too, must be fed. As our hunger keeps us forever upended, open mouthed, in a vast organic horn of nutrient, so our thirst keeps us immersed in the earth's springs and waterways, which course finally through the fluids of our bodies, and our need to pump air every instant into our lungs opens us constantly to the earth's atmosphere. We are digestive tracts, bags of water, hot-air balloons, bundles of libidinous energy through which we are tricked into propagating our species. We seem to be only fitfully conscious of our near-total dependence on the thin, spherical envelope of water, air, and soil we call the earth. There are intimations of the dependence when hunger and thirst are acute or breathing grows labored or the libidinous beast is aroused. That we are otherwise so largely oblivious of it, in our pursuit of much less vital projects, simply evidences what a small part consciousness plays in the urgent processes that bind us to the earth. The grossest philosophical error of modern times, shared by both rationalists and empiricists, is to suppose that we are self-enclosed centers of consciousness linked to the world only through the five senses. Sense perception registers only the most superficial aspects of the earthliness of our lives. All our conscious powers and volitions are dwarfed by the effects of tremendous natural forces on these earthly bodies. These forces, impervious as a capricious god to our little projects in the world, sometimes nourish us and sometimes destroy us through the very means that make us dependent on them.

This earthliness, too, is reflected in inner space, but only inadequately, for it is so ingredient in our very flesh that it cannot be objectified. The spirit does take soundings in the soils and waterways of earth, and here too it struggles to create homologies in sound and image and language. These homologies, to be sure, are created primarily not through stories but through such media as visual similacra, the pulses, harmonies and dissonances of music, the abstract language of natural scientists, and the more ecstatic theorizing of such nature mystics as Feuerbach and Nietzsche. This prodigious earthly ground of our existence does not offer promising subject matter for narrative treatment, because it is too constant. Stories are ordinarily told about events that break the cycles of constancy, usually through the actions of conscious agents. Outstanding exceptions, such as the novels of Thomas Hardy, simply prove the rule. Yet the example of Hardy suggests that the earthliness of our lives provides another necessary condition for truthtelling in narrative. Even if it is not thematized, as it is for instance in *The Return of the Native,* the earthliness of the characters in a truthtelling story awakens us to the environing field of life-supporting and death-dealing forces that are ingredient in our own bodily existence.

NARRATIVE TRUTHTELLING

It remains to reconsider the way the four spatial dimensions we have identified function as conditions of narrative truthtelling. We will take them up in reverse order.

We ended our remarks on the earthliness of human being with an apparent paradox: though it is not ordinarily a manageable subject of narrative, earthliness nevertheless grounds every true story. The solution to this paradox is the indirectness with which this grounding generally affects the action of the story. Even if it is simply taken for granted, the very fact that it is too obvious in the way the characters of the story comport themselves to need direct mention is itself powerful testimony to their essential earthliness. A story is obviously false that fails to ground character and action in the most elemental physical conditions of existence. If a high moral tone, for instance, is achieved at the cost of implicitly disembodying the characters in the story, their psychic weightlessness too will be apparent, and the morality will lack gravity as well. For the weight and density that make characters "real," independently "alive" and thus resistant to the arbitrary manipulation of a narrator, is achieved when they exhibit the mysterious opacity of earthly clay. Stories have spiritual truth to the extent that they are inspired by a spirit incarnate in this clay from which we sprang and to which, if we are fortunate, those who love us will consign us in quiet consummation. Truthtelling conforms to Nietzsche's admonition: *Bleib der Erde treu!*—stay loyal to the earth.[9]

It may be objected that this criterion of truthtelling presupposes a distinctively modern view of "nature," and of human dependency on nature in this scientifically informed sense. Certainly the particular concept of nature that has emerged from the physical sciences is of recent vintage. But ancient stories that have stood the test of time retain their ring of truth because they reflect a tragic or comic earthliness that abides through all the changes in world view. Take the canonical Gospels, for instance. They offer a particularly severe test of this proposition, since they presuppose a Weltanschauung as antithetical to the modern concept of nature as any. Certainly Nietzsche would have resisted any suggestion that the Gospels conform to an admonition of his! Hunger, sickness, and death, which from a modern point of view are simply natural conditions, are treated in the Gospels, together with sin, as signs that the world has fallen away from the condition in which it was created. In a demon-infested world, sin, hunger, disease, and death are themselves demonic forces that will be overthrown in the new kingdom that is coming. Already in the miracle stories of the Gospels these four universal plagues that afflict the children of Adam are locally and momentarily suspended in episodic anticipations of the coming kingdom: Jesus heals the afflicted, feeds large crowds with a few loaves and fishes, forgives sins, and raises Lazarus from the dead. It is anachronistic to speak of these miracles as interruptions of the natural order, because the Gospels do not even recognize any order of nature as such. The miracles are signs of a coming age in which the conditions of life will be transformed. But precisely the dramatic urgency of the longing for this transformation presupposes the universality of elemental needs that are everywhere exhibited in the Gospels. The characters in these stories, fisherfolk, prostitutes, the lame, the blind, the convulsed, are driven by manifold hungers, not necessarily including the hunger for righteousness, and they move in an atmosphere of dust, sweat, and blood. The festive moments are those in which they are feasting or bathing. These stories are good news primarily for the poor, because they live daily with hunger, sickness, deformity, and the imminent danger of death, under the pressure of sheer physical vulnerability. The gospel "message" may be otherworldly, in the sense that it promises relief, but the relief sought is also of a strictly earthly sort, a physical life in a transformed world. Meanwhile the earthbound desperation of its present condition is as vivid in the Gospels as it is in the experience of the poor in all times and places. That is a quality that gives the Gospels what Frei calls their historylike character. To inquire whether in other respects these stories are truthtelling would be a laborious task beyond our present scope. But that inquiry should not be confused with the question of their historicity, or whether they disclose esoteric knowledge. The truth of a story is in its narration.

Turning from the earthly ground of narrative truthtelling to its supercelestial height, we again find ourselves in a region that is seldom the explicit subject of narrative. But let us consider the relevance of sublime vacuity. The entropic dissipation of our homey little cosmos into this void is epitomized in every true story as an unrelieved transience. The empty sublime is the *primum mobile* that will not let the action of our stories come finally to rest. Of course, every story has to stop somehow, and traditional tales create the Aristotelian illusion of action completed. We can only smile when we hear that the lovers, after so many vicissitudes, married and lived happily ever after: The End. No need to spoil these stories by following the lovers into the new vicissitudes of marriage, but we know a white lie when we hear one. From this angle of vision there can be no convincing narrative resolutions that are both happy and definitive. Resolutions that are happy are not final, and those that are final are tragic. Hence the ironical admonition of the ancient Greeks to call no man happy until he is dead, that is, until he has suffered terminal unhappiness. Happy resolutions are temporary, their provisional status signaled by a certain irony in the story's diction, but their very transience may make the short-lived resolutions all the more sweet.

Sublimity provides a criterion of truth, in this sense, not only in literature or drama or formal storytelling but also with respect to the more inchoate narrative structures by which we give form to our individual and collective experience. We will be skeptical, we stargazers, of specious eternities in time, whether they are invested in academic tenure, or marriage, or socialism forever, or the triumph of democratic institutions—all good things and fit objects of provisional life scenarios but lures to self-deception for those who expect them to be final havens for the restless heart. Yet the pull of sublimity is not only a critical impulse. It also draws from our inner space a lyrical flight of the spirit, a vertical movement that follows the erotic perpendicular of the spire and is simultaneously a plumbing of the inner depths. This lyricism, which registers in the most visceral manner, is profoundly erotic both in its lifting beyond the stars and in its sinking into the emptiness within. It also lends its truth, at once erotic and austere, to the language of a story.

The heavenly canopy of bright spirits, spreading below the empty sublime, also contributes to the truthtelling artist and to the truthtelling construction of experience. It contributes the vital mystery of grace, without which a story has no surprises, bears no astonishment, turns nothing around. There are, to be sure, stories the force of which is precisely the relentless unfolding of the inevitable; and life is like that sometimes. But we also have the experience, which cannot be predicted, that the marvelous breaks into this grinding force of circumstance and a hopeless situation is suddenly ventilated by possibility. That is when heaven touches earth. The airy regions are full of possibility. That is the truth in the otherwise dangerous notion that destinies are determined by the heavens. A story that cannot entertain that possibility is untrue to the gift-bearing spirit, which displays its strength not by force, as is the way of the world, but by empowerments and fresh beginnings. It is not necessary that a goddess or an angel or a blessed saint actually materialize here below as a character in the story, though they sometimes do, in direct or indirect personation. But there are times when simple honesty will not permit us to withhold gratitude for the mystery that has overtaken us, heavensent, and telling such stories is itself a prayer of thanksgiving. "Whether a person is helped miraculously," says Kierkegaard's Anti-Climacus, "depends essentially upon the passion of the understanding whereby he has understood that help was impossible and depends next on how honest he was toward the power that nevertheless did help him."[10] Heaven turns to us a face like our own, transfigured, but in a manner that makes us acknowledge that its face is the prototype, ours the image. Augustine, pondering in the *City of God* how it can be that the blessed in heaven will see God when the high God is by nature invisible, concludes that they will see God in his perfected image in one another's faces.[11] So it is too that heaven sometimes condescends to us below and inspires many a magically hopeful story.

Finally, from our excursions into the upper and nether regions, we return to the social space in which most stories unfold and which all truthtelling stories must reflect. A story must not only be true to our experience of social space but must awaken us to it: to the things we know in our bones, but to which we are otherwise impervious, about the passions and delusions of the human heart, the fleshy density of family life, the ecstasies of love but also its exploitations and tyrannies, the self-protective rigidities of institutions, the madness of crowds. This list is suggestive rather than definitive. Here the true stories are those that render our shared social space with psychological and political insight communicated in the concrete detail of the telling.

I venture to say, furthermore, that the inner space of the storyteller must register some definite and intimate region of social space if her or his narrating is to be authentic in its intricacy and sureness of vision. Not many of us in this culture carry the richness of a homogeneous culture in our souls any more, as the bards of sacred space perhaps did. But without some powerful community identification, we can render only the most superficial features of the social horizon. Still, the storyteller who enjoys a strong social identity in a particular community is in a position to bring out its universal significance, with a certain contemplative irony toward the community he nevertheless continues to interiorize. It is easy to think of literary examples. Such a major American writer of this century as Faulkner, like Mark Twain before him, was affectionately rooted in a strong ethnic tradition, with a sharply defined social space, but also able to take the wryly ironical view of it. The same is true of contemporary artists as different as Alice Walker and Garrison Keillor. Such literary examples provide useful models for how to form a life of experience in a community nowadays, without either parochialism or alienation.

Truthtelling, to be sure, is not simply a matter of registering the four spatial dimensions we have identified. The meaning, as Frei has suggested, is in the specific form of the telling, and so, I should want to add, is the truthfulness. For the story itself is the locus of that homology the truthbearing spirit creates between our shared inner space and the outer space of the reality that encompasses us. The dimensions of narrative space discussed here are formal—not sufficient conditions for truthtelling but perhaps necessary conditions.

NOTES

1. Hans W. Frei, *The Eclipse of Biblical Narrative: A Study in Eighteenth and Nineteenth Century Hermeneutics* (New Haven: Yale Univ. Press, 1974), 324.

2. Ibid., 273.

3. Ibid.

4. Ibid., 279–80.

5. Mircea Eliade, *The Sacred and the Profane: The Nature of Religion,* trans. Willard R. Trask (New York: Harcourt, Brace & World, 1959), chap. 1.

6. Blaise Pascal, *Pensées,* trans. A. J. Krailsheimer (Baltimore: Penguin Books, 1966), p. 96, no. 201. There is, to be sure, some question whether Pascal is speaking for himself in this confession of dread or whether he is presenting it as the challenge of a hypothetical interlocutor. But he understands the experience.

7. Augustine *Confessions* 4.4.

8. The *de profundis* alluded to was enunciated, with the appropriate stutter, in Ray L. Hart's memorable presidential address on nothingness to the American Academy of Religion: "To Be *and* Not to Be: *Sit Autem Sermo (Lógos) Vester, Est, Est; Non, Non . . . ,"* *Journal of the American Academy of Religion* 53 (1985): 5–22.

9. Friedrich Nietzsche, *Also sprach Zarathustra,* Vorrede, vol. 2 of *Werke*

(Frankfurt am Main: Ullstein Verlag, 1976), 554; ET: *The Portable Nietzsche*, trans. and ed. Walter Kaufmann (New York: Viking Press, 1954), 125.

10. Søren Kierkegaard, *The Sickness unto Death*, vol. 19 of *Kierkegaard's Writings*, trans. and ed. Howard V. Hong and Edna H. Hong (Princeton: Princeton Univ. Press, 1980), 39.

11. Augustine *City of God* 22.19.

PART TWO

Theological applications

7

Biblical narrative and theological anthropology

David H. Kelsey

But in a certain sense theologians have to proceed in a piecemeal fashion, confronting one problem or question at a time. In doing so they must be careful not to foreclose other issues which are not at that point up for consideration. This seems a better procedure than the endeavor to reduce all questions in theology to a basic systematic position which can be applied ready-made to any and all problems that come along.[1]

There is an irony at the core of recent celebration of the importance of narrative for Christian theology. The irony is especially sharp when the celebration claims that for any theology acknowledging the authority of scripture, what is authoritative is the very narrativity of scripture—not the "content" conveyed in a narrative mode of discourse but rather scripture's narrative form and force itself. In recent theology this type of claim has been worked out in varying degrees of detail in regard to a number of traditional theological loci: Christology,[2] revelation,[3] and God.[4] The irony is this: the claims about the importance of narrative rest on claims about human personhood. But if those claims are cogent, it seems to follow that however basic scripture may be to other theological loci, in its narrativity it *cannot* serve to authorize a theological anthropology. That, at any rate, is the thesis of this essay.

My effort to show this has two parts. I begin with a sketch of claims made in behalf of the irreducible importance of narrative for theology. Two rather different types of claims will be distinguished. The irony is strongest in the type of claim largely prompted by Hans Frei's seminal work in a programmatic essay,[5] a massive account of the theological consequences of the eclipse of narrative in the history of biblical interpretation,[6] and a constructive essay in Christology.[7] Consequently it will receive primary attention. In the second part I will show why these claims about the authority of scripture's narrativity rule out, *on their own grounds,* the possibility that biblical narrative be authoritative for theological anthropology in particular. A final section will suggest an alternative way in which scripture is authoritative for theological anthropology, on grounds consonant with arguments claiming scriptural narrative's authority for some other topics.

WHY NARRATIVE?

There are, commentators often point out, two rather different kinds of claims made to celebrate the importance of narrative for constructive theology. Each brings with it important, and importantly different, implications for biblical hermeneutics and for the way in which scripture is authoritative for theology.[8] Each grounds its claims about the importance of narrative in claims about human personhood. They have in common an anthropological starting point. But they differ basically. One celebrates the importance of narrative by way of transcendentally argued analysis of human personhood which can be put to foundationalist use in theology. By contrast, the other, determinedly nonfoundationalist, rests its case for the centrality of narrative on the difficulties we face in trying adequately to describe *who* some individual person is, difficulties we face quite apart from the cogency of any analytical or speculative explanation of what it is about human persons that makes description so difficult.

The foundationalist approach argues that narrativity is the transcendental condition in consciousness of the possibility of our having the kinds of experiences we do in fact have. One universal characteristic of human consciousness is its temporal flow into the present out of the past and toward the future. As Stephen Crites put it, "The inner form of *any* possible experience is determined by the union of these three modalities in *every* experience." Crites goes on to argue that the "tensed unity of these modalities" in consciousness means that consciousness requires different types of narrative as the necessary forms for its *expression* of itself and of its "own *sense of the meaning of its internal coherence.*" The type of narrative that is transcendentally required to express our experience Crites calls "mundane story," and the type required to express our sense of our own meaning he calls "sacred story."[9] On this basis religion may be provided with a foundation in a transcendental form universal to human consciousness, namely, the narrativity of our experience of our own meaningfulness. Therewith Christianity and its theological reflections may be given a foundation as one valid instance among many of human consciousness' inescapable religiosity (even though Crites does not himself explicitly undertake this).

The nonfoundationalist celebration of narrative's importance for theology proceeds differently. Here the argument focuses on the conditions of adequate *description*, rather than the conditions of adequate *expression*, of a human person precisely in regard to his or her unsubstitutable personal identity. The superiority of narrative is said to lie in its unique power to re-present that personal identity, to make it "present" in a way, to make it available so we may know it. It is important to stress that the governing question is not the noetic question, What are the conditions of the possibility of our knowing persons, or of our experiencing persons? Nor, What are the conditions of our knowing *as* persons, or of our experiencing *as* persons? Rather, the governing question concerns modes of descriptive discourse, their genre differences, diverse types of logical force, and depth grammar: What is the best way in which to go about describing somebody's unsubstitutable identity?

One way of making the case for the superiority of narrative in describing personal identity involves two steps. First, exhibit the partial inadequacy of the available alternatives. Second, show that narrative can accomplish all that each of the alternatives succeeds in doing while overcoming the deficiency of each alternative when it is relied on alone. In an important fugitive essay that deserves to be far more widely read, Frei outlines a remarkably comprehensive and fruitful example of this line of argument.[10]

Mindful that before the overview and critique of alternative views begins it would be well to make as clear as possible what they all are

about, Frei prefaces his argument with a few remarks about the
concept of personal identity. It is not a technical concept whose home
is a formal conceptual scheme. It is a familiar concept in ordinary
language. When we try to analyze it we discover, as did Saint Augustine in regard to the concept of time, that for all our intuitive sense
that we know perfectly well what it is, it eludes clear explanation.
There is something "circular" about it, Frei remarks. That is, every
effort to explain it in other terms ends up more or less subtly using
the terms to be explained. We want to say that we are speaking not of
abstract or numerical identity in general but quite specifically "personal" identity. To explain what we mean by "personal" we say that
personal identity is an identity that involves "recollection or memory
of one's intercourse with others as well as oneself and willingness to
accept responsibility for actions in which one's own intentions have
played a prime part."[11] Such personal identity is, we want to say,
unsubstitutable by any other personal identity. And then we want to
say that we use "identity" to designate the fact that this remembering
and responsible someone is "himself and the same at an important
point as well as over a length of time." But it seems that "himself" is
simply a substitute for "is identical."

Frei does not choose to discuss the reasons for this circularity. The
fact that attempts to explain our ordinary-language concept of personal identity tend to go in circles suggests that it is a concept that
simply cannot be analyzed into logically prior, and perhaps clearer
and more precise, concepts. The concept of personal identity seems to
have the kind of logical status that P. F. Strawson argued the concept
of a person has: the status of a primitive concept, that is, a concept
used to denote that to which various (and apparently contrary) kinds
of predicates can be ascribed but which cannot itself be explained by
analysis into other more basic or primitive concepts.[12]

Thus in everyday informal uses of the concept, we want to say that
both physical and mental predicates may be ascribed to us whose
identity is distinctly personal identity. We are at once bodily and
"soulish." Furthermore, we want to say that not all our bodily and
mental states are immediately accessible to an observer. Indeed, in
virtue of our peculiar mix of physical and mental capacities, we are
capable of concealing or revealing certain of our bodily and mental
states. On the other hand, many bodily states and perhaps some

mental ones are publicly available at least to a suitably competent observer. In that sense, we want to say, our personal identity involves both "private" and "public" aspects. Moreover, the means by which we reveal bodily and mental states are socially shared languages. They include the languages of spoken and written signs, ritual gesture, bodily movement and posture, personal adornment, and significant possessions. All are languages that are communally shared, preexist and outlast us, are learned by us from the cultures in which we live, and hence shape us from infancy onward. Our personal identities are social identities, identities situated in groups of persons sharing cultures and common histories. Both individualistic and social predicates may be ascribed to our personal identities.

Now Western philosophical traditions have generated bodies of theory each designed to give a single internally coherent description of human personhood which comprehends all that we want to say about human identity (e.g., its bodiliness *and* soulishness; private *and* public dimensions; individuality *and* sociality; etc.) but with far greater rigor and precision than ordinary language allows us in our informal descriptions. For their rigor and precision these theories rely in part on schemes of concepts that are precisely designed and carefully used. The first step in an argument for narrative as the best way in which to describe personal identity is to exhibit the inadequacy of attempts to describe it by way of a theory's conceptual scheme.

Frei points out that for all their diversity, these conceptual schemes fall into three families. For the first the defining characteristic of human personhood is its capacity for *intentional action*. Perhaps this judgment is rooted in the intuition that the way to know a particular person's "unsubstitutable identity" is to know his typical action, action of which we might say, "Here he was most himself." On this analysis, intention and action are dialectically interrelated. An intention is not a "cause" of the action as its "effect." If it were, it would be describable in logical independence of its effect (and vice versa). But in fact it is not. "To describe an occurrence as an action I must describe it as explicit intention; to describe an intention as just that and not as a putative mental 'thing,' I must describe it as an implicit action." On this view, "a person's identity is constituted (not simply illustrated) by that intention which he carries into action."[13]

Conceptual schemes in which descriptions of persons as inten-

tional agents are formally elaborated with some rigor and precision
do seem able to integrate the range of things we want to say about our
personal identities when we describe them informally. The initial
insistence that intention and action are *dialectically* interrelated
stresses that a personal identity is such that both mental predicates
(e.g., intentions) and bodily predicates (e.g., bodily action) may be
ascribed to it without its being analyzable into either or both of them
(as though personhood were somehow made up out of a combination of mental substance and material substance). So too, and for the
same reason, this conceptual scheme holds together and in balance
that human persons are at once individual (only I intend my acts and
enact my intentions) and social beings (I can formulate my intentions
even to myself only by using a socially shared language; I can enact
my intentions only in and through some modification of behaviors
selected from a range of possible behaviors that are conventions
taught and learned in my society's culture). Moreover, in virtue of this
conceptual scheme's analysis of the concepts of intention and action,
it is also adequate to the dialectic between the private and public
aspects of personal identity. Intentions are private, accessible only to
the intender, until enacted in public. Indeed, an intention may be
precisely an intention so to act publicly as to obscure and conceal the
intention being enacted, so that despite public enactment it is kept
private.

But in another respect, conceptual schemes of this type are inadequate. They are powerful in descriptions of someone's personal identity as "himself and the same at an important point," namely, at the
point of the intentional action selected for description because it is an
action in which he is "most himself." But this type of conceptual
scheme is not adequate, Frei contends, to describe how someone is
"himself and the same . . . over a length of time." When we have said
all that the conceptual scheme empowers us to say by way of description of personal identity, we still feel we lack a description of the
"*ascriptive* center or focus of intentional activity."[14] How is that to be
described, that for which "I" is, in Gilbert Ryle's phrase, the "index
word"?

A second family of conceptual schemes focuses on this question. Its
task seems almost paradoxical: to describe that which is, by common
consent, persistent, ultimate, and elusive. It is persistent in that it is

simply the personal identity of someone over a length of time. It is ultimate in that, although many, sometimes apparently contrary, predicates are ascribed to it, it is not itself predicable of anything else. It is systematically elusive to self-apprehension in that every act of self-apprehending may grasp an earlier moment of the ascriptive focus of intentional action but cannot therewith *also* apprehend itself *as engaged in* self-apprehension.

This second type of conceptual scheme finds the solution of the paradox in the judgment that the defining characteristic of our unsubstitutable personal identity is its capacity for *self-manifestation*. Perhaps this judgment is an abstract generalization of the intuition that facial expressions, bodily posture, and audible speech are outward and objective expressions or manifestations of an inward and subjective state. On this analysis the persistent, ultimate, elusive ascriptive center of intentional activity is not only expressed but actually manifest, available for description, in a medium different from itself. It genuinely is self-identically present *in* this medium different from itself. It is self-manifest in self-differentiation.

The person is not to be identified exclusively with some subject that lies "behind" the self-manifestation. On the contrary, the human person is constituted by self-differentiation, constituted by the dialectical relation between inward-subjectivity and outward-objectivity. "Dialectical relation" puts it too abstractly. It is the living process that constitutes human being: consciousness as essentially and spontaneously self-expressive. Personal identity, then, simply *is* the identity of the two. To take the example of speech, my words are an objective medium different from the subjectivity that "comes to expression" in them, but I *am* the identity-in-difference of the two: "Verbal manifestation then is identity with oneself in a medium different from" onself.[15]

Like the intention-action conceptual scheme, this scheme is rooted in a presystematic judgment that a distinctive kind of vitality is at the heart of human personhood. But whereas the first kind of scheme construes distinctively human vitality as the more or less mindful enactment of more or less conscious intentions, the second kind of scheme construes it as more or less conscious but, in any case, irrepressibly spontaneous expressivity. From the point of view of the first type of scheme, the second tends to describe personal identity

more as absorbing, appreciative, and in general "aesthetic" than as
accountable and responsible, more as reactive than as proactive, and
for all its spontaneity, finally more as a receptive subject than as a
focus of limited but real power. From the perspective of the second
type of conceptual scheme, the first tends to describe personal identity as driving more toward *domination over* than toward *reciprocity
with* the "other"—as constituted by a will to power over rather than a
will to empower the "other." Personal agency is construed as "I," in
Stephen Crites's marvelous rhetorical phrase, "this tall, thin, all-too-
phallic pronoun."[16]

Conceptual schemes describing persons as expressively self-man-
ifesting in self-differentiation seem adequate to two of the major sorts
of things we want to say about personal identities when we describe
them informally, but only partly adequate to a third. Ironically, their
adequacy is challenged in regard to their handling of the polarity that
they seem to make central: the private and the public. The ascriptive
center of intentional action is constituted by consciousness, that is, by
spontaneous self-differentiating through self-manifestations of utterly
private subjectivity in entirely public objectivity. This provides in turn
a way to use the "unique location or perspective of the body that is at
once mine and myself as a paradigmatic instance of the identity-
in-difference of the elusive subject."[17] Thus by virtue of the polarity
between identity and difference, between a subject that both *has* and
is a body, this conceptual scheme can hold in coherent balance the
ranges of bodily and soulish predicates ascribed to us, neither hypo-
statizing them nor reducing one to the other. Furthermore, by virtue
of the same polarity, this scheme can hold together without self-
contradiction the individuality and sociality of human persons. One's
expressive self-manifestation is singularly one's own. But the media
in which one is self-identical-in-difference are socially shared and in
part socially constructed.

Still, conceptual schemes of this type are accused of inadequacy
precisely at the point of the contrast of private and public that they
make central. The objection is that this type of conceptual scheme
is unrealistically optimistic about the living dialectic of identity-in-
difference. The scheme seems to assume that the movement of the
living dialectic cannot malfunction, so to speak, in such a way that
the different with which the self in manifestation can be identical

turns into the utterly alien in which the self is lost. The public, the objective and outward, may be a medium that distorts rather than manifests the self. In that case, the self-in-manifestation is not an identity-in-difference but a self-manifestation in self-contradiction. In short, the objection goes, this conceptual scheme is inadequate to the reality of evil.

The third family of conceptual schemes also attempts to describe the ascriptive center of intentional activity, but in a way that is more adequate to the reality of evil. For this group too the defining characteristic of our unsubstitutable personal identity seems to be its capacity for self-manifestation. But the public world that provides the medium in which human persons are to manifest themselves radically distorts them. Instances of this family of conceptual schemes tend to locate the medium of self-manifestation in socially constructed cultural worlds rather than in the world of nature. These schemes range widely between those that stress continuity and those that stress total alienation between the medium of manifestation and the subject. But all share the view that in actual practice the subject is self-manifestation-in-alienation. On this analysis personal identity is not a living dialectic. Rather, it is a problem to be solved, a thing to be achieved. "In this world my identity is itself alienated; in this world I am without true identity. . . . My journey through that world is a journey in search of myself, constantly mirrored though not truly present to myself nor self-reconciled in the world."[18]

Conceptual schemes of this type may be even more adequate than those of the second type in their power to describe the complexity, ironies, and even tragedy ingredient in the dialectics between the private and public, the individual and social, and the bodily and soulish aspects of personal identity. But, as Frei points out, when elaborated they tend, unless checked by a counterdescription, to become inadequate to our bodiliness and our sociality. Because the scheme onesidedly stresses the social and historical world as the (alienating) medium of self-manifestation, rather than the world of nature, "it is rare that the body plays a significant part in this scheme." Furthermore, because it is the social and historical world that is both mirror and alienated distortion of the self, the significance of temporal, social events is taken to be "their subject reference rather than their public character. They are, in objectified form, the crucial stages in the transition of the subject toward full self-penetration or reconciled selfhood."[19] The ascriptive center of intentional activity thus tends to be undialectically identified with personal identity in its individuality and not its sociality.

After exhibition of the inadequacies of each of the theoretical ways of describing personal identity, the second step is to show the relatively greater adequacy of narrative. The central point, of course, is that narrative is not one more type of theory that describes personal identity by way of a conceptual scheme. Unsubstitutable personal identity does not lend itself to theoretical description. In the nature of the case a theory's conceptual scheme provides a way to describe what is universally true of all instances of personal identity. It may do this by identifying the universal transcendental conditions of personal consciousness as such, or by identifying the dynamics and processes that constitute the "personhood" of personal identity, or by identifying the curriculum through which personhood moves to actualize individuality. Precisely because of its generality, however, such a conceptual scheme cannot hope to catch precisely the unitariness of personal identity in its unsubstitutability. For the same reason, Frei argues, it is not a possible project to synthesize the several partially adequate theories into a supertheory that might overcome the partial inadequacies of each of the subordinate theories taken alone. That is not to deny that each of the theories can be used to describe human persons in regard to one aspect or another of their personhood. More than that, Frei believes, a dialectical relation or cross-reference may obtain *among* the different theoretical descriptions.[20] "But this cross reference is based on the unitariness of the self and is not simply descriptively locatable. We do not have the superdescription which would integrate the contents and descriptions."[21] Indeed, we *cannot* have the superdescription, because the basis that integrates the several families of theoretical descriptions is that unitariness of personal identity which cannot be described in general categories.

Narrative, it is claimed, is a way to describe unsubstitutable personal identity in quite a different sense of "describe." The narrative of a realistic novel or short story is a mode of discourse that holds character and circumstances together in a distinctive way. For Frei the definitive formulation is Henry James's: "What is character but the determination of incident? What is incident but the illustration of character?"[22] Thus narrative holds inseparably together in a single account both what the character did (character determining incident) and who the character is (incident illustrating character). That is to say that narrative describes a person's unsubstitutable identity both in terms of enactment of intention (what the character did) and in terms of the persistent, ultimate, and elusive ascriptive center of intentional action (who the character is).

Narrative does not describe someone's unsubstitutable identity by *explaining* the conditions of its possibility, or the dynamics constitutive of all personhood, or the necessary stages on the way to genuine identity. Rather, narrative describes someone's personal identity simply by rendering it, making it concretely present, albeit in the imaginative mode, in its concrete unsubstitutability. In that—the argument goes—lies narrative's superiority as a mode of discourse in which to describe someone's unsubstitutable personal identity.

SCRIPTURAL NARRATIVITY AND
THEOLOGICAL ANTHROPOLOGY

Each of these two kinds of claims about the importance of narrative for constructive theology is based on general, that is, nontheological, anthropological remarks. The irony is that on neither of them can a case be made for the authority of biblical narrative specifically for constructive *theological* anthropology. By constructive theological anthropology, I mean a set of theological remarks, more or less systematic, addressed to a traditional agenda of questions about human beings: What is it about us that makes it possible for us finite creatures to know the infinite God? And, given that we are capable of it, what about us accounts for the fact that mostly we do not know God and stand in need of God's gracious revelation? What does the fact of our mortality imply about our dignity and worth? What is it about us that accounts for our inexhaustible, restless yearning for some kind of fulfillment? And, notably in Western Christianity since Saint Augustine, What does our pervasive guilt-consciousness imply about our capacity for fulfillment? The underlying question that comes to expression in each of these has been, Theologically speaking, what constitutes our humanity? And the general answer, worked out in different ways in response to each question, has been, Our God-likeness, that we have been created in the image of God, a likeness deformed by sin.

Now, it is a systematic anthropological theory that is the basis for the "foundationalist" type of claim about narrative's importance. This anthropology argues not from narrative but to it. It proposes to explain why narrative is the basic mode of human self-expression, especially religious self-expression, inescapable and irreducible to any other mode of discourse. Its argument moves by a transcendental deduction from general features of our experience simply as it is given, to the conditions in consciousness of the possibility of experience's being what it is. Among those conditions, it is argued, is narrativity. That, in turn, gives guidance about what expressions of experience, that is, narratives, mean. Their meaning is precisely their function as the most appropriate mode in which to express the deep structure of our experiencing. When they are scriptural narratives, that is, sacred narratives, they function to express consciousness' sense of its own inner coherence and meaningfulness. Thus the particular narratives peculiar to the Bible, along with their images, metaphors, and concepts, are to be interpreted as instances of how sacred narratives in general "mean" by expressing human consciousness' sense of its inner coherence and meaning.

Note that this is an instance of a self-manifestation-in-self-differentiation anthropological conceptual scheme, the second of Frei's three families of theories descriptive of human nature. On this view, the persistent, ultimate, and elusive ascriptive subject of intentional action is a center of consciousness available to us only as it manifests itself by spontaneous self-expression in a medium other than itself, namely, in spoken or written narratives.

The same systematic anthropological theory can be used to generate a systematic theological anthropology. That is, it can be used to explain the meaning of traditional theological remarks addressed to the traditional agenda of theological anthropology. Thus, for example, it can show that traditional claims—about our being created in the image of God, fallen, given over to death, in sin suffering a bondage of the will and darkening of the mind, restored to the image of God by redemptive grace, etc.—are all best understood as elaborations of individual symbols collected out of the Bible and assembled in a single narrative construct, salvation history. Salvation history, in turn, is explained as the distinctively Christian version of a larger class of sacred narratives expressive of human consciousness' sense of its own inner coherence and meaning. Here theological anthropology is not authorized directly or indirectly by narrative, biblical or otherwise. It is authorized by the cogency of a systematic anthropological theory (of the self-manifestations-in-differentiation type) and its explanatory power. Theological remarks are related to biblical narratives, to be sure, but it is not a relation of "authorized by." Rather the interrelation is a function of their parallel and independent explanation by the same anthropological theory. The theory provides the basic systematic position in terms of which both the meaning of narratives and the meaning of traditional theological anthropology can be explained, a position that can in principle be equally well applied to all other topics in theology.

In contrast, it is inherent in the "nonfoundationalist" type of claims about the importance of narrative for theology to apply the claims piecemeal, confronting each theological locus independently, without assuming a priori that narrative will be illuminating or authoritative. As we have already noted, it has been shown to have impressive illuminating power when applied to constructive theological work in Christology, the doctrine of God, and the doctrine of revelation. In each case, it seems to bring with it the corollary that it is theologically more helpful to take human persons as agents, centers of power, than as patients, centers of consciousness. Nonetheless, this type of claim about the importance of narrative for theology no more allows authorization of theological anthropology by biblical narrative than does the foundationalist type of claim.

The reason lies in the nature of the case that the nonfoundationalist argument makes in its own behalf. As we have seen, its central claim is that unsubstitutable personal identity does not lend itself to *theoretical* description. It tries to show that the conceptual schemes employed by various theoretical descriptions of human personhood all fail to grasp the unitariness of a personal identity precisely in its unsubstitutability. Narrative description alone, it argues, is able to do that, not by explaining what personal identity is but by rendering one, making it present to us. But that is to say that narrative is the mode of discourse best suited to giving a *uniquely individuating* description of a person's unsubstitutable identity. Theoretical accounts explain, with varying degrees of success, what constitutes personal identity as such. By holding individual character and particular circumstances together in a distinctive way, however, realistic narrative is the mode of discourse uniquely suited to describe an individual person's *unsubstitutable* unitariness. It provides a way to give a description of some one personal identity that makes it impossible to confuse one individual with any other. And it does so without sacrificing the realities of the individual's personhood which are generally shared with all human persons. It provides the way to give a uniquely individuating description by way of close attention to these features of personhood rather than by abstraction from them.

That is precisely what makes the nonfoundationalist claims about the importance of narrative powerful for constructive theology that acknowledges the authority of scripture when it treats certain theological loci. Discussion of the significance of Jesus Christ, for example, needs to honor his unsubstitutable personal identity not only in explanation of who he is but also in explication of what he has done. An adequate Christology needs to be worked out in terms of a uniquely individuating description. So too, in a monotheistic tradition an adequate explication of the reality of God as personal (however analogical the use of "personal" may be) requires some way in which to give a uniquely individuating description of God. Furthermore, any account of that God's self-revelation in unsubstitutable and unrepeatable historical events also needs some way in which to give a uniquely individuating description of events of divine revelation.

But theological anthropology is *not* engaged in offering a uniquely individuating description of anybody. Biography and autobiography attempt to do that. Moreover, they may well be cast in theological terms and focus on the ways in which an unsubstitutable personal identity has been shaped and even constituted by its relationships with God. Witness the long and continuing tradition of "spiritual" biographies and autobiographies. Despite their temptations to uncritical hagiography, sentimental piety, and boring unreality, such narratives can be religiously and even theologically important. But they are not exercises in theological anthropology. The agenda of theological anthropology is a set of questions about human personhood that are fully as general as the questions about human being addressed by the human and physical sciences. No doubt Christian theological anthropology has a special interest in stressing that individual human persons cannot be substituted for one another. None other can be substituted for me in my living as God's creature, in my responding to neighbor and to God, in my accepting the gift of grace, in my accountability for my behavior, in my coming to personal fulfillment, or in my dying. In a way, the entire agenda of theological anthropology might be summed up in a very general way in the question, In what does our common unsubstitutability consist? On what does it rest?

There is a way of speaking about biblical narrative that might seem to refute this picture of the task of theological anthropology. It is sometimes said that the biblical story *is* the story of our lives. For the sake of the discussion we may set aside the vexing question whether the expression "*the* biblical story" can survive close scrutiny. Taken at face value, does this not suggest a way in which biblical narrative might be authoritative for theological anthropology too? Probably not. There is an ambiguity in the phrase "our lives." If it means our lives taken one by one, surely it is false on any ordinary reading of either the claim or the Bible. No one now living is a character in any part of biblical narrative. Scarcely any of the circumstances in biblical narrative now obtain. "Our lives" might, however, mean our lives collectively. Read this way, there is a measure of plausibility to the claim that the biblical story is the story of our lives. The biblical story, it might be explained, is a narrative that gives a uniquely individuating description of the communal identity of community that was the context of the lives of many of the characters who are in the biblical stories, and it continues under very different circumstances to be the context of our lives now. It is in this context that our individual personal identities are shaped. This might be developed into an argument for the authority of biblical narrative for any theological discussion of the community, that is, the people of God, or the covenant community, or, in a certain sense of the term, God's church.

Nonetheless, it does not seem to yield an argument for the authority of the biblical story for theological anthropology. When the biblical story describing a communal identity is also taken as a description of an individual identity, it becomes not a uniquely individuating description of that person but rather a quarry from which to mine archetypes that are illustrated by that person. The characters actually

rendered in the biblical story become types of which we are instances: Adams and Eves; Sarahs and Abrahams; Peters and Mary
Magdalenes; Pauls and Priscas. Although an archetype may be useful
in describing a person in certain respects for certain purposes, it
nonetheless does not give a uniquely individuating description of that
person. When the biblical story is mined for archetypes in the service
of theological anthropology, it is precisely its narrativity that is set
aside. The biblical story is not the story of our lives in a way that
might serve to authorize a theological anthropology. Indeed, it seems,
the more cogent the nonfoundationalist case for the importance of
scriptural narrative for theology, the clearer it is that the argument
does not apply to constructive theological anthropology.

SCRIPTURE, PRACTICAL THEOLOGY,
AND THEOLOGICAL ANTHROPOLOGY

If the nonfoundationalist type of celebration of biblical narrative is
cogent, what are its possible implications for constructive theological
anthropology? In the first part of this essay, I outlined the structure
that the argument in defense of this view might take; but the argument itself has not actually been made. Accordingly, what follows
inescapably has a hypothetical cast. Assuming the cogency of the
nonfoundationalist type of claim about biblical narrative's importance for theology, what follows regarding theological anthropology
in particular?

The first implication is that theological anthropology is rooted in
and ordered to practical theology. Indeed, given the nonfoundationalist view, all constructive theology is rooted in, and ordered to,
practical theology understood in a broad sense. Accordingly, scripture
helps authorize what is said in theological anthropology indirectly,[23]
insofar as scripture serves to authorize what is done in practical
theology.

This follows from the nonfoundationalist decision to eschew providing a theoretical foundation not only to claims about the importance of biblical narrative for theology but to any theological claims
whatever. On this view, there can be no theoretical foundation on
which the structure of theology can be so built that its reality claiming
and intelligibility are certified from the outset. All that the theological

enterprise can presuppose is *itself in concreto*. The constructive theological enterprise *in concreto* is simply the ongoing effort of Christian persons in community reflectively and self-critically to describe to themselves their communal self-identity, especially as that involves truth-claiming beliefs. They engage in that critical self-description as part of their living-out of their communal identity.

Hence the priority of practical theology. Christian individual and communal identity is constituted by a distinctive praxis. It is an identity that is constituted as an *active* response to something, namely, the way God actively relates to us. The way God relates to us is understood to be a calling and a sending, a vocation and a mission. The community's identity, and the identities of the persons constituting the community, are shaped as the effort to respond appropriately to this vocation and mission.

This is the context of a primary sense in which scripture functions as "authority" for Christian speech and action. Scripture is used in a wide variety of activities that constitute the common life of Christian communities: in liturgy, preaching, education, counsel, controversy, even governance. It is through these uses that the community's vocation is heard and its mission discerned. Used in these ways, scripture helps "author" Christian identity, evoking, correcting, and nurturing it.

Clearly, an adequate response to a mission consists in some kind of praxis. The identity of a Christian community is concretely real just insofar as it is being *enacted* by human persons in the world. Inevitably, as novel circumstances arise in the world, the community will face quandaries: In these new and unforeseen circumstances, what counts as *appropriate* response to God's relating to us? Given the new circumstances, are the ways in which we have been enacting our Christian identity in speech and act still appropriate and adequate, or are they in fact faithless to the identity we want to enact? A strong case could be made that the most pressing quandaries faced by Christian communities in the contemporary cultural and historical context have to do with human dignity: What does it mean to affirm the unqualified intrinsic worth of human persons? On what grounds should human life be treated with unqualified respect? Critical self-reflection on these questions within a Christian community constitutes practical theology in the broad sense. It embraces what has traditionally been called pastoral theology, social ethics, spirituality, personal ethics, etc.

Of course, discussion of these questions cannot proceed far unless there is some description available of just what "Christian identity" is. Such a description functions normatively, as a criterion over against which to judge whether the community is or is not faithful to its identity in its current forms of speech and action. The formulation of the several elements of such a description is the work of constructive theology. Constructive theology is thus rooted in and ordered to the task of practical theology.

This task includes theological anthropology as an elaboration of what must be said about human persons if God relates to us in ways that issue a call to mission to which we are capable of responding more or less adequately. As such, anthropology is indirectly authorized by biblical narratives, as they are used in the community's common life to nurture, guide, and correct Christian identity. These uses of scripture directly help to shape the identity of the community and its members. The sources, the data, so to speak, that immediately inform theological anthropology are persons in communities whose individual and common identities have in turn been partly authorized by scripture.

This brings us to the second implication for theological anthropology of the nonfoundationalist celebration of the importance of biblical narrative. In the work of constructive theology some topics have a kind of logically primary status and others are secondary. Given the nature of Christian identity, some topics in constructive theology must logically be dealt with first, when the move is made from praxis in which Christian identity is enacted to critical self-reflection in pastoral theology. And some topics are logically secondary, derivative from what has been said in elucidation of the primary topics. In the circle from praxis to theoria and back to empowered and reformed praxis, reflection on these secondary topics comes logically closer to the reengagement in praxis. Theological anthropology is one of these secondary topics in constructive theology. Indeed, where the foundationalist celebration of narrative makes anthropology *logically prior to* all other theological topics precisely because it provides the foundation on which they are to be built, the nonfoundationalist claims about the importance of narrative suggest that theological anthropology is *materially derivative from* almost all other theological topics!

Earlier I said that Christian identity is constituted as an *active* response to something, namely, the way God actively relates to us. In that case the logically primary topic in constructive theology is an elucidation of the way in which God actively relates to us—not an elucidation simply of the fact that God relates to us, but rather of the way in which God does so. This means that there is a distinctive feature of the subject matter dealt with in theology's primary or basic topics. As described by those narratives, both God and God's several modes of relating to us are marked by utter *singularity*. It is not simply that they are unique. Individual instances of the same class of things that are otherwise identical may each be unique in virtue of a location in space or time that no other instance of the same class can share. No, they are characterized by singularity in the sense in which some cosmologists speak of the moment of origin of the physical cosmos in a "big bang" as the moment of "singularity." It is not an instance of a class of events of which there logically might be other instances but of which as a contingent matter of fact there is but one instance. It is a conceptual matter rather than a matter of contingent fact that it is singular. It is such that, if it is actual, it is necessarily singular. So too with God as described in biblical literature. Surely that is part of what is correct about Saint Anselm's analysis of the concept of God. If one understands and uses the concept correctly, one understands as a conceptual (and not factual) point that one cannot intelligibly entertain the hypothesis of several Gods. It is also the point made by nonfoundationalist claims about the importance of narrative for theology. Only narrative provides the type of discourse adequate to give a uniquely individuating description of God as an unsubstitutable personal identity, that is, of God as singular.

So too the modes in which God actively relates to us. Scripture narrates a number of these. It seems a plausible proposal that these narratives group themselves into three families of stories concerning God's relating to us as our creator, that to whom we are related in radical contingency for our very reality; God's relating to us as redeemer, affirming our worth in the face of its apparent denial by evil done or evil undergone; and God's relating to us as ultimate or eschatological fulfiller, creatively overcoming the ways in which we are deformed by evil done and evil undergone.[24] As described by biblical narrative each of these modes of God's relating to us is utterly singular. None of them names a class of divine actions each embracing innumerable instances. Rather, each is a singular concrete divine intentional action that neither can be nor needs to be repeated. Once again, the subject matter of a logically primary theological topic is such that its singularity requires the uniquely individuating description only narrative can provide. Theological elucidation of such topics can only be scripturally authorized by biblical narratives.

Theological anthropology is a thoroughly theocentric description of personhood. It is derivative from, and secondary to, theological elucidation of claims about God's relating to us. It addresses an agenda of topics about human personhood generated by prior claims about God. And given constructive theology's rooting in and ordering toward practical theology, in our time theological anthropology formulates those topics in terms of quandaries about the meaning and basis of human dignity or unqualified worthiness of respect. The agenda includes a range of questions: What does it mean to say that we are related to God as creatures radically dependent on an Other both for being and for worth, and what difference does it make? What must be said about human personhood if it is also said that God relates to us as "historical redeemer" and "eschatological fulfiller"? (This is not talk simply of "divinity in general," but talk of the singular God who actively relates to us in the most peculiar way constituted by the life, ministry, crucifixion, and resurrection appearances of Jesus of Nazareth.) What is assumed about the nature of human identity if it is constituted, theologically speaking, by a relation of response to just *that* divine call to mission? What counts as an adequate response to just *that* mode of God's relating to us? What capacities are assumed in human personhood if, further, it is a relation that can consist of *in*appropriate and *in*adequate responses? What can ground persons' worthiness of respect if their response to God's relating to them is radically deformed in evil done?

Thus claims about God generate the agenda of topics on which a modest set of remarks must be made concerning personal identity. They are a *modest* set of remarks in that they need go no further than to explicate what is entailed concerning human personhood by other and prior theological discussions of God and God's relation to what is not God. Where it is not clear how theological remarks cohere with wisdom about human personhood which is well established by one or another of the human sciences, anthropology may attempt in an ad hoc way to show how the two might be understood to cohere. At least it must identify as rigorously as possible just where the inconsistency seems to lie and candidly acknowledge the unresolved tension. It is not essential to its task, however, to develop a supertheory that exhibits the coherence of all theological and nontheological wisdom about human personal identity.

Furthermore, what theological anthropology proposes is but a set of *remarks* precisely because they do not amount to a comprehensive explanatory theory about the "essential" nature of human personhood. To be sure, the remarks suggest some distinctive ways of looking at human persons: their descriptions bring to light features of personhood that other ways of looking at us may tend to obscure, and they may even help explain certain otherwise puzzling features of human behavior. Furthermore, more or less technical conceptual schemes may be used in the course of explicating these remarks. Given the rootage of constructive theological anthropology in quandaries met in the course of the enactment of Christian mission, it is likely that these schemes will tend to favor a picture of persons as modestly powerful centers of agency rather than modestly expressive subjects of experience. It could not be claimed, however, that biblical narratives themselves authorize the use of the conceptual schemes.

Thus what constructive theological anthropology has to go on is twofold. On the one hand, it has concrete communities of persons facing practical quandaries in the course of their efforts both to enact their communal and individual personal Christian identity in mission in the world and to keep that identity nurtured, corrected, and reformed. Perhaps the most pressing quandary focuses on the nature and basis of human worthiness of respect. Communal and individual identities have themselves been partly "authored" by various uses of biblical narrative in the common life of Christian communities. On the other hand, theological anthropology has in hand theological elucidations of Christian claims about God and the various modes in which God actively relates to us. Those claims have themselves been authorized by biblical narratives that give uniquely individuating descriptions of God and God's ways of relating to us. But the remarks explicated in theological anthropology are not themselves directly authorized by scripture, narrative or otherwise.

This situation is in no way evidence of some deep inner incoherence in the nonfoundationalist celebration of scriptural narrative's importance for theology. It could become that only if that celebration were itself subtly converted into a new foundationalism, perhaps a foundation laid up in divine revelation. That the nonfoundationalist claim about the authority of biblical narrativity yields a theological anthropology that is not *directly* authorized by scripture, neither by its narratives nor by anything else in it, is instead a sign that it has been faithful to its commitment "to proceed in a piecemeal fashion, confronting one problem or question at a time . . . [and] not reduc[ing] all questions in theology to a basic systematic position which can then be applied ready-made to any and all problems that come along."

NOTES

1. Hans W. Frei, "Theological Reflections on the Accounts of Jesus' Death and Resurrection," *Christian Scholar* 49 (1966): 274–75.

2. Hans W. Frei, *The Identity of Jesus Christ: The Hermeneutical Bases of Dogmatic Theology* (Philadelphia: Fortress Press, 1975).

3. Ronald F. Thiemann, *Revelation and Theology: The Gospel as Narrated Promise* (Notre Dame, Ind.: Univ. of Notre Dame Press, 1985).

4. Cf. Robert H. King, *The Meaning of God* (Philadelphia: Fortress Press, 1973); Thomas F. Tracy, *God, Action, and Embodiment* (Grand Rapids: Wm. B. Eerdmans, 1984); and in regard to God in the Old Testament, Dale Patrick, *The Rendering of God in the Old Testament* (Philadelphia: Fortress Press, 1981).

5. Frei, "Theological Reflections."

6. Hans W. Frei, *The Eclipse of Biblical Narrative: A Study in Eighteenth and Nineteenth Century Hermeneutics* (New Haven: Yale Univ. Press, 1974).

7. Frei, *Identity of Jesus Christ.*

8. See the contrasts drawn between Frei and Paul Ricoeur by Gary Comstock in "Truth or Meaning: Ricoeur versus Frei on Biblical Narrative," *Journal of Religion* 66 (1986): 117–40.

9. Stephen Crites, "The Narrative Quality of Experience," *Journal of the American Academy of Religion* 39 (1971): 301–2; my emphasis.

10. Frei, "Theological Reflections." It is "fugitive" not only by being placed in an obscure journal but also in appearing in that journal's last issue before it ceased publication. The essay is related to *Identity of Jesus Christ* as a programmatic essay is to a project worked out in accord with it.

11. Frei, "Theological Reflections," 276.

12. P. F. Strawson, "Persons," in *Minnesota Studies in the Philosophy of Science*, vol. 2, *Concepts, Theories, and the Mind-Body Problem*, ed. Herbert Feigl et al. (Minneapolis: Univ. of Minnesota Press, 1958), 330–53.

13. Frei, "Theological Reflections," 279.

14. Ibid., 280.

15. Ibid., 283.

16. Stephen Crites, "A Respectful Reply to the Assertorial Theologian," *Journal of the American Academy of Religion* 52 (1984): 139.

17. Frei, "Theological Reflections," 283.

18. Ibid., 285.

19. Ibid., 284.

20. Ibid., 276.

21. Ibid., 282.

22. Ibid., 279.

23. On the contrast between direct and indirect authorization of theological claims by appeal to scripture, see David H. Kelsey, *The Uses of Scripture in Recent Theology* (Philadelphia: Fortress Press, 1975), 139–43.

24. This rough, slightly artificial threefold factoring of biblical accounts of God's relating to us is not isomorphic with the doctrine of God's triunity. Perhaps God's triunity has more to do with the fact that each of these three ways of relating to us is an enactment of God's powerful, creative, and utterly free love.

8

Following at a distance: ethics and the identity of Jesus

From the very first, even in their crea-
tureliness, they stand in the light which is
shed by Him. But if they are in His light,
they cannot be dark in themselves, but
bright with His light. We thus ask concerning their brightness in His light.
—Karl Barth[1]

That realistic narrative is characteristic
of the Bible, and that this fact possesses
theological significance, are lessons Hans
Frei has done much to teach his contem-
poraries. Theologians who take these
lessons to heart focus often on their implications for scriptural authority. Such
concentration makes sense: the issues at
stake matter enormously to those in the
Christian comunity. I shall step outside
the circle of this discussion, however, for
two reasons. First, the issues receive extensive scrutiny elsewhere. Second, they
are by no means the only ones Frei addresses in a highly instructive way. It
would be a loss if his reflections on other
theological topics were overshadowed altogether by the debates about scriptural
authority. I propose accordingly to examine one such topic on which he likewise
proves to be an illuminating guide.

The topic concerns the relation between Christology and ethics. I shall attend chiefly to his volume *The Identity of
Jesus Christ.*[2] Here we find an abundance
of important christological claims and
also, though less explicitly, claims relevant for Christian ethics. My interest lies
primarily in normative questions: how

Gene Outka

144

we ought to understand our own identity in light of Jesus' identity; what patterns we should realize in our interactions with others, given the patterns he singularly enacts on our behalf; how far we should seek to extend these patterns in the church and in the world.[3]

The approach I shall follow interweaves three sorts of inquiry. I shall consider claims Frei makes, explore what these claims may imply, and append speculative remarks that are most charitably called extrapolations. Frei should certainly not be held accountable for this last activity, which assumes somewhat elaborate proportions at the end of the essay. And doubtless my selection and commentary throughout sometimes reflect preoccupations more nearly mine than his.

FREI'S VIEW OF
SCRIPTURAL AUTHORITY

For Frei, the Bible retains irreducibly distinctive, nontransferable authority and yet is not inerrant or simply or even predominantly propositional. It derives its authority from the events to which it is the indispensable witness and interpreter: the presence of God in Jesus Christ as the summation and climax of God's covenant with Israel. To construe this witness correctly, we must attend to it on its own terms. We must hold in abeyance (or strictly relativize) a vast store of cultural and philosophical notions insofar as they would alter such terms, and repent of our instinctive and arrogant desire to save ourselves. The knowledge of our salvation derives from a particular history that is not in the first instance our own. Indeed, we depend on that particular history not only for the knowledge of our salvation but as the decisive clue to the "one and only real world" there is. Each reader is therefore to see in the biblical narrative "his depiction, his actions and passions, the shape of his own life as well as that of his era's events as figures of that storied world."[4]

How the biblical narrative about Jesus Christ does govern our actions and passions, the shape of our lives, the events of our era, is precisely the subject I shall address here. The governance proves generally to be two-sided: we find impassable differences between Jesus and all of those who aspire to be his followers; and we discern fitting patterns of obedience despite the radical disjuncture. We must

examine both sides to see how Christology shapes our understanding
of our own identities and of our interactions with one another.

THE PATTERN OF JESUS' IDENTITY

Three aspects of the shaping will concern us. They follow from the
three interlocking features Frei locates when "we take the New Testament picture of Jesus as our norm" (63).

1. The first feature is the "cosmic scope of his redeeming activity"
(63). Such activity is an "errand of grace extended to the world"
(111). Frei notes how many strands in the New Testament point to
the unusual power, finally cosmic in outreach, that is present in
Jesus: the application to him of messianic titles, the miracles, preaching, death and resurrection, and his identification as the Son (63–64).
Whatever else the phrase "cosmic scope" might mean, it certainly
means that all human beings are included in the range of Jesus'
redemptive activity. In this activity, sharing and passivity combine.
Frei dwells on the ironic saying of the priests, scribes, and elders in
Matthew 27:42: "He saved others; he cannot save himself." Jesus
takes upon himself the pain of weaklings and outcasts and suffers for
the transgressions of many.

One contrasting case that Frei examines concerns the figure of
Jesus presented by Nikos Kazantzakis in his novel *The Last Temptation
of Christ*.[5] Though the outward events in the novel roughly approxi-
mate the Gospel narrative, the Jesus that Kazantzakis depicts shows
no comparable sharing and passivity. He is rather the superman who
does not and cannot share his struggle of agony and triumph with
others. He leaves the weak and vacillating behind. The strong are able
to see in him their supreme model for an achievement they too can
attain, but only by and for themselves. The watchword of this Jesus is,
Himself he saved; others he could not save (72).

2. The second feature is the "personal and unsubstitutable center
that is Jesus, his personal uniqueness" (64). Frei attempts to demonstrate that the Gospel story, particularly in the sequence from passion
to resurrection, presents Jesus as a singular, unsubstitutable, and self-
focused person (e.g., 52, 61). Consider, for example, how as soon as
the title of Savior is applied to Jesus, his singularity preempts the use
of the term. Any concrete duplication of him is thereby disallowed.

The New Testament story of salvation and the Savior and its story of Jesus' singular obedience exactly coincide. "The very distinctiveness of the Gospel story as a story of salvation rests wholly on the claim that the Savior is completely identical with the specific man Jesus of Nazareth" (82).

Frei offers another contrasting case from literature, Herman Melville's *Billy Budd*. Billy is interpreted as the falling and trans-figured innocent person whom evil can defeat but not corrupt. His sacrifice changes nothing materially in the world, yet its healing power touches those around him. He is then a redeeming figure of cosmic outreach. But he lacks singularity. "Billy Budd is no particular person. He learns nothing and can himself neither develop nor shape the events in which he is the chief ingredient" (68). Frei finds sin-gularity also absent from the gnostic myth, which as a loose syn-drome he takes to be "both perennial and *sui generis*" (p. x). Here the fallen and rising redeemer is no specific, individual human being but merges instead with the primordial man and our own enlightened self-presence. At the end of the day, to know our true identity is tantamount to knowing we have none. Silence lies at the end of our quest (60–61). Sheer diffusion reigns, a condition thoroughly at odds with the singular historical identity rendered by the Gospel story.

Such diffusion is also at odds with the formal ingredient in Frei's description of human identity. He does not rule out all general ap-peals to formal categories, because he is cautiously prepared to as-sume that we share with the New Testament writers some of the same kinds of identity description (46). Whatever categories are used to describe must not turn out to redescribe by importing an alien pro-gram, however; and no description is acceptable if it distorts rather than heightens the identity of Jesus disclosed in the New Testament. At least one formal description escapes these temptations: each per-son may attain singular historical identity and is thus unsubstitutable.

Both the singular and the historical aspects merit attention. To be singular one must be self-constituted: "The self is the source of its own self-relatedness; . . . nothing external to the self can constitute (though it may aid) the continuity between the past, the present, and the future that real identity requires" (39). Certainly Frei takes pains to avoid a dualistic "ghost in the machine" construal of such self-constitutedness. Identity is not a distinguishable, superadded factor "over and above all describable characteristics and the one that integrates them all"; it is instead "simply another name for the integrative pattern they form" (41). Nonetheless, the integrative pattern in question is something that only the self can bring into being.

Yet the self is likewise a historical being, and this means in part that the self is always acted upon as well as acting. Formally we must then set a limit on our own ability to identify a person. To recognize this limit permits us to see more clearly the importance of narrative interpretation. Frei writes,

> Things happen *to* a person that enter into the very identification of him; they are enacted or occur upon or through him. Do such external acts of occurrence become embodied in him? Do they become part of his identity, since they are woven into his story? Undoubtedly, yes, and in part by his own response to or incorporation of these happenings.
>
> What is to be stressed here is that our categories for identity description break down at this very point. They cannot describe how external events become ingredient in a person's identity directly, i.e., other than by his own response to them. All that one can do to describe a person in that situation of direct impact by circumstances upon him (and not as refracted through his own response) and how he becomes himself in and through these circumstances is simply to tell the story of the events. (93)[6]

Frei himself is mainly concerned to apply this observation to the Gospel story. We understand the identity of Jesus not only in the enactment of his intentions but also in the circumstances that he partly initiates and that partly devolve upon him. All these features mysteriously coincide. His passion and death incorporate what he decides, the circumstances he initiates, the circumstances to which he responds, and the external actions and events not simply occurring at his behest which he awaits and accepts (105).

3. The third feature is the pattern that unites the individuality of Jesus as Savior and the cosmic scope of his identity. Frei calls it the pattern of exchange, "particularly the pattern of *the mysterious exchange of guilt with self-sacrificing purity*" (74). Such a pattern invariably recalls the figure of the obedient and suffering servant in Isaiah 53. An entire genre of literature looks at this pattern. Frei selects Graham Greene's *The Power and the Glory* for the final contrasting case. The priest in the novel is believable only as a disciple: "He follows Christ without trying to become Christ, at a distance rather

than from too nearby, or with that intimacy of total contrast which is paradoxically one with total identity" (80). Though he is a guilty man, he is no hypocrite. His guilt includes cowardice and infidelity; he lacks the innocence of Billy Budd and the heroism of Kazantzakis's Jesus. He differs palpably of course from Jesus portrayed in the Gospels. For the priest, then, to duplicate the pattern of exchange is out of the question. Yet his lack of pretense and spiritual pride disposes him at least to humility. And this humility allows him to love his neighbor. That such love is possible at all shows that he can follow at a distance. But the love that proves possible for him shows that the distance is not overcome. His love seeks to receive as well as to give enrichment. In this love Frei locates one "common and profoundly valid way of discerning the difference between Christ and some other person who is a disciple": the priest "becomes a human being instead of a Christ figure, because he can receive and accept good" (80–81).

> Nowhere in the Gospel story is Jesus' own humanity enriched by his relation with others, and so no person who is blessed in this way can be confused with him. And yet, although Jesus does not receive enrichment at men's hands, we are commanded by him to bless our neighbors and are allowed to receive good at their hands. (81; see also 160)

JESUS AND THE BELIEVER: DIFFERENCES AND POINTS OF CORRESPONDENCE

We can now begin to develop the points of discontinuity and continuity between Jesus and ourselves. As before, I shall examine each feature in turn.

1. The cosmic scope of Jesus' redeeming activity is the first feature whose two-sided shape we must consider. One conspicuous discontinuity lies in the kind of activity he is capable of and we are not. We cannot, quite simply, be Christ figures. No reiteration of the cosmic scope of his redeeming activity is possible for us. Contrary to Kazantzakis, we must view Jesus as other than a model for what we too can accomplish if we will, at the same level or in equivalent measure. We must instead be receptive to an activity we cannot duplicate. This condition we share in common. A limit is set on our activity which all differences among us in insight and commitment, however deep and however radical, lack the power to remove. Here Frei continues a

motif of the Protestant Reformers: that of following after rather than imitating.

Ruled out as well is another claim about human accomplishment. This claim does not reach as high as a Christ figure but rather sets its sights on a variously characterized range of autonomous activity. Sometimes the activity consists in a passionate life quest. At other times it is the attainment of moral seriousness or integrity. What links the several characterizations is the claim that a specifiable kind of human accomplishment stands as the indispensable precondition for becoming a Christian. We must somehow put ourselves in the right position first if divine self-attestation is to occur. Or we must pass through a fixed experiential sequence in order for Christian faith to be meaningful and possible. Frei views the claim in all its versions as inappropriate and self-defeating. "For myself, I am quite persuaded that there is no single road to Christianity, either as a matter of universal principle or in practice" (p. xii). The right place to start is by elucidating Christian belief itself.

A possible continuity, or more modestly, a point of correspondence lies in the *range* of activity: the inclusiveness of Jesus' redeeming activity widens the scope of our own concern. "Humanity at large is the neighbor given to the church" (162). On the one side, the phrase "given to the church" points to the community that is indispensable. The church must never forsake its own mission and testimony (160). As a collective disciple it too admittedly lives under the impassable restrictions imposed on individual persons. The church can only follow Jesus and not reproduce his work; to the role of Christ figure it should not aspire. Yet it must keep its own counsels above all and not allow extraneous agendas from whatever quarter to be imposed on its life and thought. On the other side, the phrase "humanity at large is the neighbor" indicates that we are to be both committed to the well-being of humanity at large and receptive to the enrichment that neighbors outside the church so often give (160). We are directed to the providential presence of God in our public history that transcends the intramural activities of church bodies (162). We are to espouse, if you like, normative universalism. I employ this phrase here only to indicate that the point of correspondence has a material element and a justificatory element. "Universalism" refers to the widened scope itself, the material element. Each person ought to be subject to our regard; no one should be excluded from the Christian's concern. "Normative" refers to Jesus' activity as the warranting basis, the justificatory element. To widen the scope of our concern does not then require us to secure in advance from all those affected by our actions reciprocal agreements that such universalism is obligatory.

2. The second feature, Jesus' singular identity, shifts our concern from the scope and content of our interactions to the understanding of our own identity. We ask how we are to view our own identities in light of his. Here the effects of christological governance prove to be, if anything, more pronounced.

From the demonstration of Jesus' singularity, it follows necessarily that our identities must never be confused with his. The strictures against Christ figures lead unambiguously to the same conclusion. Yet to insist on differences does not mean that we are merely sent back to our limits. Instead the effects of two differences Frei introduces are affirmative rather than limiting: one clarifies our condition positively, and the other enhances the value we attach to our own identities.

The first such effect Frei registers as he denies the usefulness of "heavily freighted" identity descriptions such as "alienation":

> It follows, concerning the identity of the others for whose sakes he was obedient, that they also—in the context of this story—cannot be said to be identified as "alienated" or "estranged" or in "self-contradiction." In contrast to the Gnostics with their savior myths and to the similar traditions of modern idealist and existentialist philosophy, the story of Jesus represents at its very core an insistence that because there is at least one man, Jesus, who has an identity others have identities also; for he, as the first of many brothers, gained that possibility for them in dying and rising on their behalf. Hence, although they are sinners in need of his redemptive power, they cannot be characterized as alienated from their own identity. Whatever sin may be, it must not be confused with this clutch of cultural and philosophical notions. (138)

Jesus' identity informs us about what our own identity is and is not. Is there another way to free ourselves from a "clutch of cultural and philosophical notions" that wrongly disposes us to see our own identity as structurally alienated? We are not told. What we are told is that we depend on the identity of Jesus for liberating us from a mistaken diagnosis of our own condition. At one point the claim quoted above seems more sweeping still: Jesus' identity is the condition of the possibility of ours.

The second effect is the accentuation of our own identity: [Jesus']
specific identity is such that others cannot merge into a common indis-
tinguishable identity with him; instead they find that their own specific
and unsubstitutable identity becomes sharply accentuated by relation to
Jesus' own unique identity. (133)

Here Jesus' identity serves to foster and heighten our awareness of
our own, and to underscore the importance we attribute to it. Once
again we are not told if such awareness and importance can be
enhanced in another way; the accent falls on how deeply we rely on
Jesus.

The reliance seems so complete that one naturally asks how much
significance the formal ingredient in Frei's scheme of identity description retains.[7] His insistence that our categories of identity description
break down, on the other hand, shows no comparable sign of such
reliance. It seems to apply to us as well as to Jesus, without further
ado. So I will see the identity of the other as comprising the intentions
he or she has enacted, and also the impingement of other persons'
enacted intentions and of unintended events. I cannot finally disen-
tangle these elements; I cannot ferret out some superadded attribute
standing behind them all. That I find disentangling impossible means
that narrative is the most adequate way to view a human life. For it
captures the subtle interaction between decision and happenstance
that we invariably find when we attend to the antecedents of a
person's own history. For each of us too, therefore, to know how we
become ourselves in and through our circumstances "is simply to tell
the story of the events."

3. In the case of the third feature, the pattern of exchange, we
differ from Jesus in that we can receive and accept enrichment from
others. Barth elaborates this difference in his account of how
Christology and anthropology are related (*Church Dogmatics*, vol. 3/2).
On the one side, "we do not need to look for any other basis of
anthropology than the christological."[8] On the other, "Christology is
not anthropology."[9] The christological basis generates a claim that no
conception of human nature can be right that views human nature as
asocial or nonrelational. The "basic form of humanity" is not the
individual isolated from others but each person with others, and with
them "gladly." The notion of an eternal covenant in which God is

with us, disclosed and executed in time in the humanity of Jesus, points irrevocably to such co-presence. Moreover, Jesus' humanity is distinguished quintessentially by this: he is *for* others in the most comprehensive and radical sense. He seeks no stoical or mystic place of rest away from others. His orientation to others and dedication to their rescue are constitutive of his mission. In light of this, we cannot suppose that fidelity to him ever warrants a turning away on our part from others.

Yet two key differences between Jesus and ourselves begin also to emerge, precisely at the point of Jesus' irreversible "forness." He differs from us in the content of his mission and in the exhaustively other-regarding way in which he effects it. His mission is our deliverance and salvation. And this is his exclusive task. It is otherwise with us. First, in our own interactions with one another we cannot repeat what he does. We cannot deliver and save others. Second, our situation is not only profoundly relational, it is in addition inescapably reciprocal. Such reciprocity cannot arise in the humanity of Jesus. Barth offers this summary:

> God alone, and the man Jesus as the Son of God, has no need of assistance, and is thus able to render far more than assistance to man, namely to represent him. For us, however, humanity consists in the fact that we need and are capable of mutual assistance.[10]

This difference between Jesus' humanity and our own to which Frei and Barth both call attention is like and unlike the previous discontinuities and points of correspondence we have considered. A limit is again stressed. In our interactions we cannot save one another. Everything we accomplish stands under that relativization.

Yet the limit now permits us a distinct space. That we mutually assist and enrich one another, that I need the other as the other needs me, that neither of us can attain pure self-sufficiency, are realities we should neither seek to deny nor lament. We should in fact actively affirm them. Jesus' redemptive activity directs us toward one another and serves decisively in this way to warrant the affirmation. But his activity appears less straightforwardly the basis for reciprocity as such than it is either for inclusiveness or for singularity. Our condition of reciprocity, by no means itself corrupt, sets us apart from him by virtue of the mutual assistance and enrichment it includes.

FOLLOWING AT A DISTANCE:
SOME ETHICAL EXTRAPOLATIONS

I want finally to review the claims about christological governance so far explored, this time speculating more generally about what they may imply and what difficulties remain.

We may summarize the two-sided shape to which the claims point in this way. We honor the governance only by honoring all the differences between Jesus and ourselves. These differences, though they are all impassable from our side, vary in their effects on us. One difference discloses to us our limits: We cannot and so ought never attempt to duplicate Jesus' activity, to save or redeem or represent others. Another difference enables us to understand the positive possibilities available to us in our own identity. Indeed, perhaps these possibilities are founded in him. Yet another difference directs us to affirm a condition that is illumined by Jesus' activity but that consists in a manner of life forever distinct from his own. We must not contravene these several differences when we specify points of correspondence between Jesus and ourselves. Still our following must be discernibly patterned after him; we must show that the points of correspondence genuinely refer to him. The way we view our actions and passions, the shape of our own lives, the events of our era must display definite effects of his activity.

Let us try to say more about each of the three features in light of the injunction to follow, but to follow at a distance.

1. What is a fitting response to the *inclusiveness* of Jesus' redeeming activity? First, those in the church must test themselves at two places already mentioned. They must honor their own convictions about how to construe and justify the normative universalism that attests to this inclusiveness. And they must refuse to attribute to human accomplishment the status of an indispensable precondition for becoming a Christian. Yet they are not forced by such a refusal to oppose indiscriminately "secular ethics" of whatever stripe. Christian ethics need not jeopardize the governance in question when it assumes an attitude toward secular ethical notions more nuanced than that of opposition in principle.[11] Certainly it must take pains not to depend on any de facto moral and political agreements it may share with the surrounding culture; it should retain perpetually a certain critical

distance from that culture. Yet criticism of secular moralities must always be possible but not always necessary. It should remain free to forge various temporary alliances and ad hoc conjunctions. Indeed, it has a positive responsibility to make the most of whatever agreements there may be between believers and nonbelievers.

Second, if normative universalism answers the question "Who is my neighbor?" it does not thereby answer the question "What am I to do and refrain from doing to my neighbor?" How do we ensure that the weak and vacillating are not effectively left behind? What attitudes should we adopt and what gestures of respect should we pay in order seriously to include them? From such questions, tiresomely familiar and notoriously difficult as they are, christological governance does not spare us. How far we can appeal directly to the narrative of Jesus as we articulate our answers is also a familiar debate in the Christian tradition. Our answers must reflect first and last the most perspicacious reading of the Bible of which we are capable. This reading, though authoritative, may be supplemented by the use of the practical reason to review the body of relevant verdicts the tradition has reached in the past, critically reasserting, revising, and extending them.

Third, we must estimate the final significance of our actions on the neighbor's behalf. The most transparently loving actions are subject to this estimate, and not only those we perform in perplexity. Suppose we do all in our power to overcome economic deprivations, psychic sufferings, the plight of outcasts, the hostility of enemies. Are these redemptive works? Do they have at least positive material connections with redemption? Assuredly we must see these involvements as providentially ordered, as part of a mysterious pattern of meaning. For the view before us, however, we must also see them as unfinished (160–61). They are not themselves to be conflated with the redemption already accomplished once for all. When we release our works from the weight of a final seriousness they cannot bear, we may be able to display a certain lightness in the way we comport ourselves, a lightness that resembles only superficially the frivolous or the complacent.

2. What is a fitting response to the affirmative effects on our identity of Jesus' *singularity*? Two broad possibilities suggest themselves. First, to deny that we are structurally alienated disposes us to

hold together as an object of judgment the self and its actions. These are not doomed to be incongruous. Frei directs his own attack against the philosophical and theological analysts of alienation who find all "manifestations"—words, names, the web of social institutions and cultural life—to distort the "true subject-self" (98–99). Against such a view he maintains a compatibility between inwardness and outwardness. His attack can be readily applied to versions of the alienation view which abound in moral and political thought. And generally in our moral judgments of action the compatibilist position inclines us, I think, to count changes actually effected in the world and not only intentions. To count both represents a refusal to allow intention to float freely and inscrutably behind mere "external" behavior. The compatibilist position also encourages us to appraise positively our involvements in public and, specifically, political life. These involvements are not incurably distorting. We may seek our identities in their midst and not at their edges and boundaries.

Second, the impetus from Jesus' identity always goes toward accentuation of our own, and away from merger either with his or with one another's. His governance in this case never signifies a domination that blurs or rubs out our distinctive features. A radically irreducible first-personal element is not only preserved but promoted. In this case what attitudes and actions on our part correspond to his governance? One answer seems obvious. We are to preserve and promote the specific and unsubstitutable identity each of us has. No person is to be regarded as interchangeable with another. Each has an identity we cannot exhaustively measure or compare or classify with others'. A further answer, less obvious but still probable, is this. The particular individual is not to be subsumed within the life of any larger entity, for subsumption pulls us back toward merger and interchangeability. On this ground we may resist wholly submerging the individual in society for the sake of the well-being of the society itself.

In addition to these two broad possibilities, suppose we ask what we might infer from Frei's observation that a limit is set on our ability to identify a person, the recognition of which underscores the importance of narrative. How, for example, might my perception of the neighbor I am to love be influenced? Two inferences appear likely.

First, my love must include, at a minimum, respect for the neighbor as he or she *happens to be*. I am to regard what the other has undergone, what he or she has suffered as well as decided. The effects of what happens to a person, sometimes what tragically assails him or her, and not only the other's autonomous choices, must come within the range of my concern. Second, my love for the neighbor must involve the honoring of an entire lifetime. And this seems to imply that the other's specific actions acquire their significance from the overall story of his or her life. At the very least I often need to know the neighbor's history to determine whether particular obstacles faced or pains endured are to be counted as victories or defeats. It is arguable "that most good and ill fortune has as its subject a person identified by his history and his possibilities, rather than merely by his categorical state at the moment. . . ."[12]

Such influences aid me in loving my neighbor appropriately. That the other's history has value I affirm by virtue of Jesus' identity.

3. We come now to the last feature. What is a fitting response to Jesus' "forness" given our condition of *reciprocity?* I observed that christological governance operates less straightforwardly here. "Less straightforwardly" means that we are thrown back on our own re-sources to a greater degree as we try both to understand the internal dynamics of the condition and to judge what behavior is appropriate to it. Jesus' identity does less demonstrable work as we undertake these tasks. David Kelsey finds that such a shift in degree occurs in Barth,[13] and it seems a similar shift occurs in Frei. When Barth addresses the subject of our reciprocity or co-humanity, he uses common-sensical observations acquired from everyday experience as "data," and relies on the New Testament identity descriptions of Jesus as "backing." The patterns of mutual enrichment in which we live furnish canons of what to expect and not to expect that Jesus' "forness" warrants generally but does not guide specifically.

This shift in degree is subject to diverse and sometimes rival assess-ments. I shall distinguish three such assessments that recur in the tradition. First, we may effectively call the shift into question. Often we do this by retaining a normative link between Jesus' "forness" and the manner of life that marks his followers. This link seems too close to accommodate the shift. Though our manner of life cannot redeem, the aspiration to be sheerly other-regarding, to see in this pattern the correct point of correspondence, is not misguided. Barth may himself reforge this link when he writes about Christian discipleship and about Christian love or agape (*Church Dogmatics*, vol. 4/2). To be a disciple is to leave oneself behind and heed the command of Jesus above all else. It is to be freed from the rule of creaturely attachments, the so-called given factors or natural orders, where reciprocity or mutual assistance hold sway. Self-giving service to Jesus requires one to abandon the friend-foe distinction, to break out from the captivity of family and clan, even to refrain from the displays of devoutness that the world of piety expects.[14] And when Barth explores Christian love he commends "self-giving" and "interposition" on the neighbor's behalf, a standing surety for him or her.[15] A nonredemptive "forness" obtains.

Second, rather than retain the closer link, we accept that the condition of reciprocity differs normatively from Jesus' "forness." Still the normative difference yields no final incompatibility. Though christological governance indeed operates less straightforwardly when we consider reciprocity, we may actively affirm the latter condition on its own terms. Often the condition is grounded in a doctrine of creation. It stands as our lot.

Third, again we accept the normative difference. But now our acceptance is tainted by regret. Even when we describe reciprocity in ideal terms its distance from Jesus' "forness" makes tension unavoidable. Moreover, and this is decisive, we can never honestly content ourselves with an ideal description. For we know that our life of mutual assistance and enrichment is shot through with vulnerability and loss and wasted opportunities. We suffer the absence of assistance and enrichment in concrete circumstances, just as we fail to provide them. We turn accordingly to assertion and counterassertion, in order to compensate, redress, to repair again to tolerable levels. There is sadness in this turning, but resolution too because we must fight the truly intolerable. We accept a lesser state than Jesus' "forness." His state shows ours as shadowed. And if this is so, perhaps because it is so, our light depends all the more on his. We may still affirm the most succinct meaning of christological governance: Emmanuel.

NOTES

I have benefited from reactions and suggestions offered by Richard Fern, Timothy Jackson, David Kelsey, Cyril O'Regan, William Werpehowski, and especially Susan Owen.

1. Karl Barth, *Church Dogmatics*, vol. 3/2, trans. Harold Knight et al. (Edinburgh: T & T Clark, 1960), 225.

2. Hans W. Frei, *The Identity of Jesus Christ: The Hermeneutical Bases of Dogmatic Theology* (Philadelphia: Fortress Press, 1975). Page references to this volume will be given in parentheses in the text.

3. A richly comprehensive study is James M. Gustafson's *Christ and the Moral Life* (New York: Harper & Row, 1968).

4. Hans W. Frei, *The Eclipse of Biblical Narrative: A Study in Eighteenth and Nineteenth Century Hermeneutics* (New Haven: Yale Univ. Press, 1974), 3.

5. It is clearer for my purposes to reverse the order in which Frei discusses the novels by Melville and Kazantzakis.

6. William Werpehowski first brought home to me in conversation the importance of this passage. I shall not venture here into the forest of other literature on the significance that narrative allegedly has for theology and ethics; for an earlier discussion, focusing on Stanley Hauerwas, see Gene Outka, "Character, Vision, and Narrative," *Religious Studies Review* 6 (1980): 110–18. For representative discussions in theology, see George W. Stroup, *The Promise of Narrative Theology: Recovering the Gospel in the Church* (Atlanta: John Knox Press, 1981), and Ronald F. Thiemann, *Revelation and Theology: The Gospel as Narrated Promise* (Notre Dame, Ind.: Univ. of Notre Dame Press, 1985). For a thorough study in ethics, see Paul T. Nelson, "Narrative and Morality: A Theological Inquiry" (diss., Yale Univ., 1984); this will soon appear as a book published by Pennsylvania State Univ. Press.

7. We can distinguish two questions. The first is whether the view about human identity put forward by a believer in the syndrome labeled, e.g., gnostic (and perhaps by certain forms of Buddhism) intrudes on the integrity and flow of the Gospel narrative. The second is whether the gnostic or Buddhist view goes wrong at a "formal" level. We can answer the first question affirmatively and leave the second open or regard it as unintelligible. How would we proceed to show that the gnostic or Buddhist view of "true identity" is formally mistaken? What theological significance would this procedure have? In any event, if Frei must err in either of two directions—by retaining the singularity of Jesus' identity or by retaining formal identity description—he prefers unhesitatingly, I think, to err in the former direction. He avoids impressively the danger he fears most: domination by any independently founded hermeneutical theory or philosophical system.

8. Barth, *Church Dogmatics* 3/2:208.

9. Ibid., 222.

10. Ibid., 262.

11. For elaboration of the view that Christian ethics should resist cultural assimilation and yet make the most of whatever material overlaps there may be, see Gene Outka, "Discontinuity in the Ethics of Jacques Ellul," in *Jacques Ellul: Interpretive Essays*, ed. Clifford G. Christians and Jay M. Van Hook (Urbana: Univ. of Illinois Press, 1981), 216–18.

12. Thomas Nagel, *Mortal Questions* (Cambridge: Cambridge Univ. Press, 1979), 5.

13. David H. Kelsey, *The Uses of Scripture in Recent Theology* (Philadelphia: Fortress Press, 1975), esp. 169, 179. Kelsey notes that his appraisal refers to the structure of the overall argument in vol. 3/2 of the *Church Dogmatics* but not in vol. 4.

14. Karl Barth, *Church Dogmatics*, vol. 4/2, trans. G. W. Bromiley (Edinburgh: T. & T. Clark, 1958), 533–53.

15. For an account of Barth's stress not only on self-giving but on interposition *(Einsatz)*, where one becomes the "guarantor" of the other, see Gene Outka, *Agape: An Ethical Analysis* (New Haven: Yale Univ. Press, 1972), 208–9.

9

The story-shaped church: critical exegesis and theological interpretation

George Lindbeck

For many of Hans Frei's readers, his greatest contribution has been to make possible the restoration of the christologically centered narrative sense of scripture to its traditional primacy. His *Eclipse of Biblical Narrative*, they believe, has shown how the confusion in the last two centuries of biblical studies, between the narrative and historical (i.e., "factual") senses, has resulted in gross misunderstandings of premodern interpretation as this was generally practiced up through the Reformation. On their view, the opposition between historical-critical and premodern exegesis is as misconceived as that between evolution and Genesis. They are inclined to think that Frei's work marks the beginning of a change in biblical interpretation as decisive—though in a different direction—as that occasioned by Albert Schweitzer's *Quest of the Historical Jesus*.

This essay assumes this assessment and turns to further questions. Granting the compatibility of premodern narrative interpretation and modern historical-critical study, what more can be said about their relation? Are they logically independent, or does historical criticism make a difference to narrative meaning?

I shall discuss this issue in reference to the topic of the church.[1] The conclusion will be that classical narrative reading, in combination with historical-critical awareness, makes the church as the New

Testament presents it look more like Israel, including Israel *post Christum*, than Christians have customarily supposed. This change occurs only when the two approaches are conjoined: when pursued independently, no such result need follow. The importance of their interaction in this instance, however, cannot be generalized. Both historical criticism and classical narrational interpretation are piece-meal procedures, and the revisionary force of combining them varies from topic to topic. Thus all that this essay claims is that in some areas, of which ecclesiology is one, a renewed focus on narrative meanings, together with critical awareness of how they functioned, provides scriptural authorization (but not directives) for major changes in theological interpretations.

The task of supporting this claim is both the exegetical-historical one of determining what the text meant and the theological one of interpreting what it means. (This is an inadequate way of stating the contrast between exegesis and theology for many purposes, but not, I think, for our present ones.) We shall in the first two sections stipulate what for our purposes are the crucial differences between historical and theological interpretation, comment on the relation between classical narrative hermeneutics and other approaches, and in view of both these points, sketch an exegetical account of biblical narrative ecclesiology. This will provide the basis for a discussion in the third section of later distortions of this ecclesiology, and the possibilities of its reappropriation in a critically corrected form.

HISTORY, THEOLOGY, AND
NARRATIVE MEANING

History interprets what the text meant, and theology what it means. More fully, historians, insofar as their work is theologically relevant, describe the religiously significant functioning of a text in its original setting, and theologians make proposals about how the text should be understood and used so that its present meaning may be faithful to its original one. In stipulating this distinction, I simply assume what I take to be the contemporary commonplace that, for example, the stories that expressed and molded the communal self-understanding of early Christians need to be retold and reinterpreted if they are to function appropriately in later periods. In brief, what the

Bible properly means theologically is the right application of what it meant historically.

The notion of right application, it should be noted, includes the possibility of no application at all. The biblical tolerance of slavery, for example, is now almost universally regarded by Christians as totally and permanently inapplicable. Conceivably the same holds for what scripture meant by the church. Perhaps faithfulness to the central meaning of scripture, to Christ, requires that Christians now substitute some quite different way of thinking about Christian community. I shall later have more to say about that. For the moment I shall simply posit that part of the practice of reading a text as authoritative, even in the minimal sense of "classic," is that what it meant does have present relevance unless there are good reasons for supposing the contrary. The burden of proof is on those who deny applicability. Paul himself recognized this, for otherwise he would not have accepted the burden of arguing at length that the scriptural requirement of circumcision no longer held, at least for Gentiles.

Exegetical and theological interpretation interact. If a certain kind of meaning seems important for understanding what a sacred text meant, the inclination is to think it theologically important also, and vice versa. One powerful post-Reformation tendency has been to give factual meanings both exegetical and theological primacy. The extreme conservative version of this outlook holds that everything depends on the complete reportorial and scientific accuracy of scripture; for the liberal version, the critical reconstruction of, most notably, the historical Jesus is crucial. In contrast, there are also other outlooks, invariably susceptible to both liberal and conservative uses, for which doctrinal, or moral, or existential, or symbolic, or narrational meanings were or are religiously more important. From these perspectives, Enlightenment-spawned debates over factuality are of secondary interest even historically. For example, if one focuses on symbolic meaning, questions regarding the import of patriarchal images of God may seem historically as well as theologically more significant than the issue of whether the whale swallowed Jonah or whether claims about the resurrection are empirically meaningful in the sense, for example, of falsifiable. The decision between these orientations is not usually a historical-critical matter. It rather depends, as David Kelsey has argued, on an unformalizable global assessment (discrimen) of what once was or now is the religiously most intelligible, efficacious, and faithful way of reading the text.[2]

Perhaps, however, there is a partial exception to this. The claim to primacy of the narrative meaning of the stories about Jesus for scripture as a whole is embedded in the way these stories are told in the Gospels and is sometimes explicit as well as implicit in other New Testament writings. This is a historical judgment, not simply a critically unassessable discrimen. The stories in their narrative function unsubstitutably identify and characterize a particular person as the summation of Israel's history and as the unsurpassable and irreplaceable clue to who and what the God of Israel and the universe is. They interpret the Hebrew Bible in terms of christological anticipations, preparations, and promissory types. Jesus' story fulfills and transforms the overall biblical narratives of creation, election, and redemption, and thereby specifies the meanings of such concepts and images as Messiahship, Suffering Servanthood, Logos, and divine Sonship. He is the subject, everything else is predication. Some New Testament writings may not clearly exhibit this pattern (Luther would cite James), but insofar as they are treated as parts of a narrationally and christologically unified canon, they are submitted to the same hermeneutical rule. If one characterizes the literal sense as that which a community of readers takes to be the plain, primary, and controlling signification of a text (a less problematic move than appealing to authorial intention or to some property ingredient in the text), then, as Frei has suggested in a recent article,[3] the narrative meaning of the stories about Jesus was the uniquely privileged *sensus literalis* of the whole of scripture for the groups by and for whom those stories were composed. It continued to be so for the later generations who added the New Testament canon to the Old, and it remained the dominant view, if Frei's *Eclipse* is right, until the post-Reformation era, when primacy began to be accorded to rationalistically doctrinal, pietistically experiential, and empiricistically factual meanings. Thus there are historical-critical grounds for reading the Christian Bible in chiefly (though not, of course, exclusively) narrational terms if one wants to know what it originally meant.

This, as we have indicated, does not settle the question of what the Bible means—of how what it meant historically should now be theologically applied. But before we turn in the third section to that issue, we must ask about what it meant. Detailed exegesis, needless to say, is out of the question. I shall simply comment on the tacit rules or principles (perhaps we could even say "grammar" or "doctrines")[4] that structured the biblical pattern of thinking about the church.

EXEGESIS AND THE
BIBLICAL STORY OF THE CHURCH

The first and, in a narrative approach, tautological rule for reading is that the church is fundamentally identified and characterized by its story. Images such as "body of Christ," or the traditional marks of "unity, holiness, catholicity, and apostolicity," cannot be first defined and then used to specify what is and what is not the church. The story is logically prior. It determines the meaning of images, concepts, doctrines, and theories of the church rather than being determined by them. Just as the story of the Quakers is more fundamental than descriptions such as "church of the poor" or "church of the wealthy" (for they have been both), and the story of the French is more fundamental than "monarchy" or "republic" (for France has been both), so also in the case of the church.

A corollary of this priority of story is that "church" ordinarily refers to concrete groups of people, not to something transempirical. An invisible church is as biblically odd as an invisible Israel. Stories of the biblical realistic-narrative type can only be told of agents and communities of agents acting and being acted upon in a space-time world of contingent, unpredictable happenings. The primacy of narrative thus implies that exalted concepts and images such as "holy" and "bride of Christ" usually refer to empirical churches in all their actual or potential messiness.

For the early Christians, in the second place, Israel's history was their only history. They did not yet have the New Testament or later church history as sources. Thus for the writings they produced, the Hebrew scriptures (usually in the Septuagint form) were the sole ecclesiological text. This is the second rule for reading what they say about the church.

A third rule is an extension of this second one. Not only was Israel's story their only story, but it was the whole of that story which they appropriated. It was not only the favorable parts, the Old Testament histories of faithful remnants, that they applied to themselves. All the wickedness of the Israelites in the wilderness could be theirs. They might rebel as did Korah (Numbers 16), or perish for fornication as did three and twenty thousand in the desert (Numbers 25). These happenings, Paul tells his readers, are types *(tupoi)* written for our admonition (1 Cor. 10:5–11). As of old, judgment continues to begin in the house of the Lord (1 Peter 4:17), and the unfaithful church can be severed from the root no less than the unbelieving synagogue (Rom. 11:21). There is nothing in the logic of this hermeneutic to deny that the bride of Christ, like the betrothed of Yahweh (Ezekiel 16 and 23), can be a whore worse than the heathen. The typological transfer is not actually made,[5] but then, the responsible narrative exegete will note, situations as extreme as the one Ezekiel confronted did not develop until later in church history.

Thus, despite most later exegesis, the relation of Israel's history to that of the church in the New Testament is not one of shadow to reality, or promise to fulfillment, or type to antitype.[6] Rather, the kingdom already present in Christ alone is the antitype, and both Israel and the church are types. The people of God existing in both the old and new ages are typologically related to Jesus Christ, and through Christ, Israel is prototypical for the church in much the same way that the exodus story, for example, is seen as prototypical for all later Israelite history by such prophets as Ezekiel. Christ is depicted as the embodiment of Israel (e.g., "Out of Egypt have I called my son"; Matt. 2:15), and the church is the body of Christ. Thus, in being shaped by the story of Christ, the church shares (rather than fulfills) the story of Israel. The communal fulfillment will take place in God's kingdom which, though already actualized in the crucified, resurrected, and ascended Lord, is only anticipated in the communities that witness to him before and after his first coming. Something like this is the pattern structuring much, at least, of the New Testament churches' appropriation of what for them were the only extant scriptural stories of God's people.

From this it follows, fourth, that Israel and the church were one people for at least many early Christians. There was no breach in continuity. A new age had begun, but the story remained the same, and therefore also the people it identified. The French remain French after the revolution, the Quakers remain Quakers after becoming wealthy, and Israel remains Israel even when transformed by the arrival of the eschaton in Christ. The church is simply Israel in the time between the times. The continuity of the story and the identity of the people are not broken.

Discontinuity and nonidentity are problems in the New Testament, not for the church per se but for unbelieving Jews, on the one hand, and gentile Christians, on the other. The apostle Paul says of the first group in Romans 11 that they have been cut off, but that this can happen does not differentiate them from Christians. Christians also, as we have already noted, can be severed from the root. They can, in the even more vigorous language of Revelation, be spewed forth, expectorated (3:16). Yet when this occurs, it does not alter the identity of the people of the promise. "The gifts and the call of God are irrevocable" (Rom. 11:29). The identity of the chosen people in the new age as in the old depends utterly on God's election, not at all on its own faithfulness or unfaithfulness. For the one New Testament writing in which the problem is directly addressed, Judaism after Christ is as inalienably embraced as the church in the continuous overarching story of the single people consisting of faithful remnants and unfaithful masses which stretches from the patriarchal period to the last days. Unbelieving Jewry will ultimately be restored.

So strong was this sense of uninterrupted peoplehood that the only available way to think of gentile Christians was, in Krister Stendahl's phrase, as "honorary Jews."[7] The uncircumcised, "alienated from the commonwealth of Israel," have become "fellow citizens of the household of God," "fellow heirs, fellow members of the body, fellow partakers of the promise" (Eph. 2:11, 19; 3:16). This inclusion of the Gentiles is represented in Ephesians as the most wondrous aspect of the work of Christ. Where there were two, there is now one, the new man in Christ (2:11—3:11). Thus has begun the inclusion of all humankind in God's people, the promised ascent of the nations to worship in Zion, the crowding of the Gentiles into the heavenly Jerusalem. But Zion does not change identity: the gates of the new Jerusalem are marked with the names of the twelve tribes (Rev. 21:12). The inclusion through Christ of the uncircumcised in the one eternal covenant constituted, for the early Christians, not the formation of a new people but the enlargement of the old.

This enlarged people, to be sure, is also said to be Spirit-filled. For many later Christians, ranging from papalists to anti-institutional spiritualists, this has been the major reason for thinking of the church as discontinuous with Israel.

When one looks at the function of the New Testament references to the Holy Spirit, however, one discovers that they often serve to distinguish the believing church from the unbelieving synagogue in the new age.[8] This age is indeed the epoch in which the words of Joel come true, in which the Spirit is poured forth on all flesh, and sons and daughters prophesy (Acts 2:17ff.). The faithful are Spirit-filled as they were not before, and it is therefore this gift that now most sharply differentiates them from the unfaithful. But the Spirit also spoke through prophets before Christ, and it departs from the faithless in the present as it did in the past. Faithful Israel *ante Christum* is more Spirit-filled than the faithless church, and the same can be true of synagogue *post Christum*. There are strands of thought in the New Testament suggesting this, even though there are no explicit claims. First, those who have not heard the message live theologically in the time before Christ, incapable of either acceptance or rejection (Romans 10). Second, if one adds, as later history testifies, that Jews for the most part do not and cannot hear because of Christian persecution, it follows that Judaism, living theologically before Christ, can on occasion be more Spirit-filled than Christianity. Whether or not this reasoning holds,[9] it is clear that the Spirit-wrought holiness of the church is a relational attribute referring to what God is making and will make of it, not to an inherent property. Pentecost marks the beginning of the age of unheard-of possibilities, gifts, and callings, not the formation of a new people.

Narrative interpretation, it will be observed, presses the exegete toward finding the same basic understanding of the church in all the New Testament literature. The variations from book to book can be construed as arising from changes in circumstance and application. When Paul was preoccupied by the persecution of the church in Thessalonica (1 Thess. 2:14–16), for example, he seemed to contradict what, as we have noted, he later wrote about unbelieving Israel in Romans. But even if in fact he changed his mind, it is misleading, on a narrative approach, to describe this as a change in his ecclesiology (or "Israelology," as it could just as well be called). The normative story remained exactly the same (for that, in Paul's thinking, was to be found in scripture, not in his head), as did also the procedures for applying it. But situations alter, and the faithful use of the ancient tales to shape the unfolding story of the nascent church required new and surprising twists and turns. It is of the very nature of narratives to subsume variations that outside their narrational context are contradictions. Desert wanderers settle in the promised land, and those liberated from Egypt are repeatedly enslaved. This compatibility of contrary descriptions does not imply harmonization: the differences are real. Further, some differences, such as the "sectarianism" of the Johannine communities and the "Platonism" of Hebrews, may under some circumstances be church-dividing. Only those exegetes, however, who focus on theological ideas, such as Ernst Käsemann, will risk judgments that they must always be so.[10] Those for whom narrative meaning is primary and who try to understand this in the context of social history will be more cautious. Even if one reads the New Testament writings as discrete literary units rather than in their canonical unity, their ecclesiological agreement from the perspective we have outlined is considerable.

It is hard to see how it could have been otherwise. Early Christians were a variegated Jewish sect, no more (and perhaps less) remote from the thought world of "normative Judaism" (if there was such a thing) than the Essenes, the Qumran community, or at the other extreme, intellectual Hellenists like Philo. They adhered to a crucified and resurrected Messiah who authorized them, some of them believed, to welcome the uncircumcised into their fellowship, but they were also deeply committed to maintaining their legitimacy as Jews. All the categories they possessed for communal self-understanding were derived from their only scriptures, the Hebrew Bible, and they interpreted this as Jews. It was natural that they should understand their communities as *ecclesia*, as *qahal*, the assembly of Israel in the new age. (For once, philology and etymology cohere with broader historical considerations.)[11] Thus the story of Israel was their story, and they had good reason for construing it in terms of the principles of the continuity of the narrative, the unity of the people, and the possibility of churchly unfaithfulness which we have described.

The historical-critical contribution to this description is basically the negative one of removing interpretive prejudices and making it believable that these principles did indeed guide the New Testament

uses of Israel's story. There is nothing novel in the details of the
interpretation I have offered. These are for the most part com-
monplaces of New Testament scholarship. What is different is the
significance the details acquire for understanding biblical ecclesiology
when narrative meaning is taken as primary. Then something like the
reading suggested in this section is both the plain and critical account
of what the church meant in the early Christian writings.

THEOLOGICAL INTERPRETATION

The question of what the church means in these same writings is
quite different from, and for the most part only indirectly related to,
what was meant (even, in some cases, to what the interpreter thinks
was meant). It is this bearing of critical exegetical findings on theological interpretation which will concern us in this last section in reference, first, to principles; second, to past ecclesiologies; and last, to
present and future possibilities.

As has already been emphasized, what the Bible means does not
necessarily correspond imitatively to what it meant; or to put this
same point in uncompromisingly theological language, what God
said in scripture is not necessarily what he now says. The proper
theological interpretation is one that is intelligible, efficacious, and
scripturally faithful, but the conditions for intelligibility and effica-
ciousness change, and faithfulness is not equivalent to reiteration.
Departures from the story-shaped understanding of the church may
thus at times be desirable even for those who hold to the primacy of
narrative meanings.

This is so because on a narrative construal, it will be recalled, the
controlling *sensus literalis* is the narrative meaning of the stories about
Jesus. Meanings contrary to this sense must be excluded. Thus when
the biblical narrational understanding of the church engenders
meanings inconsistent with the Jesus story, the narrative must be
altered or abandoned. A nonbiblical way of describing the church
may in changed circumstances better accord with the christological
center.

The history of ecclesiological reflection in its entirety can be in-
voked to illustrate these principles. Modifications of the biblical story
of the church started in the very first generations. The hardening of

the opposition between synagogue and church led even Jewish Christians, as such documents as the *Letter of Barnabas* testify, to reject the notion that unbelieving Jews remained part of God's people. Faithfulness became the mark of election, and election, conversely, became conditional on faithfulness. The doctrines of predestination and salvation *sola gratia,* insofar as they persisted, tended to be applied only to individuals and not to communities. Heretical groups were more and more regarded as not really the church at all. They were not seen after the fashion of the ancient prophets as the adulterous spouse whom the Lord may cast out for a time but never divorce.

A second development was that the church quickly became wholly gentile, and the New Testament awareness of the church as, sociologically speaking, a Jewish sect disappeared. It became intellectually and practically difficult for gentile Christians to think of themselves as naturalized citizens in the continuous, uninterrupted commonwealth of Israel. Thus not only was the synagogue excluded but the one people of God was broken into two peoples, the old and new. This created the problem of how to relate them, and the solution was to read the scriptures as if Israel were the type no longer simply of the coming kingdom and of its instantiation in the person of Christ but also of the church, which thus became the antitype, the fulfillment. The more unsavory aspects of the history of Israel were no longer genuinely portions of the history of the church but were projected exclusively on the synagogue.

These modifications, it will be observed, are quite explicitly changes in the canonically unified and authorized narrative pattern[12] rather than simply new applications. Yet despite the monstrous offspring they ultimately engendered, they cannot be flatly condemned as simply unfaithful. They were the historically (i.e., contingently) necessary conditions for the church's appropriation of Israel's story. Without that appropriation, we may plausibly speculate, Gnosticism would have wholly triumphed, the Marcionite rejection of Israel's scriptures and Israel's God would have become universal among Christians, and the Nazi heresy that Jesus was not a Jew would have become orthodoxy from the second century on. Because the modifications were the only available alternative to utter subversion of the christological center, they can be regarded, despite their magnitude and consequences, as scripturally faithful interpretations of the story of the church.

Such excuses become increasingly inapplicable, however, after the empire was converted and persecuted Christians became the persecutors. Anti-Semitism was the paradigmatic problem, but it needs to be seen as an acute manifestation of a more general disease. The dissonance between antitypical claims to fulfillment and empirical reality was the central difficulty. The church was now a *corpus mixtum* composed overwhelmingly of visible sinners rather than visible saints. The pressure was great to refer its high claims not to the overall pattern of communal life but to segregated aspects: to pure (ultimately infallible) doctrines, to uniquely (and in vulgar understanding, magically) efficacious sacraments, and to divinely established institutions. Even these developments, to be sure, did not always function antiscripturally. They might be compared, perhaps, to the Israelite monarchy, to which God consented *contre coeur* (1 Sam. 8), and yet which he also mightily used to preserve his people and prepare for the Messiah (Jesus sprang from the Davidic line). In somewhat similar fashion, one could argue, the imperial church preserved the faith amid barbarian chaos, converted Europe, and was the cradle of the first civilization to become worldwide (whether there is anything messianic about Western-spawned modernity is another question). The antitypical pretensions of Western ecclesiastical establishments (from which Reformation churches were by no means wholly exempt) could not help evoking sectarian reactions (which, incidentally, have not been so strong in the East, where Caesaropapism, whatever its faults, muted churchly arrogance).

The sectarian solutions to the church's dilemma have on the whole been less biblical, but not uniformly less faithful to scripture, than the earlier catholic ones. They have been less biblical because for the most part they have no longer understood God's people in terms of Israel's story but have rather modeled themselves after New Testament depictions of fervent first-generation communities, especially as found in Acts. Yet however unbiblical one may think the ecclesiology of, for example, the Quakers, it is hard to deny that such groups have at times been faithful remnants amid the faithless masses. Insofar as they are protest movements against Constantinian churches, the sects are in general scripturally justified, but they are also deeply problematic. The intense effort to make the empirical reality of Christian communities conform visibly to images of antitypical fulfillment can have consequences in some ways worse than institutional triumphalism. The arrogant self-righteousness of the company of the visibly holy may on occasion compare ill with the concern for publicans and sinners sometimes found in churches that conceive of themselves as arks of salvation, as hospitals for sick souls.

The difficulties in traditional ecclesiologies, whether Catholic, Reformation, or sectarian, have led in recent centuries to new ways of thinking about the church that depart even further from biblical patterns but that, once again, can have scriptural authenticity. Not only is Israel's story abandoned but also the referential primacy of empirical communities. Something other than these communities is really the church, is really the subject of the claims to antitypical fulfillment, with the result that ecclesial arrogance of either the catholic or sectarian types is no longer theologically legitimate.

For example, the church is characterized denotatively (not simply connotatively, or predicatively, or in some promissory or other illocutionary mode) as event, or mission, or liberating action, or the new being in Christ, or the fellowship of the Spirit, or the communion of Christ's justifying grace which works in anonymously as well as explicitly Christian ways. For the most part, any suggestion that the church is invisible is stoutly resisted. Rather, it necessarily takes visible form, and in some interpretations, referential primacy is accorded to what is empirically or experientially identifiable (e.g., event, mission, or liberating action). Nevertheless, however observable or experienceable the main referent may be, it is not first of all a people. It is not empirical churches in all their crass concreteness. These latter are rather imperfect manifestations, realizations, participations, or thematizations of the church's true, eschatological reality.

Thus in terms of our earlier exegesis, what for the Bible are predicates are in these modern approaches turned into subject terms. The reference of these terms is not an agent or community of agents of the kind whose identity is rendered by realistic narratives, and it must therefore be described in some other way than by telling its story. Systematic ecclesiology replaces the narrational variety. This is what has happened in our day in almost all major theological outlooks, whether Catholic or Protestant.[13]

Yet, to return to the starting point, these unbiblical ways of thinking about the church are not, for all that, unfaithful. They eliminate occasions for anti-Semitism and ecclesial arrogance by making the antitypical church something other than the empirical churches. In this and other respects they may be more genuinely Christian than their predecessors. It would be artificial but not impossible to write a history of ecclesiology in which increasing departures from the Bible were correlated with increasing closeness to Christ. In this area, whatever might be true of others, neither conservatives nor progressives mean by the church what scripture meant, and the re-recognition of the original narrative pattern (assuming that that is what we have described) does not by itself mandate a return. The Bible may for our times be no more adequate concerning the church than concerning slavery.

Yet the exegetical findings do make a difference. For one thing, they block eisegesis. Possibilities that were once excluded because of theologically biased readings of what scripture meant once again become options. As we earlier put it, the burden of proof is on those who think that what scripture meant is now inapplicable. Perhaps it is, but this needs to be shown, and in trying to show it, if that is what theologians try to do, they will find themselves struggling with a way of thinking about the church that has been unknown and unimaginable for nearly two thousand years.

They may even begin wondering whether what "church" once meant it can now mean again. In some respects, the present situation is more similar to the first century than to the intervening periods. Christendom is passing and Christians are becoming a diaspora. The antagonism of the church to the synagogue has been unmasked (we hope definitively) for the horror it always was. Christian pretensions to fulfillment have become obnoxious to vast numbers of Catholics and Protestants alike. Some of the reasons for distorting the story are disappearing, and perhaps its original version is again applicable.

Certainly there are reasons for wanting to apply it. The empirical churches are losing the loyalty and devotion of their members. Special-interest enclaves are replacing comprehensive communities as the locus of whatever shreds of communal identity the isolated individuals of our society retain. The conviction that the churches even in their crass concreteness have a place in God's plans has weakened. All these considerations call for a return to Israel's story as the template by which the church shapes its own history. It needs to understand itself as a witness that God has irrevocably chosen to testify to his glory in both its faithfulness and unfaithfulness, in both God's mercy and God's judgment. It needs to acknowledge that its election despite unfaithfulness is the source of its identity. Such convictions have made of Jews the great exception to the sociological and historical generalizations that apply to other nations, and have enabled them, despite their dispersion and small numbers, to be a major force in history (not least, it should be recalled, when they were wholly in the Diaspora). History shows that Israel's story has unique ability to confer communally significant meaning on whatever happens: it has, one might say, unrivaled power to encode successfully the vicissitudes and contradictions of history. Christianity, it can be argued, has urgent need to make greater use of that same tale if it is to be comparably tenacious and flexible in maintaining its identity as a people irresistibly called (and ineluctably failing) to witness by self-less service of all humankind to the universal yet thoroughly particu-lar God of Abraham, Isaac, Jacob, and Jesus.

It must be added, however, that there are as yet few signs that this is happening. On the right, apocalyptic conservatism is on the rise, but this, despite its often ardent support for the Israeli state, not only thinks of Christianity as the replacement of Judaism but also restricts the church to the company of the datably converted. On the political left, liberationists selectively appropriate episodes from Israel's his-tory, especially the exodus, but use these as legitimating precedents for their own campaigns, not as shapers of a comprehensive commu-nity of sinners and saints, oppressors and oppressed, tyrants and liberators. More generally, despite such dubious phenomena as Jews for Jesus, Christianity continues for the most part to be as gentile in its self-understanding as ever, and few Christians are in the least inclined to think of themselves as even remotely analogous to a Jewish sect or honorary Jews. As long as this is the situation, a biblically Israel-like understanding of the church will not be intelligi-ble, efficacious, or scripturally appropriate.

Frei's metahistorical critique of biblical criticism helps free the exegete to find the biblical meaning of the church in the story of Israel as appropriated by the early Christians. This recovery of what was meant creates the permanent possibility of an ecclesiological revolution, but whether the possibility will be exploited is a question beyond the scope of this essay. In the meantime, whether Frei knows it or not, and whether we thank him or not, his work is a challenge to all those concerned with what Christian community is and should be.

NOTES

1. Frei's sole *ex professo* comments on the doctrine of the church (in *The Identity of Jesus Christ: The Hermeneutical Bases of Dogmatic Theology* [Philadelphia: Fortress Press, 1975], 157–64) are only tangentially related to the present essay but are, I believe, consistent with it.

2. David H. Kelsey, *The Uses of Scripture in Recent Theology* (Philadelphia: Fortress Press, 1975).

3. "The 'Literal Reading' of Biblical Narrative in the Christian Tradition: Does It Stretch or Will It Break?" in *The Bible and the Narrative Tradition,* ed. Frank McConnell (New York: Oxford Univ. Press, 1986), 36–77.

4. See George A. Lindbeck, *The Nature of Doctrine: Religion and Theology in a Postliberal Age* (Philadelphia: Westminster Press, 1984), esp. chaps. 1, 4, and 5, for discussions of the similarities of doctrines and grammatical rules.

5. To be sure, 2 Cor. 11:1–4 explicitly evokes the possibility of the church betrothed to Christ becoming a whore; and gross actual or potential unfaithfulness is also in view in Galatians, in Hebrews, and as we shall later note, in Revelation (see esp. 2:4, 20–23; 3:15–19). (I am indebted to Richard B. Hays for suggesting this note as well as for help at other points in this essay.)

6. The kind of work that James Samuel Preus has done in his *From Shadow to Promise: Old Testament Interpretation from Augustine to the Young Luther* (Cambridge: Belknap Press of Harvard Univ. Press, 1969) needs to be extended more fully to specifically ecclesiological themes. It is noteworthy that even as recently as the Second Vatican Council the relation of Israel and the church was said to be that of type and antitype.

7. Krister Stendahl, *Paul among Jews and Gentiles, and Other Essays* (Philadelphia: Fortress Press, 1976), 37.

8. Jacob Jervell, "Das Volk des Geistes," in *God's Christ and His People: Studies in Honour of Nils Alstrup Dahl,* ed. Jacob Jervell and Wayne A. Meeks (Oslo: Universitetsforlaget, 1977), 87–106. Jervell's argument amply supports the statement in the text that the references to the Holy Spirit "often" function in this way, but perhaps not his much stronger claim that they almost always do so indirectly even if not directly.

9. Given the dependence of this reasoning on a hypothesis about how the

New Testament texts apply in a situation of Christian persecution of Jews that was wholly outside the purview of the early church, it is more properly characterized as theological than exegetical interpretation (as Richard Hays has pointed out to me), but in an exploratory essay such as the present one the untidiness of making this theological point in an exegetical discussion is perhaps excusable.

10. Ernst Käsemann, "The Canon of the New Testament and the Unity of the Church," in *Essays on New Testament Themes* (Naperville, Ill.: Alec R. Allenson, 1964), 95–107, is often cited in this context. Those who disagree with Käsemann about the contradictions of New Testament ecclesiologies—such as the Roman Catholic scholar Raymond Brown—nevertheless in the absence of a narrative approach fail to find much unity. From the perspective of this essay they confuse disparateness of situations and applications with an ununifiable disparateness of views of the church.

11. Krister Stendahl's summary of the philological and exegetical evidence in *Die Religion in Geschichte und Gegenwart*, 3d ed., 3:1297–1304, is a gem of concise exposition.

12. One can, to be sure, proof-text later Christian understandings of the relation of Israel and church, as Richard Hays has reminded me in a written memorandum: "See, e.g., Matthew's distinctive 'moral of the story' to the parable of the vineyard-tenants (21:43) and his version of the parable of the marriage feast (22:1–10)." Giving hermeneutical priority to such passages, however, makes a canonically unified reading impossible. If e.g., Matt. 21:43 is the last word on Israel and the church, then Romans 9—11 makes no sense; but if the passage from Romans is taken as the interpretive key, then the verse from Matthew retains its force as the description of a temporary situation.

13. Karl Barth, despite popularizing the nature of the church as event, is in large part an exception to this generalization. The story-shaped people of God, embracing both Christians and Jews, is usually referentially primary in the later volumes of the *Church Dogmatics*. It is well to observe in this connection, however, that the popularity of the designation "people of God" in recent ecclesiology (manifesting itself not least in the second chapter of Vatican II's *Constitution on the Church*) does not necessarily indicate a return either to narrative or to denotative concreteness. Often "people of God" is treated as an attributive rather than denotative term. Thus, e.g., Paul Minear discusses it as an "image" of the church logically comparable to others such as "body" or "bride" of Christ (*Images of the Church in the New Testament* [Philadelphia: Westminster Press, 1960], 66–104). In such an approach, "people of God" becomes competitive with other attributions, and warnings against overemphasis may seem appropriate (as in fact happens in Raymond E. Brown, *The Churches the Apostles Left Behind* [New York: Paulist Press, 1984], 60, 83). Nils A. Dahl (*Das Volk Gottes: Eine Untersuchung zum Kirchen- bewusstsein des Urchristentums*, 2d ed. [Darmstadt: Wissenschaftliche

Buchgesellschaft, 1962]) is one author who in practice recognizes that "people of God" in the Bible, like "America" in ordinary usage, is usually a denotative term, and that when the biblical phrase is employed in this way, it makes no more sense to inveigh against overuse than in the case where "America" or "church" is employed referentially in discourse.

10

The church as God's new language

In itself, recognition of the theological significance of narrative is not very important. After all, stories do not save. God saves. Moreover, God's salvation is witnessed and embodied in a particular historic people called the church. I have chosen, therefore, to begin this essay with a sermon to remind us that the emphasis on narrative for theological reflection is unintelligible when abstracted from an ecclesial context. Too often, I fear, the very sophisticated hermeneutical analyses of the formal significance of narrative are attempts to substitute a theory of interpretation for the church.[1] Therefore, both the form and content of the following sermon are meant to exhibit why the questions of the truthfulness of Christian convictions cannot be abstracted from the ecclesial and moral context.

A PENTECOST SERMON

Genesis 11:1–9
Acts 2:1–21
John 15:26—16:11

At Pentecost we celebrate the birth of the church by the Holy Spirit. Pentecost is the climax of the Christian year, for only now are we able liturgically to tell the whole story of God's redemption of his creation. All is finally summed up through God's new creation of the church. By creating this timeful people God has storied the world, since now we have everything necessary to know the

Stanley Hauerwas

179

time in which we live. For God saves by making possible the existence of a people who are formed by his time so that the world can
know that we are creatures of a good creator.

The grand sweep of the texts for today reminds us that the salvation
wrought by God in the death and resurrection of Jesus of Nazareth is
cosmic in scope. All nature has now been renewed—returned to its
ordered relation to God. The mighty wind that gave birth to the
church involves the affairs of nations and empires. That wind created
a new nation that was no longer subject to the constraints of the past.
Salvation cannot be limited to changed self-understanding or to
insuring meaningful existence for the individual. Salvation is God's
creation of a new society that invites each person to become part of a
time that the nations cannot provide.

For we believe that at Pentecost God has undone what was done at
Babel. In Genesis we are told that originally the whole earth had one
language though few words. That such was the case allowed for
unusual cooperation as people migrated together seeking a good
place to live. Finding the land of Shinar, they discovered how to make
bricks and became builders. As the son of a bricklayer, I think I have a
deep appreciation for that achievement. Making bricks, while simple
enough, makes possible shelter, the home, and that wonderful complex phenomenon we call the city. Please note that God does not
object to people using their creative energies to embellish creation: he
wants us to make bricks. We are invited to plant vineyards and
cultivate the soil that our lives might be less subject to chance.
Equally important is our capacity for concerted effort, through which
community is formed in the effort to discover the goods we share in
common.

The problem at Babel was not human inventiveness but that our
forebears used their creative gifts to live as if they had no need to
acknowledge that their existence depended on gifts. Thus the people
said, "Come, let us build ourselves a city, and a tower with its top in
the heavens, and let us make a name for ourselves, lest we be
scattered abroad on the face of the earth." It was not technology that
was the problem but the assumption that God's creatures could name
themselves—insuring that all who came after would have to acknowledge their existence. They thus erected a tower, an unmistak-
able edifice, so they would never have to fear being lost in this vast

world. God acknowledged our extraordinary power as, seeing the accomplishments of this united people, he feared they would now think that nothing they proposed was impossible. Such is the power of human cooperation.

So God confused their language and people could no longer understand one another. Confused, they were scattered across the earth, abandoning all attempts to build the one city of humanity. Condemned to live as separate peoples isolated into homes, lands, and histories, no longer able to cooperate, people lost the ability for concerted action so necessary for the grand project of "making a name for themselves."

God's confusing the people's language, as well as his scattering of them, was meant as a gift. For by being so divided, by having to face the otherness created by separateness of language and place, people were given the resource necessary to recognize their status as creatures. God's punishment was the grace necessary to relearn the humility that ennobles.

But our parents refused to accept this gift as gift and instead used their separateness as a club, hoping to force all peoples to speak their tribe's language. Thus at Babel war was born as the fear of the other became the overriding passion that motivated each group to force others into their story or to face annihilation. The killing begun in Cain was now magnified as humankind's cooperative ability unleashed a destructiveness that was as terrible as it was irrational. Humans became committed to a strategy of destroying the other even if it meant their own death. Better to die than to let the other exist. To this day we thus find ourselves condemned to living in tribes, each bent on destruction of the other tribes so that we might deny our tribal limits. Our histories become the history of war as we count our days by the battles of the past.

Babel is the climax of the primeval history, for after scattering humankind over the face of the earth, God no longer acted toward humankind as a unity. Rather he called Abraham out of his tribe and promised to make of him a great people. In calling Abraham, God created a rainbow people so that the world might know that in spite of our sinfulness God has not abandoned us. The history of Abraham's people is, of course, one of unfaithfulness as well as faithfulness, yet his people remained faithful enough so that they might be truthful about their unfaithfulness.

The faithfulness of Israel is manifest in its unwavering conviction that the main character of the story it tells of the world is not Israel itself but God. As Robert Alter has reminded us, the very narrative art of Israel involves the ability to destabilize any monolithic system of causation in favor of a narrative account of the world. Such an art reflects the profound belief that God, not humanity, is the ultimate determinant of human history. Israel developed the means to be a faithful storyteller just to the extent that it resisted the temptation to resolve the tension between the divine promise and its failure to be fulfilled, and the tension between God's will and human freedom.

Thus the call of Abraham foreshadows God's care for all creation through the existence of a people who can stand as a light to the nations. For again we are reminded that God's salvation is not simply knowledge, not even the knowledge captured by a story, but that rather his salvation is the creation of a people who have the capacity to be timeful. To be timeful means to be capable of rest, of worship, in a world bent on its own destruction.

It is only against the background of Babel, therefore, that we can understand the extraordinary event of Pentecost. The sound that was like the rush of a mighty wind signaled a new creation. The fire of the Holy Spirit burned clean, making possible a new understanding. The Jews of the Diaspora heard these Galilean followers of Jesus telling of the mighty works of God in their own language. The promised people themselves who had been scattered among the tribes, learning their languages, were now reunited in common understanding. The wound of Babel began to be healed first among the very people God had called into the world as a pledge of God's presence.

The joy of that healing surely must have made the people ecstatic. It is literally a joy not possible except by God's creation. It is a joy that comes from recognizing that we have been freed from our endless cycle of injury and revenge. It is the joy of unity that we experience all too briefly in moments of self-forgetfulness. It is no wonder, therefore, that some onlookers attributed this strange behavior simply to consumption of potent wine.

Peter denies that wine was the cause, by pointing out that the people could hardly be drunk, since this was only the third hour of the day. Yet what happened was a matter of time, for this reconstitution of our unity portends the last times. Thus Peter reminds his hearers that this extraordinary creation is what is to be expected at the end time:

And in the last days it shall be,
  God declares,
that I will pour out my Spirit upon
  all flesh,
and your sons and your daughters
  shall prophesy,
and your young men shall see
  visions,
and your old men shall dream
  dreams,
yea, and on my menservants and
  my maidservants in those days
I will pour out my Spirit; and they
  shall prophesy.
And I will show wonders in the
  heaven above
and signs on the earth beneath,
blood, and fire, and vapor of
  smoke;
and the sun shall be turned into darkness
and the moon into blood,
before the day of the Lord comes,
the great and manifest day.
And it shall be that whoever calls
  on the name of the Lord shall be saved.
                (Acts 2:17–21; cf. Joel 2:28–32)

This is strong apocalyptic language, but it is necessary if we are to appreciate the significance of the new creation at Pentecost. Creations are, after all, not everyday affairs. They are dramatic in their power to make and consume time. For this new creation born through the power of the Spirit does not make irrelevant all that has gone before nor make indifferent all that comes after. Rather this apocalyptic time places all history in a new time—the time made possible by the life, death, and resurrection of Jesus of Nazareth.

Some have suggested that the so-called delay of the Parousia, that is, the sheer continuation of history after Pentecost, creates an impossible problem for Christians. For it seems that the end did not come.

This, however, is to forget that the apocalyptic expectations created in the early Christian community drew on the conviction that in Jesus of Nazareth, Israel's cosmic desires were being fulfilled. Apocalyptic does not deny the continuation of the history of creation but rather reminds us that it is historical exactly because it has an end. That end Peter now proclaimed to be present at Pentecost.

Peter proclaimed the presence of the end time, to better his ability to recognize that the fiery Spirit was so timeful, because he knew it as the same Spirit that rested on Jesus of Nazareth. Thus following Peter's appeal to Joel's prophecy of the last days, he said,

Men of Israel, hear these words: Jesus of Nazareth, a man attested to you by God with mighty works and wonders and signs which God did through him in your midst, as you yourselves know—this Jesus, delivered up according to the definite plan and foreknowledge of God, you crucified and killed by the hands of lawless men. But God raised him up, having loosed the pangs of death, because it was not possible for him to be held by it. (Acts 2:22–24)

The Spirit, to be sure, is a wild and powerful presence, creating a new people where there was no people, but it was a spirit known then and now. For the work it is doing is not different from the work that was done in Jesus of Nazareth. Therefore, in John, Jesus tells his disciples that he must go so that the Counselor, the Spirit of truth, might be present to bear witness to him. Moreover that same witness that the Spirit makes to Jesus transforms the witness of the disciples, for they are now able to see what they have seen from the beginning but not seen at all.

In this transformation of the disciples we see the central theme of the gospel. To be a disciple of Jesus, it is not enough to know the basic "facts" of his life. It is not enough to know his story. Rather, to be a disciple of Jesus means that our lives must literally be taken up into the drama of God's redemption of his creation. That is the work of the Spirit as we are made part of God's new time through the life and work of this man, Jesus of Nazareth.

That is why the Trinity is such a central affirmation to sustain the Christian life. The Trinity is not metaphysical speculation about God's nature in and of itself but is rather our affirmation that God has chosen to include us in his salvific work. Thus the Spirit proceeds from the Father so that Jesus might continue to be present with us. It is this Spirit received at Pentecost that made the affirmation possible that in Jesus of Nazareth we have seen time renewed by the end time's having come.

After Pentecost we can better understand how Jesus' life was from the beginning integral to God's life. For creation itself heralds the presence of this Jesus. From the beginning God's being as Trinity, rather than being a denial of time, is an affirmation of God's time-fulness. Thus even at Babel God says, "Let us go down," prefiguring even then the necessary sacrifice of his Son so that the world might be judged, and if judged, redeemed. For in that sacrifice we are given the grace to know our sin, and judgment is made on the rulers of this world who rule by fraud and fear.

It is no wonder, therefore, that being made part of that judgment by the Spirit at Pentecost, we may well be thrown out of synagogues and even killed. Moreover, those who do the killing will think they are serving God, not knowing or acknowledging that we now know that God is the Father because we have beheld his Son. Jesus tells us such hard truths even before we have experienced them, because we can learn such truths well only by remembering them in the light of our living faithfully to the Spirit's call. Such a faithfulness no doubt will challenge the powers of this world who continue to believe that we lack an alternative to war and violence.

The unity of humankind prefigured at Pentecost is not just any unity but that made possible by the apocalyptic work of Jesus of Nazareth. It is a unity of renewed understanding, but the kind of understanding is not that created by an Esperanto that denies the reality of other languages. Attempts to secure unity through the creation of a single language are attempts to make us forget our histories and differences rather than to find the unity made possible by the Spirit through which we understand the other as other. At Pentecost, God created a new language, but it was a language that is more than words. It is instead a community whose memory of its Savior creates the miracle of being a people whose very differences contribute to their unity.

We call this new creation the church. It is constituted by Word and Sacrament, for the story we tell, the story we embody, must not only be told but be enacted. In the telling we are challenged to be a people capable of hearing God's good news so that we can be a witness to others. In the enactment, in Baptism and the Eucharist, we are made part of a common history that requires continuous celebration to be rightly remembered. It is through Baptism and Eucharist that our lives are engrafted on the life of the One that makes our unity possible. Through this telling and enactment, we become, like Israel, peculiarly a people who live by our remembering the history of God's redemption of the world.

The creation of such a people is indeed dangerous, as we know from Babel. For the very strength that comes from our unity has too often led the church to believe that it can build the tower of unity through its own efforts. Not content to wait, in time we try to make God's unity a reality for all people through coercion rather than witness. Remembering the church's relation to the Jews is particularly painful in this respect. Such a history of unfaithfulness has led many to downplay the peculiar mission of the church to witness to the world the reconstitution of humankind through the life, death, and resurrection of Jesus of Nazareth.

Pretension and presumptuousness, however, cannot be defeated by false humility. Rather, our task is to be what we were made to be at Pentecost: a people so formed by the Spirit that our humility is but a reflection of our confidence in God's sure work. Without such confidence, the church is constantly tempted to self-righteousness and self-aggrandizement. But we have a sure check against such temptations by the very Savior who has made us what we are. For how can we be prideful when the very God we worship is most fully manifest on a cross?

There is no way, if we are to be faithful to God's gift at Pentecost, that the church can avoid calling attention to itself. To be sure, like Israel, the church has a story to tell in which God is the main character. But the church cannot tell that story without becoming part of the tale. The church as witness to God's work for us in Israel and in Jesus of Nazareth means that here the teller and the tale are one. For this is not just another possible story about the way the world is; it is the story of the world as created and redeemed by God. That story, the story of the world, cannot be told rightly unless it includes the story of the church as God's creation to heal our separateness.

After all, as Christians we confess, "We believe in one holy catholic and apostolic church." That surely seems an odd thing to do, even given the eschatological nature of the claim, since why do we need to confess belief in something we can to some extent see and experience? That we do so is a recognition that the church, catholic and apostolic, is not our creation but God's. Moreover, it is not a creation that God completed at a point in time and does not need to continue. Rather it is our belief that what God did at Pentecost he continues to do to renew and to sustain the presence of the church so that the world might know that there is an alternative to Babel.

So as we celebrate Pentecost may our joy be so manifest that some may even mistake our behavior for that produced by "new wine." For we are a people of God's time and we rejoice in the knowledge that we are not condemned to repeat the past. That means that we really do have an alternative to Babel, to the fear of one another, and finally then, to war. Even more happily it means that insofar as we are the church we do not just have an alternative but we are the alternative. Not only do we have a story to tell but in the telling we are the story being told. So as we move once again to the feast of the new age, let us praise God for the creation of his church. Amen.

THE END OF NARRATIVE THEOLOGY?

I would not want questions about the possibilities and limits of narrative for theological reflection to be determined or judged by whether it translates into good sermon practice; even less would I want it to be judged by reference to my sermon in particular. I am not even sure how good or bad a sermon of mine may be: it is certainly short on contemporary examples. But I did try to write the sermon drawing on what I have learned about the narrative character of theological convictions from Hans Frei, as well as from David Kelsey, George Lindbeck, Ronald Thiemann, and James McClendon, among others.[2] Though the sermon itself does not tell a story, in it I boldly interrelate the birth of the church, the primeval history in Genesis, and the life, death, and resurrection of Jesus in a way that presumes they are narratively interrelated.

Yet why should I have chosen those particular texts? The answer is quite simple: I did not choose them. They were the lectionary texts given me by my church for Pentecost. I was therefore authorized by the church to hold them up authoritatively for the whole church. But why choose the form of a sermon in the first place?[3] Could you not as easily make a case in a Barth-like fashion by doing systematic reflection on scriptural texts? Of course the answer is yes, except that I lack Barth's knowledge of scripture, as well as his genius.[4]

But there is a still more significant reason for using a sermon, which I hope the sermon itself exhibits. Part of the difficulty with the rediscovery of the significance of narrative for theological reflection has been too much attention on texts qua texts. It is no doubt significant to rediscover the literary and narrative character of the texts of the Bible. That is particularly the case if one is interested in redirecting the attention and method of those engaged in the scholarly study of the Bible.[5] But the emphasis on narrative can only result in scholarly narcissism if narrative texts are abstracted from the concrete people who acknowledge the authority of the Bible.

I suspect this is the reason that Professor Frei has begun to feel uneasy with some aspects of the upsurge of interest in narrative for theology. Having been one of the prime movers behind that development, Frei, it seems, may now be ready to declare an end to the story of "narrative theology." Moreover, given the extraordinary diverse claims made in behalf of the importance of story, one cannot help being sympathetic to Frei's attempt to distance himself from the groundswell for narrative.

Elie Wiesel's story of the great Baal Shem Tov and his followers is certainly a good story, but one can be told once too often that "God made man because he loves stories."[6] After the initial enthusiasm over rediscovering the significance of stories, one begins to feel the need for some good old-fashioned arguments that are more scholastic in form. Those satisfied with Wiesel's claim would do well to read his later book *Souls on Fire*, where he tells the same story of how it fell to Israel of Rizhim to avert disaster when all he could do was tell the story of what the Baal Shem had done. Following the story, with its optimistic claim of the sufficiency of stories, Wiesel notes that such stories are no longer sufficient, because "the threat has not been averted. Perhaps we are no longer able to tell the story. Could all of us be guilty? Even the survivors? Especially the survivors?"[7] Of course, Wiesel is not retreating from his earlier claim of the significance of stories, but his later gloss is a sobering reminder that when we have said "story" we have just begun, not ended, the project.

Frei has a deeper concern about the enthusiasm for narrative as the key to all theological work, than the confusing and contradictory claims made in the name of narrative. He rightly fears that the theological construal of scripture as a narrative of God's work in behalf of his creation might be qualified by claims of the narrative quality of existence or the self. When narrative becomes a general category prior to the theological claim, Frei suspects a masked form of another kind of foundationalism or susceptibility to the deconstructionist critique. He notes the irony that even the New Criticism movement turned its own insight concerning the integrity of the individual text into a "general theory of meaning, literature, and even culture," thus creating a "scheme embracing a whole class of general meaning constructs."[8]

The point Frei is making is very similar to his earlier argument that because a Christ figure must be constituted by universal redemptive scope, an unsubstitutable personal identity in which the scope is enacted, and a pattern enacted by that person's history, any Christ figure's identity is already preempted by the one who is the Christ of scripture.

> In short, there can be no Christ figure because Jesus is the Christ, unless an author depicts the figure in terms of a particular identity and pattern wholly different from that of Jesus' story. But in that case it would not make any sense to talk of a Christ figure at all. To speak of Christ involves an enormous claim—a claim so large that it is made exclusively of whomever it is made. The claim is that in *one unique case* identity and presence are so completely one that to know who he is is to confront his presence. In him and in him alone, so the claim goes on, are also to be found these three elements by which the "Christ figure" is identified.[9]

This stress on the irreducibility, or unsubstitutability, of Jesus accords with Frei's reasons for qualifying some of the claims for "realistic narrative" made in *The Eclipse of Biblical Narrative*. Even though his primary thesis concerning the narrative character of the scripture has been fruitful for recent biblical scholarship,[10] Frei argues that to be convincing, the emphasis on realistic narrative must reflect the authority structure of a community's tradition.[11]

Thus narrative as a category does not precede the content of the Christian witness. Jesus is prior to story, though Jesus' life and resurrection can be displayed only narratively. Yet the

reason why the intratextual universe of this Christian symbol system is a narrative one is that a specific set of texts, which happen to be narrative, has become primary, even within scripture, and has been assigned a literal reading as their primary or "plain" sense. They have become the paradigm for the construal not only of what is inside that system but for all that is outside. They provide the interpretive pattern in terms of which *all* of reality is experienced and read in this religion. Only in a secondary or derivative sense have they become ingredient in a general and literary narrative tradition.[12]

Frei's position in this respect seems quite similar to his interpretation of Barth's theological project as one of conceptual description. He notes that Barth took the classical themes of "communal Christian language molded by the Bible, tradition and constant usage in worship, practice, instruction and controversy, and he restated or redescribed them, rather than evolving arguments on their behalf."[13] Therefore the style of Barth's *Dogmatics* is integral to Barth's theological position. For by his lengthy and leisurely unfolding of Christian language, Barth was attempting to "recreate a universe of discourse, and he had to put the reader in the middle of that world, instructing him in the use of that language by showing him how—extensively, and not only by stating the rules or principles of the discourse."[14]

Of course, by associating Frei's basic intent with that of Barth, I may only be confirming some of the deepest suspicions of Frei's critics. For it would then appear that all the talk about the importance of narrative, particularly in the form of a denial of any foundational starting point, is in fact a cover for a confessional starting point that results in a fideistic theology. Narrative, therefore, becomes but a way for Barthians, reinforced by Wittgensteinian "language game" analysis, to avoid dealing with the veridical status of theological claims.

It is not my place to defend Frei from this charge, since he is more than capable of defending himself. But I believe that the sermon with which I began, in both its form and its content, at least helps throw a different light on Frei's position. Narrative is but a reminder that the church is a community that lives by memory. Hence the alternative Thiemann notes between narrative as a transcendental quality of

experience and as a literary form that demands appropriate interpretive approaches for proper reading turns out to be a false choice.
According to Thiemann, when the former predominates, narrative is
seen as useful for theology primarily as a means for capturing the
temporality of human existence. When the latter predominates, narrative is employed as a useful tool for the interpretation of the biblical
writings through redescription.[15] Thiemann rightly thinks that Frei's
project builds on the second conception of narrative, but if I am right
about the significance of my sermon, such an interpretation of Frei
(an interpretation that Frei himself may share) will understate the
significance of his achievement. I must try to explain why that is the
case.

THE SIGNIFICANCE OF WHERE AND
HOW THE STORY IS TOLD
AND OF WHO TELLS IT

As I suggested above, the difficulty with the suggestion that theology's task is largely one of conceptual redescription is that one is
unsure how questions of truth can ever be raised. As long as one
remains in the "language game" what one says may seem intelligible
and even significant,[16] but by the very nature of the "game" one will
not be permitted to ask questions external to the narrative. So the
narrative, particularly the biblical narrative, threatens to create a
world that "overcomes our reality."[17] But the very power of the
narrative to engulf us makes us doubt its veracity, since we have no
means to check its truthfulness. It may be true that the biblical
accounts are only historylike, but does not that history finally have to
refer in a way that makes it liable to standard forms of reference?

Frei's position might be liable to such a critique if he assumed that
narrative, in particular biblical narrative, was in and of itself intelligible. In fact he has never done that but has reminded us that

> when Christians speak of the Spirit as the indirect presence now of Jesus
> Christ and of the God who is one with him, they refer to the church. The
> church is both the witness to that presence and the public and commu-
> nal form the indirect presence of Christ now takes, in contrast to his
> direct presence in his earthly days. In the instance of the church, refer-
> ence to the Spirit means affirmation of the spatial, temporal basis of

Christ's indirect presence in unity with his presence in and to the shape
of public events of the world and of human history.[18]

In philosophical terms Frei's appeal to the church as the subject as
well as the agent of the narrative is a reminder that the narrative does
not refer but that rather people do. To isolate biblical narratives in and
of themselves would be equivalent to considering the truth or falsity
of sentences separate from their context of utterance.[19] Once this is
understood, Frei's proposal cannot be seen as an attempt to avoid
realist claims but must be recognized as an attempt to situate the
context of those claims. It is to remind us, as Janet Soskice has
argued, that strictly speaking, not words and sentences refer but
rather speakers using words and sentences.[20]

As Soskice notes, one of the attractive features of such an account
of reference is that it has a significant social aspect since the notion of
membership in a linguistic community becomes crucial—whether
that community is one of science or the church. Appealing to Hilary
Putnam, Soskice notes that the realist explanation "is not that language mirrors the world but that *speakers* mirror the world; i.e. their
environment—in the sense of *constructing a symbolic representation of
that environment.*"[21]

There is no way such a theory can avoid the importance of experience, on which reference is grounded, but each speaker in the community need not have had the particular experience necessarily embodied by different aspects of the language. For good communities
depend on "what Putnam has called a 'division of linguistic labour,'
that is, we rely on authoritative members of our community to
ground referring expression. We refer to Columbus when we mention
his name, because we have heard the name from others, who heard it
from others, etc., going back to Columbus himself."[22] Thus each
speaker of a particular linguistic community is connected through the
members of that community, living and dead, to a range of experience
exceeding the speaker's own.

And so there follows the necessity of the sermon as the communal
action whereby Christians are formed to use their language rightly.
For it must be remembered that it is not the preacher who makes the
sermon efficacious. To think that would be but the form of *ex opere
operato* applied to the preached word. Rather for the preached word to

be God's Word, the Holy Spirit must make us a body of people capable of hearing that Word rightly. Put differently, the preached word's power is its capacity to create a people receptive to being formed by that Word.

The sermon is a churchly event, even when it is used to witness to those not Christian, as it proclaims the power of God to create a new people by being made part of God's continuing story. Yet Christians confess that any valid continuation of the story must take its form from the story of Jesus Christ. As Frei observes, in this respect the

> relation between the church and Jesus Christ is somewhat like that between Israel and Jesus. To describe the people of Israel is to narrate its history. And to identify that people with the identity of Jesus Christ is to narrate the history of Jesus in such a way that it is seen as the individual and climactic summing up, incorporation, and identification of the whole people, by which the people receive their identification. The church likewise moves toward an as yet undisclosed historical summing up that must be narrated, though it cannot yet be because the story is unfinished and the new Israel's Kingdom of God not yet climaxed or visible in our midst.[23]

The emphasis on narrative, therefore, is not first a claim about the narrative quality of experience from some unspecified standpoint but is rather an attempt to draw our attention to where the story is told, namely, in the church; how the story is told, namely, in faithfulness to scripture; and who tells the story, namely, the whole church through the office of the preacher. For as we see from the sermon above, the story is not self-referential but rather creates a people capable of being the continuation of the narrative by witnessing to the world that all creation is ordered to God's good end. The church is the necessary context of inquiry for the testing of that narrative. The church must always remain open to revision since the subject of its narrative is easily domesticated.

Thus once we recognize that the church is crucial for the intelligibility of the story that Christians have to tell, we do not have to choose between narrative as a transcendental category of experience and narrative as a literary form illuminative of scripture.[24] For example, it is obvious that not all of scripture is narrative in form, but the issue is not which form is predominant but how the content of the scripture is properly displayed. I have suggested that the church is the community that is at once the storyteller and a character in the story that is required by the Christian affirmation of God's redemption of the world through the people of Israel and the cross and resurrection of Jesus of Nazareth.

Moreover, the church is crucial for sustaining claims of the narratability of the world. Our experience, of the world as well as of ourselves, is open to narrative construal, but experience in and of itself does not entail the form of narrative or the kind of story Christians learn to tell about the world and our place in it. The church is, therefore, an ontological necessity if we are to know rightly that our world is capable of narrative construal. Without the church the world would have no history. Such a claim is not just a "confessional" stance but the most determinative realist claim Christians can possibly make.

Which brings us back to Babel. If I have been right, we are in a position to appreciate why the faithfulness of the church is crucial for the destiny of the world. To be sure, God's kingdom is more determinative than the church, yet at Pentecost God storied a people with gifts so that they might be capable of witnessing to the world the renewal of our unity made possible in Jesus of Nazareth. The church's theological witness cannot, therefore, avoid being a challenge to the conventional wisdom of the world. For the church is involved in nothing less than offering an alternative to war by providing the world with a history by our willingness as Christians to respond to Jesus' command "Go therefore and make disciples of all nations, baptizing them in the name of the Father and of the Son and of the Holy Spirit, teaching them to observe all that I have commanded you; and lo, I am with you always, to the close of the age" (Matt. 28:19–20).

NOTES

I am indebted to Michael Cartwright, Greg Jones, Richard Lischer, and Dennis Campbell for their criticisms and suggestions.

1. Even a book as rich as Robert Alter's *The Art of Biblical Narrative* (New York: Basic Books, 1981) remains formal insofar as he seems to assume that the examination of the form (or art) of narrative will reveal the meaning of the text. It is unfair, however, to accuse Alter of formalism without attending to his claim that the narrative art of the Bible is tied to the monotheistic

convictions and the correlative understanding of human nature (see, e.g., pp. 25, 91, 115, 126). That said, it is still the case that Alter owes us a more thorough account of the relation between form and content than he provides in his book. I am grateful to Michael Cartwright for pointing out the formal nature of Alter's analysis.

2. For Frei's work, see *The Identity of Jesus Christ: The Hermeneutical Bases of Dogmatic Theology* (Philadelphia: Fortress Press, 1975); *The Eclipse of Biblical Narrative: A Study in Eighteenth and Nineteenth Century Hermeneutics* (New Haven: Yale Univ. Press, 1974); and "The 'Literal Reading' of Biblical Narrative in the Christian Tradition: Does It Stretch or Will It Break?" in *The Bible and the Narrative Tradition*, ed. Frank McConnell (New York: Oxford Univ. Press, 1986), 36–77. See also David H. Kelsey, *The Uses of Scripture in Recent Theology* (Philadelphia: Fortress Press, 1975); Ronald F. Thiemann, *Revelation and Theology: The Gospel as Narrated Promise* (Notre Dame, Ind.: Univ. of Notre Dame Press, 1985); and James William McClendon, Jr., *Ethics: Systematic Theology,* vol. 1 (Nashville: Abingdon Press, 1986). By listing these together I do not mean to imply that they are in agreement or even constitute a common position in general. In fact, however, they share enough that they can generate a good argument, for which we should be grateful.

3. The reader is reminded that the sermon cannot be isolated from the liturgical actions of prayer, praise, and Eucharist. The whole liturgy enacted over the whole Christian year developed over a lifetime is the presumption necessary to enable one sermon to concentrate on a few texts and specifiable topics. The traditional issue of the relation of Word and Sacrament becomes even more pressing once the narrative character of Christian convictions is acknowledged.

4. David Ford's *Barth and God's Story: Biblical Narrative and the Theological Method of Karl Barth in the "Church Dogmatics,"* 2d ed. (Frankfurt am Main: Verlag Peter Lang, 1985), is an extremely enlightening treatment of Barth from this perspective. Ford notes that "Barth's comprehensive alternative world of meaning is an overarching story which is not the traditional one from creation to parousia but is the lifetime of Jesus Christ. A doctrine of time based on an interpretation of the resurrection supports the inclusiveness of that stretch of time, and the Old Testament history and all world history are 'figured' into it" (p. 165). Such "figuring" depends on an account of the church that Barth largely fails to develop.

5. This issue is complex, since it is often not easy to separate claims about the scripture as canon from the narrative character of scripture. See, e.g., Charles Wood's suggestions in *The Formation of Christian Understanding* (Philadelphia: Westminster Press, 1981), 100. See also Colin E. Gunton, *Enlightenment and Alienation: An Essay towards a Trinitarian Theology* (Grand Rapids: Wm. B. Eerdmans, 1985), 111–55.

6. Elie Wiesel, *The Gates of the Forest*, trans. Frances Frenaye (New York: Holt, Rinehart & Winston, 1966), xii.

7. Elie Wiesel, *Souls on Fire* (New York: Vintage Books, 1972), 168.

8. Frei, "'Literal Reading' of Biblical Narrative," 66. Frei continues, "There may or may not be a class called 'realistic narrative,' but to take it as a general category of which the synoptic Gospel narratives and their partial second-order redescription in the doctrine of the Incarnation are a dependent instance is first to put the cart before the horse and then cut the lines and claim that the vehicle is self-propelled.'

9. Frei, *Identity of Jesus Christ*, 65.

10. E.g., see R. Alan Culpepper, *Anatomy of the Fourth Gospel* (Philadelphia: Fortress Press, 1983); David Rhoads and Donald Michie, *Mark as Story* (Philadelphia: Fortress Press, 1982); Jack Kingsbury, *Matthew as Story* (Philadelphia: Fortress Press, 1986); and Dan O. Via, *The Ethics of Mark's Gospel—In the Middle of Time* (Philadelphia: Fortress Press, 1985). I suspect Frei would be less sympathetic to Via's approach, since he tends to assume that a general hermeneutical theory is needed in order to translate the biblical claims into existential truths.

11. Frei, "'Literal Reading' of Biblical Narrative," 68. The general argument by Charles Wood is obviously along these lines. What is frustrating about Frei's (and Wood's) position is the failure to specify the liturgical context through which such consensus is formed. This is not just a genetic point, for without the liturgy the text of scripture remains just that—text. It is important to remember that before the church had the New Testament it nonetheless worshiped and prayed to God in the name of Jesus of Nazareth. In effect, the worship of the church created scripture, though, once formed, scripture governs the church's worship. For a fascinating account of the development of the Christian interpretation of the Bible, see James Kugel and Rowan Greer, *Early Biblical Interpretation* (Philadelphia: Westminster Press, 1986). In particular, see Greer's discussion of Irenaeus's method that at least in principle requires scripture to be interpreted in a temporal way (pp. 168–76). Greer notes that Irenaeus tended to qualify this emphasis by using "type" to refer to an earthly representation of a heavenly reality. I think typological interpretation is unavoidable, but the crucial question is what controls the types. Originally I had written the sermon using the first person in relation to the story of Babel—e.g., "So God confused our language." Although I certainly think we continue to live out Babel's history, I am equally convinced that we also indicate that it is a time that is theologically in our past. Thus I tried to relate the texts temporally rather than contemporaneously.

12. Frei, "'Literal Reading' of Biblical Narrative," 72. While Frei is certainly right to emphasize the "plain sense" as primary, I think that he does not sufficiently note that the "plain sense" is that determined through the corporate life of the Christian community.

13. Hans Frei, "An Afterword: Eberhard Busch's Biography of Karl Barth,"

in *Karl Barth in Re-View*, ed. H.-Martin Rumscheidt (Pittsburgh: Pickwick Press, 1981), 110.

14. Ibid., 111.

15. Thiemann, *Revelation and Theology*, 83.

16. Much silliness has been written for and against the theological use of Wittgenstein's "language games." For an insightful and careful account of Wittgenstein on this matter, see James Edwards, *Ethics without Philosophy: Wittgenstein and the Moral Life* (Tampa: Univ. Presses of Florida, 1982, 1985), 123–42. Equally important is Joseph M. Incandela, "The Appropriation of Wittgenstein's Work by Philosophers of Religion: Toward a Reevaluation and an End," *Religious Studies* 21 (1985): 457–74.

17. Frei, *Eclipse of Biblical Narrative*, 3. How the gospel "engulfs" the world is not by denying the reality of our diverse narratives but by providing an invitation to be part of a new people. The imperial character of the story that the church embodies requires witness, not coercion. Precisely because the content of the story requires us to recognize our fallibility, we cannot anticipate how God will use our witness in relation to the diverse stories of the world. Indeed the story we believe to be entrusted to the church does not displace all other stories, for it does not pretend to tell us all that is worth knowing about our existence: it tells us only what we need to know about God's saving work.

18. Frei, *Identity of Jesus Christ*, 157. John Milbank, of the University of Lancaster, puts this point forcefully in "An Essay against Secular Order" (unpub.), when he says, "If we are to say 'salvation is a fact,' 'salvation has appeared on the historical stage,' then we have to enunciate, not just an ecclesiology, but also an ecclesiology which recounts and resumes the church's *actual concrete* intervention in the human social order, where the rules of 'non-interference' have not really applied" (p. 13).

19. Janet Martin Soskice, *Metaphor and Religious Language* (Oxford: At the Clarendon Press, 1985), 86.

20. Ibid., 135–36.

21. Hilary Putnam, as cited by Soskice (ibid., 136).

22. Ibid., 145. That is why questions of authority are unavoidable in any community. In the church it is the responsibility of those we invest with authority to direct our attention to those without whom we could not exist as church—i.e., the saints.

23. Frei, *Identity of Jesus Christ*, 159. Again as John Milbank says, "The church is not primarily a *means* of salvation, but rather a *goal* of salvation insofar as it is nothing other than the community of reconciled. Our way back to God is through our incorporation into the historical body of the redeemed" (p. 8).

24. As Greg Jones argues, "It is certainly true that there is a narrative quality to human life that is morally significant. But that is not the primary claim Christians are concerned to make. It is rather that the biblical *narrative*

seeks to incorporate all people into God's narrative. Thus there is a strong
sense in which the narrative of a single human life does not begin with birth
and end with death: for by being incorporated into the life of Christ the
narrative of a single human life begins at creation and ends with the consummation of the Kingdom. It is by being incorporated into the Church that it is
possible to develop the virtues necessary to live truthfully and morally.
[Therefore] the narrative of the Christian tradition is a way of displaying two
claims: on the one hand it displays the continuing embodiment of the
community through the ages (thus showing that the claim is not a utopian
fantasy), and on the other hand it displays the claim that each person's
salvation is indispensable to the salvation of everyone else, even the dead"
("Alasdair MacIntyre on Narrative, Community, and the Moral Life," in
Modern Theology, forthcoming).

Selected bibliography of works by and about Hans W. Frei

WORKS BY FREI

Books

The Eclipse of Biblical Narrative: A Study in Eighteenth and Nineteenth Century Hermeneutics. New Haven: Yale Univ. Press, 1974.

The Identity of Jesus Christ: The Hermeneutical Bases of Dogmatic Theology. Philadelphia: Fortress Press, 1975.

Articles

"Niebuhr's Theological Background" and "The Theology of H. Richard Niebuhr." In *Faith and Ethics: The Theology of H. Richard Niebuhr,* ed. Paul Ramsey, 9–116. New York: Harper & Bros., 1957.

"Religion: Natural and Revealed." In *A Handbook of Christian Theology: Definition Essays on Concepts and Movements of Thought in Contemporary Protestantism,* ed. Marvin Halverson and Arthur A. Cohen, 310–21. Cleveland: World Pub. Co., 1958.

"Theological Reflections on the Accounts of Jesus' Death and Resurrection." *Christian Scholar* 49 (1966): 263–306.

"The Mystery of the Presence of Jesus Christ." *Crossroads* 17/1 (January–March 1967): 69–96; 17/2 (April–June 1967): 69–96.

"Feuerbach and Theology." *Journal of the American Academy of Religion* 35 (1967): 250–56.

"Karl Barth" and "Albrecht Ritschl." In *Encyclopaedia Britannica* (1969).

"Karl Barth: Theologian." *Reflection* (Yale Divinity School) 66/4 (May 1969): 5–9. A slightly different version of this essay appears in *Karl Barth and the Future of Theology: A Memorial Colloquium Held at the Yale Divinity School, January 28, 1969,* ed. David L. Dickerman (New Haven: Yale Divinity School Assn., 1969), 5–12.

"German Theology: Transcendence and Secu-

larity." In *Post-War German Culture,* ed. S. Scher and C. McClelland, 98–
  112. New York: E. P. Dutton & Co., 1974.
"An Afterword: Eberhard Busch's Biography of Karl Barth." In *Karl Barth in
  Re-View: Posthumous Works Reviewed and Assessed,* ed. H.-Martin Rumscheidt,
  95–116. Pittsburgh Theological Monograph Series 30. Pittsburgh: Pick-
  wick Press, 1981.
"In Memory of Robert L. Calhoun, 1896–1983." *Reflection* (Yale Divinity
  School) 82/1 (November 1984): 8–9.
"David Friedrich Strauss." In *Nineteenth Century Religious Thought in the West,*
  ed. Ninian Smart et al., 1:215–60. New York: Cambridge Univ. Press,
  1985.
"The 'Literal Reading' of Biblical Narrative in the Christian Tradition: Does It
  Stretch or Will It Break?" In *The Bible and the Narrative Tradition,* ed. Frank
  McConnell, 36–77. New York: Oxford Univ. Press, 1986.

Book Reviews

Jürgen Moltmann, *The Theology of Hope.* In *Union Seminary Quarterly Review*
  23 (1968): 267–72.
Eberhard Busch, *Karl Barth: His Life from Letters and Autobiographical Texts.* In
  New Review of Books and Religion 1/4 (December 1976): 6; *Virginia Seminary
  Journal* 30 (1978): 42–46; *Religious Education* 73 (1978): 728–29; *Histor-
  ical Magazine of the Protestant Episcopal Church* 51 (1981): 109–21.

REVIEWS OF
"THE ECLIPSE OF BIBLICAL NARRATIVE"

Boobyer, G. H. *Scottish Journal of Theology* 28 (1975): 578–80.
Borsch, Frederick H. *Religious Education* 70 (1975): 571–72.
Brown, Colin. *The Churchman* 89 (1975): 72–73.
Bruce, F. F. *Christian Scholar's Review* 5 (1975): 199–201.
Dillistone, F. W. *Journal of Theological Studies* 26 (1975): 223–24.
Drake, Robert R. *Westminster Theological Journal* 38 (1975): 94–97.
Duffy, Eamon. *Journal of Ecclesiastical History* 26 (1975): 442–43.
Duke, James O. *Encounter* (Christian Theological Seminary) 38 (1977): 296–
  306.
Evans, C. F. *Times Literary Supplement* 73 (1974): 1320.
Keck, Leander E. *Theology Today* 31 (1975): 367–70.
Kelly, Justin J. *Theological Studies* 36 (1975): 155–58.
Klaaren, Eugene M. *Union Seminary Quarterly Review* 37 (1983): 283–97.
MacIntyre, Alasdair. *Yale Review* 65 (1976): 251–55.
Murphy, Roland E. *Catholic Biblical Quarterly* 37 (1975): 573.
Nineham, Dennis. *Theology* 79 (1976): 46–48.
Pratscher, W. *Theologisch-praktische Quartalschrift* 123 (1975): 191–92.
Reardon, Patrick Henry. *Review for Religious* 34 (1975): 175.
Riches, J. K. *Religious Studies* 12 (1976): 117–19.

Schäfer, Rolf. *Theologische Literaturzeitung* 101 (1976): 49–50.
Steiner, George. *Philosophy and Literature* 1 (1977): 238–43.
West, Cornel. *Union Seminary Quarterly Review* 37 (1983): 299–302.
Wood, Charles M. *Interpretation* 30 (1976): 80–82.
Yu, Anthony C. *Journal of Religion* 58 (1978): 198–203.

REVIEWS OF "THE IDENTITY OF JESUS CHRIST"

Ambrozic, A. M. *Catholic Biblical Quarterly* 37 (1975): 387–88.
Butterworth, Robert. *Religious Studies* 11 (1975): 481–82.
Duke, James O. *Encounter* (Christian Theological Seminary) 38 (1977): 296–306.
Evenson, George O. *Lutheran Quarterly* 27 (1975): 274–75.
Jenson, Robert W. *Interpretation* 30 (1976): 83–85.
Keck, Leander E. *Theology Today* 32 (1975): 312–20.
Meitzen, Manfred O. *Dialog* 15 (1976): 227–28.
Robinson, William D. *Expository Times* 87 (1975): 27.
Tassone, Salvatore. *Horizons* 2 (1975): 259–60.
Via, D. O. *Perspectives in Religious Studies* 4 (1977): 281–83.
Wiles, Maurice. *Journal of Theological Studies* 27 (1976): 261–62.
Young, Warren C. *Foundations* (Baptist) 19 (1976): 84–86.

Names and subjects

Allegory. *See* Interpretation, allegorical
Alter, Robert, 29–30, 41 nn. 19, 25; 182,
194–95 n. 1
Angels, 105–8, 116
Anselm of Canterbury, Saint, 139
Anthropology, theological, 121–43
Anti-Semitism, 171–72, 174
Apocalyptic, 77 n. 18, 175, 183–84
Apologetics, 86
Archetype, 7
Aristotle, 109
"As," 85, 86–93, 96 n. 33
"As if," 46, 53, 83, 86–93. *See also* Fiction
Aspect, dawning of an, 85. *See also* Gestalt
Auerbach, Erich, 27–28, 29
Augustine, Saint, 110, 116, 124, 131
Authority, concept of, 20 n. 12, 43, 50–52,
55–56, 57 n. 25
Axis mundi, 102, 104, 109

Baal Shem Tov, 188
Baptism, 186
Barbour, Ian G., 96 n. 31
Barnabas, Letter of, 171
Barr, James, 55, 57 n. 25
Barth, Karl, 144, 160 n. 15, 188, 190, 195
n. 4
on Christian love, 157–58
on Christology and anthropology, 152–53
on the nature of the church, 177 n. 13
Barton, John, 50, 52
Bernstein, Richard, 26
Biblical theology movement, 44
Braithwaite, Richard, 88
Brown, Delwin, 7, 13, 14, 19 n. 4
Brown, Raymond E., 177 nn. 10, 13
Buddhism, 109
Bultmann, Rudolf, 44

Canon, 19 n. 1, 53–54, 62, 69
"curse of the," 42

extrabiblical, 19 n. 3
function of the, 72–74
intertextuality of the, 16
narrative reading of the, 45–48
"working," 40–41 n. 15
Cartwright, Michael, 195 n. 1
Childs, Brevard, 90, 96 n. 36
Christ figures, 149–51, 189
Christological governance, 144–60
Church, doctrine of the, 161–78,
     179–98
Classic, 55, 163
Communal practice, 60–66
Comstock, Gary, 95 n. 14, 142 n. 8
Crites, Stephen, 122–23, 128

Dahl, Nils A., 177–78 n. 13
Dante, 107–8
Deconstructionists, 22, 24, 25–27,
     39 n. 6. *See also* Derrida,
     Jacques
Derrida, Jacques, 25–26, 60, 64
Descartes, René, 26, 40 n. 11
Diaspora, 174
DuPlessis, Rachel Blau, 19 n. 2
Duck-rabbit figure, 85, 88–89, 92

Ecclesiology. *See* Church,
     doctrine of the
Edwards, James, 197 n. 16
Eliade, Mircea, 102
Empiricism, 82
Enlightenment, 26, 163
Enûma Elish, 101–2
Ethics
     secular, 154–55
     theological, 144–50
Eucharist, 186, 195 n. 3
Evans, Christopher, 42, 56 n. 2

Fact-fiction duality, 84, 88, 90, 94,
     99. *See also* Fiction
Faith, 30–31, 35, 39. *See also*
     Fideism

fides qua creditur, 55
fides quae creditur, 55
Faulkner, William, 117
Fenton, John, 57 n. 26
Feuerbach, Ludwig, 112
Fiction, 79–96. *See also* Fact-fiction
     duality
Fideism, 86, 91–92, 95 n. 14, 96
     n. 37, 190
Ford, David, 195 n. 4
Formalism, 99, 194–95
Foucault, Michel, 60, 64
Foundationalism, 26, 40 n. 12, 87,
     122–23, 132–33
Frei, Hans W., 13, 16–17, 50, 92, 95
     n. 14, 114, 117, 175–76, 196
     n. 10
     Eclipse of Biblical Narrative, 28–29,
          43, 59, 79–80, 96 n. 36, 97–99,
          122, 143 n. 8, 144, 161, 164,
          189, 197 n. 17, 200–201
     on fiction, 81, 82–83, 91
     Identity of Jesus Christ, 28–29, 82–
          83, 122, 144–60, 176 n. 1, 201
     on literal sense, 20 n. 10, 39 n. 6,
          41 n. 18, 59–60, 96 n. 36, 190,
          196 nn. 8, 11, 12
     on narrative theology, 187–91
     on personal identity, 121–43
     on scriptural authority, 145–46
Fundamentalism, 5, 48, 79–80

Gamble, Harry Y., 16
Gellner, Ernest, 81–82, 89
Genre, 14–16
Gestalt, 85, 89
Gestalt switches, 92
Gnosticism, 77 n. 21, 147, 151, 171
Greene, Graham, 148–49
Greer, Rowan, 196 n. 11
Gustafson, James M., 159 n. 3

Habermas, Jürgen, 19 n. 5
Hardy, Thomas, 112

Ogden, Schubert M., 11, 19 n. 5
Oral tradition, 70–71

Paradigms, 86, 87–88, 91–92
Parousia, delay of the, 183–84
Pascal, Blaise, 108–9, 117 n. 6
Pattern. *See* Gestalt
Paul (apostle), 163
Pentecost, 168, 179–87, 194
Plain sense. *See* Literal sense
Plato, 107, 109–10
Pluralism, 22–24, 81–82, 84, 85, 88, 89, 93
Positivism, 86
Postliberal theology, 50. *See also* Lindbeck, George
Preus, James Samuel, 176 n. 6
Promises, 37–39
Prototype, 7
Putnam, Hilary, 192

Reciprocity, 148–49, 152–53, 157–58
Regnum gratiae, 93–94
Relativism, 22, 28, 81–82, 84, 86, 90, 91
Religious studies, 92–93
Ricoeur, Paul, 89, 142 n. 8
Rorty, Richard, 39 nn. 8, 10; 60
Ryle, Gilbert, 126, 147

Sadducees, 77 n. 20
Schüssler Fiorenza, Elisabeth, 7, 13, 19 n. 3
Science, 86, 87–88, 96 n. 31
Scriptural authority, 10–12
Scripture
definition of, 19
nonscriptural uses of, 6
Second Vatican Council, 176 n. 6, 177 n. 13
Seeing-as. *See* "As"
Sensus literalis. *See* Literal sense

Singularity, 133–34, 139
of Jesus, 146–48, 151–52, 155–57, 189
Smith, Wilfred Cantwell, 96 n. 33
Soskice, Janet Martin, 192
Spirit, 31, 100–101, 115–16. *See also* Holy Spirit
Stendahl, Krister, 90, 167, 177 n. 11
Strauss, David Friedrich, 98
Strawson, P. F., 124
Sykes, Stephen, 52

Theology
conservative, 3, 5, 9, 81, 175. *See also* Fundamentalism
definition of, 60–61, 93
liberal, 3, 5, 8, 50, 80, 81
liberation, 5, 175
narrative, 187–91
practical, 137–38
Thiemann, Ronald F., 45–47, 49, 187, 190–91
Thomas Aquinas, Saint, 109
Trinity, doctrine of the, 143 n. 24, 184–85
Truth, narrative, 79–96, 97–118
Twain, Mark, 117
Typology, 166, 195 n. 4

Unitarians, 56 n. 3
Unsubstitutable identity, 133–34, 139

Vaihinger, Hans, 83, 86–87
Vatican II, 176 n. 6, 177 n. 13
Via, Dan O., Jr., 196 n. 10

Walker, Alice, 117
War, 181
Watt, E. D., 20 n. 12
Welker, Michael, 96 n. 31
Werpehowski, William, 159 n. 6

Scripture references